Everythi

"Perhaps no part of the Bible is more relevant to the modern human heart than Ecclesiastes. In this brilliantly crafted book, Bobby Jamieson brings this ancient wisdom to the deepest questions of life. *Everything Is Never Enough* would be deeply valuable purely as a work of commentary on the message of Ecclesiastes, as it is filled with clarifying insights about the meaning of the book. But it is also a tremendous accomplishment as a pastoral application to modern life and culture, engaging with modern sociology and speaking directly to the questions we all ask. It is clearly written, a pleasure to read, and edifying, and it ultimately points us to Jesus. In short, this is a thrilling book that deserves a wide readership."

—Gavin Ortlund, pastor, speaker, and author of *Why God Makes Sense in a World That Doesn't*

"Do you feel thwarted and cramped by the ambient lameness of the modern world and suspect the problem goes deep? In *Everything Is Never Enough,* Bobby Jamieson brings an ancient text to bear on the challenge of living fully. The result is fresh, direct, and enlivening. With the ancient author, Jamieson helps us see the gifts that God is 'constantly flinging' at us."

—Matthew B. Crawford, writer and fellow at the Institute for Advanced Studies in Culture at the University of Virginia

"When I opened this book, I had no idea what to expect. Now that it's finished, I can't quite believe what I've read. *Everything Is Never Enough* is many things at once, but above all, it is a marvel. It is beautifully, clearly, and movingly written. It is a searching commentary on the most challenging book of the Bible. It is an invitation to anyone curious enough about life to be dissatisfied with it to press on that bruise, to learn from the pain, to see beyond it to its sources—both without and within. I am overwhelmed and impressed, not to mention jealous, that Bobby Jamieson is this learned, this wise, this incisive. I'm glad to know that in this time and place there is a pastor theologian with such chops, preaching and teaching the Word week in and week out. I have no doubt that Qohelet would be proud because Jamieson knows already that his words are straw, even absurd, without the gift of knowing God. I cannot wait to recommend this book to every one of my students."

—BRAD EAST, associate professor of theology at Abilene Christian University and author of *Letters to a Future Saint*

"Few books in history have examined the subject of happiness more insightfully and honestly than Ecclesiastes. In this thoughtful and often sparkling introduction, Bobby Jamieson shows us why its ancient wisdom is exactly what we need today and how we might live in ways that benefit from it."

—ANDREW WILSON, teaching pastor at King's Church London

"I want to read everything Bobby Jamieson writes, and I think you should too. A scholar's mind, a pastor's heart, and a poet's pen. If I wasn't so helped by him, I'd be jealous! There's some strange comfort, too, in knowing that he's wrong at points. Even when you disagree with him, however, you're a better thinker for having read his work. Relish this book with an open Bible that you might see the world more clearly, enjoy God's gifts more fully, and fear God more completely."

—James M. Hamilton Jr., professor of biblical theology at Southern Baptist Theological Seminary and senior pastor at Kenwood Baptist Church

"Bobby Jamieson is an expert guide through Ecclesiastes. As any scholar or pastor will know, the book of Ecclesiastes can feel like a whirlwind of topics and a constant whiplash of perspective. Nevertheless, we instinctively know there's treasure to be found here. That treasure is more easily discovered and experienced with Jamieson's work. Apart from regular interpretative insights and application to our modern cultural setting, the real strength of his text is the interpretive grid that Jamieson calls the "three-story building," which provides the reader with a helpful way of keeping Ecclesiastes together in our imagination. As a pastor, I'm excited to get this book into the hands of my congregants. As a father of young adults and teenagers, I'm excited for my children to read and grow in how to live faithfully in this world."

—John Starke, lead pastor of Apostles Uptown in New York City

"Along with a wildly heterogeneous body of biblical criticism and commentary over the centuries, Ecclesiastes has occasioned an equally varied tradition of engagement directed not at scholars and students but at 'ordinary readers,' however defined. Bobby Jamieson's *Everything Is Never Enough* is the best book in this vein I've seen since Jacques Ellul's *Reason for Being.*"

—JOHN WILSON, contributing editor at Englewood Review of Books and senior editor at Marginalia Review of Books

Everything Is Never Enough

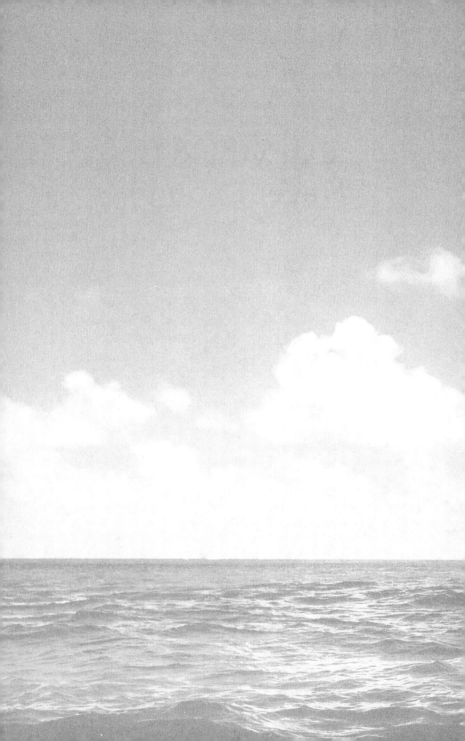

Everything Is Never Enough

Ecclesiastes' Surprising Path to Resilient Happiness

BOBBY JAMIESON

WATERBROOK

WaterBrook
An imprint of the Penguin Random House Christian
Publishing Group, a division of Penguin Random House LLC
1745 Broadway, New York, NY 10019

waterbrookmultnomah.com
penguinrandomhouse.com

A WaterBrook Trade Paperback Original

Library of Congress Cataloging-in-Publication Data
Names: Jamieson, Bobby, author.
Title: Everything is never enough : Ecclesiastes' surprising path to resilient happiness / Bobby Jamieson.
Description: Colorado Springs : WaterBrook, [2025] | "A WaterBrook trade paperback original." | Includes bibliographical references.
Identifiers: LCCN 2024034809 | ISBN 9780593601310 (trade paperback ; acid-free paper) | ISBN 9780593601327 (ebook)
Subjects: LCSH: Happiness—Religious aspects—Christianity. | Bible. Ecclesiastes.
Classification: LCC BV4647.J68 J33 2025 | DDC 223/.806—dc23/eng/20241125
LC record available at https://lccn.loc.gov/2024034809

Printed in the United States of America on acid-free paper

1st Printing

The authorized representative in the EU for product safety and compliance is
Penguin Random House Ireland, Morrison Chambers,
32 Nassau Street, Dublin D02 YH68, Ireland.
https://eu-contact.penguin.ie

Book design by Jo Anne Metsch

For details on special quantity discounts for bulk purchases,
contact specialmarketscms@penguinrandomhouse.com.

To Drew Bratcher,
for showing me the fence,
and to Matt McCullough,
for telling me to swing for it.

CONTENTS

PREFACE

Shouldn't You Be Happier?

Shouldn't you be happier? If you're reading this book, you can read. Just two hundred years ago, only 12 percent of people in the world could read.

If you're reading this book, you have enough time to spare from prolonging your own and others' survival to do something as biologically unessential as scanning your eyes over thousands of little marks on paper.

If you're reading this book, you or someone you know had enough disposable income to buy this book—or maybe a library let you walk away with it for free, for a time. That you hold this book in your hands is a modest sign of wealth, whether your own or your community's.

If you kept counting, I'm sure you could tally many more, and more significant, blessings, privileges, pleasures, and possibilities. Seen in light of the circumstances of many around the world, and certainly in light of history, you have it pretty good. Better than many. Better, probably, than your grandparents. As historian of happiness Darrin McMahon puts it, "Those who enjoy bemoaning their fate must acknowledge that on average they can do so for far longer and in far greater comfort than ever before."

And yet. Given all that you have, all that you know, all that you can do, and all the options you can choose from, do you feel like these advantages should do more for your well-being than they do? Does it feel like you should be happy, you want to be happy, and you try to be happy, but somehow you can't?

One way to be unhappy is to lack what you most want. Another is to get all you could possibly want and discover that everything is never enough.

■ ■ ■

Happiness sometimes seems as hard to define as it is to experience. But when people talk about happiness, they usually mean one of two things—or both.

First, there is happiness in an objective sense: Happiness is whatever it means for life to have value and meaning and purpose and coherence. According to this objective sense, which has deep roots in ancient philosophy, to be happy is to live a good life. In this view, happiness is human flourishing.

Second, there is happiness in a subjective sense: To be happy is to enjoy your life, whether in part or in whole, for a moment or over decades. To be happy is to feel good. Modern discussions of happiness typically give priority to this subjective sense.

The first perspective sees happiness as a form of health: What health is to the body, happiness is to the soul. The second treats happiness as a mood. The same external conditions might not produce the same response in everyone.

The subtitle has tipped you off that this book is about happiness. Throughout, when I speak of happiness, I mean to include both senses, but the first is primary. While enjoyment is an ingredient in a good life, it is also, and more basically, a by-product, like heat from fire. One of happiness's many paradoxes is that you don't get happy by aiming at happiness but by leading a life worth living. So the question "How can I be happy?" opens downward onto a deeper one: "What makes life worth living?" To see happiness accurately, you have to see through it to deeper-down bedrock.

Because of happiness's see-through character, because it depends on and derives from bigger and better realities, this book will say surprisingly little about happiness directly. But, indirectly, every word aims to help you not only understand happiness but become happy.

▪ ▪ ▪

You want to be happy. In one way or another, everything you do is motivated by the desire to be happy. You might not think that you brush your teeth in order to be happy, but if you'd be less happy with cavities and fillings, my point stands.

This book wrestles with the biblical book of Ecclesiastes, an ancient work of philosophy written by someone who relentlessly sought to observe, understand, and especially experience everything that could possibly lead to lasting happiness. Ecclesiastes tells the story of someone who saw it all, got it all, experienced it all, and in the end found fault with it all. Like Bono, despite all these "alls," the author of Ecclesiastes still didn't find what he was looking for. In fact, he found that having it all won't make you happy. He found that everything is never enough.

Ecclesiastes is surprisingly unreligious—even irreligious. Much of Ecclesiastes observes and evaluates life: success and failure, fulfillment and disappointment, desire met and unmet. God is nowhere to be found throughout much of Ecclesiastes, and he hardly shows up in the first part of this book. Anyone with eyes can agree with what the author of Ecclesiastes sees in his survey of life under the sun. Much of what he sees are problems that have no easy or obvious solutions. Yet he does turn, frequently, from happiness's problems to its solutions, from its lack to its ever-flowing sources. My hope is that, regardless of your stance on religion or God or the Bible, you'll find the author's diagnoses of this world's problems, and your problems, so compelling that you'll approach his answers with an open mind.

▪ ▪ ▪

Ecclesiastes was written well over two thousand years ago and is arguably the Bible's only work of philosophy. Its primary author and protagonist is identified not by name but by title, "Qohelet." (Pronounced like "Go yell it.") We know little about Qohelet. In the book's first chapter, he tells us that he is a son of David and was king in Jerusalem, but that may be a dramatic persona rather than a historical claim.

The Hebrew word *qohelet* names an activity. The word is somewhat obscure, but it likely refers to gathering, presiding at, or instructing an assembly. Qohelet is a teacher, someone who made a living speaking publicly; many translations and commentators call him "the Teacher" or "the Preacher." The sociologist Richard Sennett observes, "The good teacher imparts a satisfying explanation; the great teacher . . . unsettles, bequeaths disquiet, invites argument." Through years of studying and teaching Ecclesiastes, I have found Qohelet to be both a good teacher and a great teacher. I hope you will too. But I have to warn you, Qohelet does far more unsettling than satisfying. He disquiets more than he quiets.

Ecclesiastes is a strange book. It sets contradictory statements side by side without warning or framing. Its literary structure defies tidy analysis. It makes stunning, sweeping claims: Qohelet has seen it all, devoured it all, considered it all, and now he declares his verdict on it all. This little book has a huge scope and confronts huge questions. Does life have a meaning? What is the good life? How can I be happy? Those questions are all ways of getting at the main point of Ecclesiastes, which is also the main point of this book.

Because Ecclesiastes is such a strange book, your reading of this book will be greatly enriched by reading Ecclesiastes. I would encourage you to read the whole thing several times as you read this book. It may be weird, but at least it's short. To orient you to the book as a whole, and to what Qohelet is doing throughout, here are five metaphors to keep in mind.

First, Ecclesiastes is a quest. Qohelet sought to discover and analyze everything that people do. He amassed wisdom as if it were a fortune. He examined by experience a dizzying array of pleasures "till I might see what was good for the children of man to do under heaven during the few days of their life." In brief, and cliché as it might sound all these centuries later, Qohelet went on a quest for the meaning of life. In the book's first two chapters, Qohelet set himself an experiment: to experience and evaluate all possible sources of satisfaction and significance. More broadly, throughout the book's first six chapters, Qohelet carries out a program of observation and evaluation. In addition to many sources of pleasure, he assesses work, money, possessions, status, and power. This questing mode lasts for roughly half the book; after the sixth chapter, the balance shifts from mostly observation to more instruction. And at the end of the seventh chapter, Qohelet reflects on his whole journey, accenting its disappointments. Since Ecclesiastes is a quest, in this book we will retrace Qohelet's steps and walk them with him. The switchbacks and sore ankles and blisters are all part of the point.

Second, Ecclesiastes is a question. There are far more questions than answers in this book. The first half of the book is driven by the question, "What does man gain by all the toil at which he toils under the sun?" The question that closes the book's first half, and names one of the chief goals of Qohelet's quest, concerns not gain but good: "Who knows what is good for man while he lives the few days of his vain life, which he passes like a shadow?" A series of "who" questions haunts the book:

> Who knows whether the spirit of man goes upward and the spirit of the beast goes down into the earth?

> Who can bring someone to see what will happen after their life?

> Consider the work of God: who can make straight what he has made crooked?

> That which has been is far off, and deep, very deep; who can find it out?

In other words: Who knows what happens to you after you die? Who knows what happens to the world after you die? Can you fix what's wrong with this world? Who knows the deep causes and consequences of everything?

Better a good question than a bad answer. Qohelet's questions prod like a finger in the ribs to wake you up when you overslept your alarm.

Third, Qohelet is a stand-up comic. Not literally, of course. But Qohelet's way of investigating the world and his style of speaking are strikingly similar to modern comedians who are often called "observational," such as Jerry Seinfeld. Every observational comic squints to bring part of life's picture into sharper view. Each adopts a certain point of view; they speak from a certain persona. Their goal is to reveal the truth from surprising angles. They sneak up and catch you off guard in order to wound from behind. Stand-up comics traffic in hyperbole. They don't pause for footnotes or qualifications. They tell the truth, but not the whole truth, and both you and they know it. They draw caricatures so that the truth beneath pops out. For instance, consider Jerry Seinfeld's description of being a father.

> When I say I love being a parent,
>
> I certainly don't mean to give you the impression that I am in any way effective at it.
>
> I tell my kids to do things.
>
> But they say, "No."
>
> And so I have been reduced to threats, fear and intimidation.
>
> I have become a small-time mob boss around my house.
>
> I figure out what they like, and then I threaten to hurt those things.
>
> "I notice you're becoming quite fond of that little stuffed Curious George
>
> that sits in the corner of your room.
>
> It would certainly be a shame if something were to suddenly happen to him.
>
> He sits so close to the stairwell.

> And with you being at nursery school all day.
> He seems so vulnerable.
> I was just looking at the box he came in,
> and I think I noticed the word 'flammable.' "

Fourth, Qohelet is a philosopher at a party. Everyone else is trying to have the kind of good time that allows them, however briefly, to forget their problems, their failures, and their mortality. Qohelet wanders over, sits down next to you, stares in your eyes, and says, "Death comes to us all." Qohelet is the ultimate buzzkill. His questions and provocations and pronouncements are like a five-thousand-degree furnace that turns all superficial solutions to ash.

Fifth, Qohelet is a photographer. More specifically, Qohelet is like a photographer circling a globe and taking snapshots as he goes. Then he assembles the snapshots into a collage, but the order of the arrangement is tough to discern. You can make out the subject of each photo, but it's hard to tell how they fit together. Each photo shows you a picture, but none of them is the whole picture, and it's hard to assemble the big picture from the little pictures.

▪ ▪ ▪

Each of those five metaphors helps us grasp something of what Qohelet is doing. But we need to consider one more, which will help us see how his wildly divergent thoughts fit together into a coherent whole. This image will help us fit the whole book of Ecclesiastes into a structure we can navigate without getting lost.

Namely, Ecclesiastes is like the view from a three-story building. You and Qohelet enter the building on the ground floor. This is where he stays for most of the book. Looking out from a floor-to-ceiling window, Qohelet's far-seeing eyes take in the whole of human life from its own level. He weighs the merits of work, sex, food and drink, wealth, power, and many other possible sources of meaning and satisfaction. He finds them all wanting and pronounces them all "absurd"—*hevel* is the Hebrew keyword. (It rhymes with *level.*) Qohelet sounds embittered and defeated, even depressed. At one point he tells us that he hates his life and that he gave his heart up to despair.

But at several points in the book—seven, to be precise—Qohelet climbs up a set of stairs to the second story. From up here, he surveys the same territory, considering many of the same subjects—work, wealth, food and drink—and he pronounces them good. He sees rich opportunities for enjoyment and tells us to get busy enjoying them with statements such as, "There is nothing better," "What I have seen to be good and fitting," "And I commend joy," "Go, eat your bread with joy," and "So if a person lives many years, let him rejoice in them all." In these seven passages, Qohelet surveys the same territory but sees something astonishingly different. He sees the same subjects yet comes to the opposite conclusion. Here on the second floor he says that everything is a gift. What accounts for the radical difference between the view from the first floor and the view from the second? We'll get to that.

But first, we need to go with Qohelet to the third floor. He comes here only a few times, gives no warning before he does, and never stays long. To get to the third floor, we enter an elevator. Qohelet pushes a button, and the elevator rises fast and long. When you emerge and approach the window, the view is striking and strikingly different. Qohelet only stays long enough to point out two crucial reference points: one, fear God because, two, he is going to judge all that you do and all that everyone ever does.

Accounting for the contradiction between what Qohelet concludes on the first and second floors is the key challenge in interpreting the whole book. And, in my view, the key to solving that puzzle is to consider the vantage point Qohelet sees from. While on the ground floor, Qohelet investigates through observation, experience, and reflection. He is constantly telling us what he saw, what he turned to consider next, what he inwardly mused on, and what he concluded from it all. To put it in the language of epistemology (the branch of philosophy that considers how we know what we know), we can say that on the ground floor, Qohelet operates empirically. He gathers evidence from his senses, adds to it by personal experience, and draws conclusions based on what he sees and does and suffers. What he knows, down on the ground floor, is what anyone can know who is willing to look long and hard enough. What Qohelet tells us from the first floor is the truth, but it is not the whole truth.

On the second floor, Qohelet also tells us what he saw or perceived. But in the seven second-floor passages, what Qohelet means by "saw" is not so much "observed" as "concluded." He is not observing surfaces but discerning depths. He concludes that life is good, that life is a gift, and that the threads that compose the fabric of our lives are each themselves gifts. The key difference between the first floor and the second floor is that, on the second floor, Qohelet brings God to bear. Specifically, he considers all of life through the lens of its being created by God and sustained by God. For Qohelet, to say that life is a gift is not a vague, wishful metaphor but the strict and sober truth. Because life comes from God's hand, and all the good things in life do too, both life itself and its million small good things are gifts. Seeing that and living accordingly makes the crucial difference between despair and delight.

Qohelet's discussions from the first floor and the second floor fill up the bulk of the book. They function like parallel tracks. Neither one cancels the other or erases the other. Even though all things are absurd, all things are gifts. That all things are gifts does not make them any less absurd. These two key themes—all is hevel, all is gift—are like two magnetic poles with opposite charges. The two stories are distinct but not separate. If you collapse either into the other, you distort Qohelet's message. And the brief visits to the third floor, for their part, extend and intensify the view from the second floor. If God is the creator of all, then he is also the judge of all, and in addition to receiving his gifts with gladness, you should obey him with reverence.

Another way to account for the difference between the first floor and the second floor is to consider two key points from the Bible's account of the origin and fate of the whole universe in the first four chapters of the book of Genesis. Genesis 1 and 2 teach that this world is the good creation of a glad and generous God. Genesis 3 and 4 teach that through humanity's disobedience to God's command, we were plunged into ruin and misery, the whole created order was cursed along with us, and human society has been disintegrating in various disheartening ways ever since. This world is good but fallen, beautiful but broken, a gift but absurd. From the ground floor, Qohelet looks at all of life through the lens of Genesis 3 and 4. From the middle floor, he looks at all of life through the still-relevant lens of Genesis 1 and 2.

For most of the book, Qohelet looks out the ground-floor window. At regular intervals, forming seven transition points in the book's structure, he climbs up to the second floor. So, the book toggles between the first two stories with occasional furtive forays to the skyscraping third story.

▪ ▪ ▪

No matter what minute you're living in, Ecclesiastes has an uncanny way of seeming up-to-the-minute. For long years now, people who view themselves as "modern" have been surprised by how modern Ecclesiastes sounds. Ecclesiastes is like one of those creepy paintings where the eyes follow you across the room. Somehow, whatever strange and sad places the modern world pushes you into, you find Qohelet there waiting for you. How did he know that I'd feel so empty the day after my birthday? How could he have guessed that getting a perfect new job would only leave me feeling more stressed and anxious?

The modern world is the world Qohelet surveys and censures, only more so. What Qohelet considers when he studies his largely agrarian, perhaps rapidly urbanizing, ancient Near Eastern society is not merely a socioeconomic condition but the human condition. Modernity accelerates and intensifies certain aspects of the human condition, but it is still the human condition that modernity is accelerating and intensifying. Wherever we go, there we are.

▪ ▪ ▪

To uncover ways in which Ecclesiastes speaks precisely to our moment, I have enlisted the help of expert critics of modernity, especially sociologists, and especially Hartmut Rosa. In Qohelet's quest for the meaning of life, he evaluates not merely individual experience but the way the world works: how power corrupts, how incentives skew perverse, how good intentions backfire. Qohelet's observational program has much in common with the research agenda of modern sociology. Although not all sociologists would agree, Hartmut Rosa says, "In my view, sociology is born out of the diffuse but probably universal basic human perception that 'something is wrong here.'" Qohelet's research agenda springs from the same source.

Who is Hartmut Rosa, and why have I given him a prominent place as a dialogue partner? Rosa is a German sociologist whose career began with a study of the political thought of Charles Taylor. He has spent decades not only diagnosing the ills of late modernity but developing what he calls "a sociology of the good life." Rosa argues that late modernity is defined by the phenomenon of "social acceleration": Both individuals and institutions have to constantly strain, strive, gain, grow, and reinvest capital, not in order to get ahead but in order not to fall behind. As we will see throughout this book's first part, Rosa's thick description of current economic structures and rhythms of life uncovers many causes of the angst, alienation, and absurdity that the modern world multiplies. Rosa provides striking insight into the modern strains of the human ills that Qohelet diagnoses. Rosa's and Qohelet's judgments of what's wrong with the (modern) world sound in haunting harmony.

Not only that, but Rosa has articulated a positive vision of the good life, against the backdrop of modernity's acceleration and alienation, which he calls "resonance." As we will see in this book's second part, especially in chapter 19, Rosa's "resonance," well, resonates with Qohelet's summons to enjoy present gifts. Throughout this book, I gratefully draw on Rosa's insights, along with those of other sociologists and cultural theorists such as Richard Sennett and Byung-Chul Han. And, at the end of this book's second part, I suggest ways that Ecclesiastes' diagnosis and prescription dig deeper and see farther than Rosa does.

■ ■ ■

What is true of Ecclesiastes is true of this book too: You have to let it hurt you before it will heal you. Ecclesiastes demolishes before it rebuilds; so does this book. Ecclesiastes spends more time demolishing than rebuilding; so does this book. A doctor can only begin their healing work once they've diagnosed you, and the diagnosis often alarms. A friend who's going to try to help you restore a broken relationship has to first point out the mess you've made but haven't yet seen the full scope of.

Ecclesiastes tries to convince you that many of this world's most common promises are false friends and you should break up with them. As one scholar comments about the bleak poetry of T. S. Eliot, "The statement of a terrible truth has a kind of healing power."

A sad truth stated starkly is like a flood that washes away all of and only what deserves to be destroyed. In the words of Franz Kafka, "If the book we're reading doesn't wake us up with a blow on the head, what are we reading it for? . . . But we need the books that affect us like a disaster, that grieve us deeply. . . . A book must be the axe for the frozen sea inside us."

Why? Because, although we labor to forget it, this world is irretrievably broken.

GROUND FLOOR

Absurd

"A Memory of the World Unbroken"

Michael Chabon, "Wes Anderson's Worlds"

The world is so big, so complicated, so replete with marvels and surprises that it takes years for most people to begin to notice that it is, also, irretrievably broken. We call this period of research "childhood."

There follows a program of renewed inquiry, often involuntary, into the nature and effects of mortality, entropy, heartbreak, violence, failure, cowardice, duplicity, cruelty, and grief; the researcher learns their histories, and their bitter lessons, by heart. Along the way, he or she discovers that the world has been broken for as long as anyone can remember and struggles to reconcile this fact with the ache of cosmic nostalgia that arises, from time to time, in the researcher's heart: an intimation of vanished glory, of lost wholeness, a memory of the world unbroken. We call the moment at which this ache first arises "adolescence." The feeling haunts people all their lives.

▪ ▪ ▪

The most we can hope to accomplish with our handful of salvaged bits—the bittersweet harvest of observation and experience—is to build a little world of our own.

■ ■ ■

"For my next trick," says Joseph Cornell, or Vladimir Nabokov, or Wes Anderson, "I have put the world into a box." And when he opens the box, you see something dark and glittering, an orderly mess of shards, refuse, bits of junk and feather and butterfly wing, tokens and totems of memory, maps of exile, documentation of loss. And you say, leaning in, "The world!"

1

Hevel (I): Uncontrollable

"For my next trick," says Qohelet, "I have put the world into a book." And when you open the book, you see something dark and glittering, an orderly mess. Tokens and totems of memory you thought you had erased. Documentation of loss you have not yet suffered.

Will you lean in or look away? Will you meet Qohelet's stare?

Qohelet's book is the bittersweet harvest of observation and experience. He stakes his credibility on the breadth of his program of inquiry into the nature and effects of mortality, entropy, heartbreak, violence, and failure. Our researcher learned all their bitter lessons by heart. He says, "I applied my heart to seek and to search out by wisdom all that is done under heaven. . . . I have seen everything that is done under the sun." Later he reiterates, "I turned my heart to know and to search out and to seek wisdom and the scheme of things, and to know the wickedness of folly and the foolishness that is madness." Twenty-seven times he tells us that he saw; the objects of his sight include "everything," "all the oppressions that are done under the sun," that "the race is not to the swift, nor the battle to the strong," and that "folly is set in many high places."

Qohelet does not merely observe the full sweep of human life; he passes judgment on it, most often with a single word: *hevel.* This one-word verdict opens the book and closes its body, bracketing the whole. This word punctuates Qohelet's reflections as a tolling refrain. The problem is that the book's most important word is also its most difficult to translate. You might recognize the King James Version's rendering of the opening thesis, "Vanity of vanities, saith the Preacher, vanity of vanities; all is vanity."

The most concrete sense of hevel is "breath, air, vapor." Because exhaled breath is weightless and apt to vanish, other Old Testament writers often use hevel metaphorically, to characterize something as insubstantial, ineffective, or worthless. For ancient Israel, a political alliance with Egypt would be hevel, offering empty help. When a sage contrasts female piety and beauty, the latter is hevel because it is superficial and fleeting. The theological reasonings of Job's friends are hevel because they miss their mark. Human life is hevel since, like breath, it quickly disappears. A new car is hevel since the moment you drive it off the lot it starts losing value. Beauty is hevel since age never subtracts wrinkles; it only adds them.

Ecclesiastes uses hevel in all these senses and more. And throughout the book Qohelet custom molds hevel. He presses the word into a new shape, rendering it a fitting term of art to deliver his pitiless verdict on all of life. You could translate Qohelet's opening thesis in half a dozen ways, each granting some purchase on his point, none exhausting it:

"Meaningless! Meaningless!" says the Teacher. "Utterly meaningless! Everything is meaningless."

Perfectly pointless, says the Teacher, perfectly pointless. Everything is pointless.

"Absolute futility," says the Teacher. "Absolute futility. Everything is futile."

"Utterly enigmatic," says Qohelet, "utterly enigmatic, everything is enigmatic."

"Complete hot air!," says Qohelet, "Complete hot air! It's all hot air!"

Utterly absurd, said Qohelet, utterly absurd. All is absurd.

Meaningless, pointless, futile, enigmatic, hot air, absurd. We will meet all these nuances and others in the following chapters, as Qohelet delivers blow after blow to our sense of what's worth living for. Here in this chapter, we will treat one aspect of hevel as a key that opens the door to the house Qohelet is building. Life is hevel because, in a sense far more fundamental than you want to admit, life is uncontrollable.

Can you control the wind? Or a pea-soup fog? Or your breath after you exhale?

■ ■ ■

We had to drive at a walking pace. The headlights were little help. My friend Nick half jogged in front of the car, his shadow against the fog marking a road I couldn't see. In a car that could safely travel at seventy miles per hour, on a twisting mountain road above Santa Barbara that could accommodate thirty, we were making three. A fog so solid it might have been a billion-cubic-inch pillow filled the air.

Four friends, my brother, and I had just begun a hundred-mile trip back to downtown Los Angeles. At our speed, even traversing the asphalt on hands and knees might have been better for morale. Since there was only one way off the mountain, we couldn't go around the fog. Since the fog was so thick, we couldn't see through it. And we had zero chance of controlling it.

What do you try to control? What happens when you can't?

According to sociologist Hartmut Rosa, the central drive of modernity is to "make the world engineerable, predictable, available, accessible, disposable . . . in all its aspects." In a word, controllable. We want to control everything, down to the temperature of the room I'm in as I write and the one you're in as you read. Rosa states, "The history of our modern relationship to the world is a history of conquering and dominating the night with electric light, the sky with airplanes, the seas with ships, the body with medicine." The compounding discoveries of science serve mastery. We want to know so that we can control.

We especially want to control life itself, to tame the intolerable unpredictability of how it begins and ends. Why has euthanasia gained so much popular support and legal sanction in the West in recent decades? Because certain suffering of uncertain depth and length conflicts with the dream and demand of control. And we employ a range of complex, expensive technologies in the hope of creating new lives that enter our lives only when career plans permit. In America alone, ten million women daily dose sterility to "control" birth. As Rosa observes, through these technologically aided efforts, "modern society has found ways to make children more 'accessible.'" Just when we want children to exist, we beckon them; otherwise, we keep them from entering the world and scrambling our schedules. Rosa comments, "Childlessness or having an abundance of children is no longer a 'fate' given to us as a kind of task or challenge to which we must listen and respond in terms of how we live our lives; it is instead either a plan or a mistake."

More and more of modern life is lived under this clinical light of control: Life is no longer a challenge that summons but a job whose success proclaims a plan well executed or whose failure means someone is at fault. Whenever disaster occurs, like a hurricane demolishing a city, investigations are opened so that we can find someone to blame. Rosa notes, "We seek out guilty or responsible parties wherever accidents and misfortunes occur, on the assumption that the conditions that produced them were 'essentially' controllable. *Someone must be responsible for this.*"

As a result of this dominant desire to dominate, "for late modern human beings, the world has simply become a point of aggression. Everything that appears to us must be known, mastered, conquered, made useful." A fact that escapes explanation, a force that won't be tamed, a reality that can't be utilized or optimized—modern persons encounter each not as a given but as an affront. Because the world resolutely resists our efforts to control it, we experience the world as hostile. Painfully often, the world does not do what you want; instead, it does the very thing you hate, spawning tornadoes, recessions, wars, cancer. From this hostility between self and world comes what Albert Camus has called "the absurd": "He feels within him his longing for happiness and for reason. The absurd is born of this confrontation between the human need and the unreasonable silence of the world." The world has always resisted our efforts to control it, but the more you expect to be able to control, the more you will resent the uncontrollable. The more dominant you expect to be, the more the world's resistance will rankle.

When we try to control the world, resistance is not its only response; it also goes silent. The bitter paradox of control is that "it is only in encountering the *uncontrollable* that we really experience the world. Only then do we feel touched, moved, alive. A world that is fully known, in which everything has been planned and mastered, would be a dead world." In the most meaningful experiences, something in you resonates with something or someone in the world. The wire connecting you and the world starts to hum. A masterful sunrise; a series-winning shot; a look that says all you need to hear; hearing, live, the opening chords of your favorite song: None of these would cause the skin on the back of your neck to tingle if they lacked the uncontrollable. You can't control the sun, the shot, the look, the song. If you could, their meaning would splatter then disappear, like water from a burst balloon. Yet, as Rosa argues, the driving urge of modernity is to control it all, to render the world "a series of objects that we have to know, attain, conquer, master, or exploit. And precisely because of this, 'life' . . . always seems to elude us. This in turn leads to anxiety, frustration, anger, and even despair."

▪ ▪ ▪

Anxiety, frustration, anger, and even despair. How many of those can you find in Qohelet's summary of his observational enterprise?

> And I applied my heart to seek and to search out by wisdom all that is done under heaven. It is an unhappy business that

God has given to the children of man to be busy with. I have seen everything that is done under the sun, and behold, all is absurd and a striving after wind.

What is crooked cannot be made straight,
and what is lacking cannot be counted.

I said in my heart, "I have acquired great wisdom, surpassing all who were over Jerusalem before me, and my heart has had great experience of wisdom and knowledge." And I applied my heart to know wisdom and to know madness and folly. I perceived that this also is but a striving after wind.

For in much wisdom is much vexation,
and he who increases knowledge increases sorrow.

The world Qohelet surveyed is not our present control-obsessed regime. The ancient Near Eastern life he led was more obviously subject to powers no one dreamed of trying to control, like sun, wind, rain, disease, drought, and famine. Yet Qohelet is vexed by the world's uncontrollability. In addition to pronouncing everything hevel, he calls all human activity "a striving after wind," a chasing after what one can never capture. Striving after wind is trying to control the uncontrollable.

What Qohelet considers and catalogues is the human condition as it has been for as long as anyone can remember. The condition Rosa diagnoses is modern, but its roots are ancient. Modernity has intensified the possibilities and problems of control, but it did not create them. When we look through Qohelet's eyes, layers of familiar purpose and reassurance disappear, and we feel something akin to Camus's account of natural beauty:

> At the heart of all beauty lies something inhuman, and these hills, the softness of the sky, the outline of these trees at this very minute lose the illusory meaning with which we had clothed them, henceforth more remote than a lost paradise. The primitive hostility of the world rises up to face us across millennia.

When Qohelet judges that "what is crooked cannot be made straight," he asserts that there are wrongs we lack the power to right. There are dislocations—of cause and effect, work and wealth, desire and payoff, power and justice—that we can't slip back into their proper sockets. There are wounds in the world that no human surgery can heal.

This is why Qohelet declares that more wisdom brings more vexation, irritation, and provocation. More knowledge means more sadness. Why doesn't more wisdom make you happier? Because wisdom is consciousness without control. In an uncontrollable world, wisdom tells you more about what's wrong without giving you any more ability to fix it. Knowledge is not always power. Sometimes knowledge can't even buy you a meal.

> Again I saw that under the sun the race is not to the swift, nor the battle to the strong, nor bread to the wise, nor riches to the intelligent, nor favor to those with knowledge, but time and chance happen to them all. For man does not know his time. Like fish that are taken in an evil net, and like birds that are caught in a snare, so the children of man are snared at an evil time, when it suddenly falls upon them.

Qohelet's point is not that the fastest runner always loses but that the fastest runner doesn't always win. The same is true for the strong in a fight, and the smart in many situations, whether trying to make money or friends. Skill does not guarantee success. The fastest runner might trip; the best-qualified applicant might get passed over for someone's college friend's child. Fortune mocks. Despite your cherished illusion that you are the master of your fate, you are subjugated to powers clear beyond your control: time and chance.

No matter how meticulously you prepare, you don't control whether you'll win the race or the fight. You don't control whether you'll land the contract or get the nod. But most of all, and worst of all, you don't control the time of your death. So often the time seems cruelly untimely. When is it timely for a bird to be snared? The modern West's control complex catechizes you to think of yourself as the captain of a vessel cutting a razor-straight course through life's succession of storms. But you're not the captain; you're not even on the boat. In the end, you're a fish in the ship's net.

Time and chance harass all. Annie Dillard sees it: "That it's rough out there and chancy is no surprise. Every live thing is a survivor on a kind of extended emergency bivouac." In Qohelet's survey of everything under the sun, he discovers a world that slips out from all our efforts to control it. Poet Amit Majmudar says, "Reality escapes hope the way wet soap slips the squeeze." A wise person dies a fool's death; a painfully prepared inheritance passes to an incompetent heir; the guilty are declared innocent, and the innocent guilty; a fortune disappears in one bad deal; someone gets everything they could want except the ability to enjoy it.

▪ ▪ ▪

To desire control is to grasp at guarantees. You want to be certain that the dollar you feed in will send a snack through the slot. You want a sure return on investment, a guaranteed payout. But this life is full of everything except guarantees. Accidents aplenty, unfair outcomes, chances just missed, disasters that no one saw coming.

You can't make that woman love you or this child succeed or that plan prosper. Striving for control is like constantly clenching your teeth, jaw, neck, and shoulders. The effort you spend hurts you and hinders your chances of success. Life demands that you bend, but grasping for control leaves you brittle.

The first step that sets an addict on the path to recovery is realizing they've lost control. Control itself is like a drug: It at once enhances your self-perception and diminishes your abilities. Give up control, and your eyes and head start to clear. Weight lifts off. You find more in yourself and your life to laugh at. You learn to focus not on what you can't do but on what you can. Letting go of control is like taking a deep gulp of air after you've held your breath too long. Happiness comes not from controlling your life but from realizing that everything you care about most is entangled with forces beyond your control.

▪ ▪ ▪

Of the maladies that still afflict us, perhaps the one that most cruelly mocks our pretensions of control is cancer. It is always an evil time when cancer's snare catches, but some times feel more evil than others. Kate Bowler is a historian of American religion at Duke Divinity School. In 2015, Bowler was thirty-five, married, and the mother of a young son when she was diagnosed with stage 4 stomach cancer. Among many other thefts, cancer stole from her any sense that she was in control. The obligation to make something of yourself may be the prime moral directive of modern society. But an aggressive cancer not only forbids you from making something of yourself; it also makes you into something you'd never choose to be.

> I have a terrible premonition that at the end of this—once every stone is upturned and every drug tried—my family will have nothing left. I feel like an anvil dropped, crushing everything on its way down. I know it like I know the weight of my son's sleeping body in my arms. I will be the reason for the tall paper stacks of bills on the desk in the study, the second mortgage on my parents' aging home, the slope of their backs as they walk a little more heavily. They will carry my death in their checkbooks, vacations deferred, sleepless nights, and the silence of Sunday morning prayers when there is no daughter left to pray for. I am the death of their daughter. I am the death of his wife. I am the end of his mother. I am the life interrupted. Amen.

What are you to those you love most? What will you be to those who most love you?

Another way to state the "categorical imperative of late modernity" is this: "Always act in such a way that your share of the world is increased." The relentlessly repeated mantra of modern life is that the more of the world you bring within your effective influence, the better your life will be. Rosa calls this the "Triple-A Approach" to the good life: "The modern way of acting and being-in-the-world is geared towards making more and more of its qualities and quantities available, accessible and attainable." The life modernity molds us to live aims at making more and more of the world "knowable, calculable, disposable." To make more of the world available, accessible, and attainable is to bring it increasingly under the control of your mind and power.

Rosa concludes, "In this way, the world is turned into a disposable place, with money, education and technology supplying the charms for incessantly increasing our reach and scope." More money, education, and technology each mean more control. More control means more life. This has become the dominant principle in all our decision-making. But what happens when your share of the world collapses overnight? What question would you ask then? Bowler reflects,

> Control is a drug, and we are all hooked, whether or not we believe in the prosperity gospel's assurance that we can master the future with our words and attitudes. I can barely admit to myself that I have almost no choice but to surrender, but neither can those around me. I can hear it in my sister-in-law's voice as she tells me to keep fighting. I can see it in my academic friends. . . . "When did the symptoms start?" they ask. "Is this hereditary?" Buried in all their concern is the unspoken question: Do I have any control?

2

Gain

Qohelet searched for something you and I search for too. In all his relentless investigation of life under the sun, he wasn't just questioning, he was questing. Everywhere he went, he looked for lasting good. Gain that doesn't desert you. Satisfaction that doesn't slip away. Is there any job that doesn't get old? Any reward that doesn't fade?

What if you got the best job and the best house in the best neighborhood? What if you had the best family and took the best vacations and got all the recognition and money you could ever want? Would any of it keep you full? Would it last?

Qohelet sets up his quest in the book's third verse. Immediately after stating his thesis that the whole of human existence is hevel, he asks: "What does man gain by all the toil at which he toils under the sun?"

Qohelet likely takes his Hebrew word for "gain," *yitrôn,* from the world of commerce. The term marks profit: "It is what one carries away from a deal, or what one has left when accounts are settled and the books are closed." In his quest for gain,

Qohelet applies a stringent standard. The deal he wants to carry something away from is life itself. The accounts to be settled and the books to be closed comprehend the whole span of our brief existence. Add up all of a life's credits and debits. What is left for you when every gain has been added and all losses have been subtracted?

Don't forget death. What does death do to your closing balance?

■ ■ ■

Let's head outside. Shut the door on the indoors and climb to the top of a hill to breathe air not circulated by a machine. Take a long look; take it all in.

> A generation goes, and a generation comes,
>   but the earth remains forever.
> The sun rises, and the sun goes down,
>   and hastens to the place where it rises.
> The wind blows to the south
>   and goes around to the north;
> around and around goes the wind,
>   and on its circuits the wind returns.
> All streams run to the sea,
>   but the sea is not full;
> to the place where the streams flow,
>   there they flow again.
> All things are full of weariness;
>   a man cannot utter it;
> the eye is not satisfied with seeing,
>   nor the ear filled with hearing.

What has been is what will be,
    and what has been done is what will be done,
    and there is nothing new under the sun.
Is there a thing of which it is said,
    "See, this is new"?
It has been already
    in the ages before us.
There is no remembrance of former things,
    nor will there be any remembrance
of later things yet to be
    among those who come after.

This poem, which immediately follows the book's introduction and is structured like an ascending-then-descending staircase, starts by staging the changeless earth as a mute backdrop to the flicker of each passing generation. Roughly three generations are alive at any time. In less time than it takes to blink your eyes twice, verse 4 says, "A generation goes." Blink once, two and a half billion people are gone. Blink again, another two and a half billion. Blink a third time, and no one alive today is left on the planet. Having been assembled from dust, each generation at its close returns its dust to the earth, and the bodies of the next generation are made from the same dust. Humanity is not being renewed but recycled; our life cycle is an earth cycle because it is a dust cycle. Verse 11 correspondingly evokes the oblivion of everyone about everything. Let the clock run long enough, and everyone who comes after will have forgotten everyone who came before.

Do you beg to differ? As evidence will you propose, say, the American founders? We still read their words and visit their preserved homes and maintain the monuments we erected to them. Permit me a couple counter-counterexamples. For instance, Cai Lun (蔡伦, also called Jingzhong) and Dennis Ritchie. Lun, a court official of the Eastern Han Dynasty in the second century A.D., invented paper and the modern printmaking process. Ritchie was one of the chief architects of Unix and the C programming language. Unix underlies all major operating systems save one, and they are all largely written in C. Each man left a bigger and better impact on the world than most anyone could reasonably hope to. But, before reading this paragraph, had you heard of either? You could be forgiven for forgetting, or never hearing about, Cai Lun. But Ritchie died a week after Steve Jobs, and few noticed.

What about your own great-grandparents? How many of the eight can you name? If you can name any, can you say anything more about who they were or what they did? It will not take long for time to deposit enough fine particulate matter to fill every print your feet press into the earth. The outer brackets of Qohelet's poem ask, "What gain are you seeking?" and answer, "If you're seeking an enduring legacy, keep looking."

Each of the poem's nature vignettes displays action that is not merely repetitive but profitless. All settings reset; all patterns restart. No amount of energy can make the needle stay pegged; it always falls back to zero. Not innovation and newness but repetition and alreadyness are signatures of the human condition. If the gain you seek is progress, keep looking. Would satisfaction count as gain for you? No matter: You won't find it. Like the sea that can always receive more streams without filling up, your eyes and ears will never receive enough pleasurable sensations to satisfy you.

Qohelet constructs this diorama of net-zero recurrence not as proof but as illustration. Like these powers of nature, no human effort can notch a net gain. Like the natural forces that sustain it, human life is a treadmill. Nature's movement without progress mirrors our work without gain. When you look through Qohelet's eyes at the natural world, he wants you to see your life. Do you? If not, some examples might close the gap.

Later, Qohelet tells us that he systematically examined sources of enjoyment by experiencing each. He lapped up laughter, pleasure, and wine. He completed ambitious projects: houses and vineyards, gardens and parks and orchards. He amassed an unprecedented and unparalleled fortune. He abstained from no lawful gratification, and he enjoyed them all: "I kept my heart from no pleasure, for my heart found pleasure in all my toil, and this was my reward for all my toil." Qohelet enjoyed equally his work and its rewards. But, for reasons he withholds, for no external cause that he specifies, at the end of all this, the work, wealth, and pleasure proved an inadequate return. "Then I considered all that my hands had done and the toil I had expended in doing it, and behold, all was absurd and a striving after wind, and there was nothing to be gained under the sun."

Why are you so often disappointed by your work's results and rewards? What do you hope to gain from work that it never gives?

A man heaped up an inheritance, saving it, he thought, for his son. Then he lost it all in one disastrous venture. Here is where that leaves him: "As he came from his mother's womb he shall go again, naked as he came, and shall take nothing for his toil that he may carry away in his hand. This also is a grievous evil: just as he came, so shall he go, and what gain is there to him who toils for the wind?" But it isn't only this ill-fated investor who will carry nothing away. You, too, will exit life's stage as naked as you entered it. What is obviously true for this poor man is also true, though less obviously, for each of us.

Who toils for the wind? Not just the one who finds failure but the one who achieves smashing success, since death reclaims without remainder all work, all pleasure, and all profit. There is no walking away while you're ahead; whenever you leave the table, the house claims all your winnings.

In a couple places, Qohelet uses this keyword *gain* in what seems a more promising, positive sense: "Then I saw that there is more gain in wisdom than in folly, as there is more gain in light than in darkness." Better to see where you are going than to flail around in the pitch black. No surprise there. "And yet I perceived that the same event happens to all of them. Then I said in my heart, 'What happens to the fool will happen to me also. Why then have I been so very wise?' And I said in my heart that this also is absurd." The relative gain of wisdom is canceled by the absolute zero of death.

Later Qohelet observes that "wisdom is good with an inheritance" and thereby "an advantage." Like money, wisdom's gain is that it preserves its possessor. But how reliable is that protection? "Consider the work of God: who can make straight what he has made crooked?" God sprinkles days of joy and misery in a scatterplot we can't pattern. Those plot points include tragically early deaths for virtuous people and decades of untroubled prosperity for the immoral. So what gain is wisdom? Or work, wealth, or pleasure? Relatively, something; absolutely, nothing.

■ ■ ■

But maybe Qohelet is eccentric. Maybe his problem isn't the world but himself. Where did he get this desire for gain that will withstand even death's all-withering blast? Maybe he needs to diminish his desire to an order the world can fill. Maybe.

■ ■ ■

Nothing stays put. Three days ago, for the first time I can remember, I lost my keys. Two younger sets of hands had touched the keys that morning, but the movers of those hands credibly disclaim responsibility. The last to touch the keys says she put them in the tray on the kitchen counter. I believe her. Still, when I went to look, the keys weren't there. You leave your keys where you need them, and they walk off.

Satisfaction is a retreating horizon. You might row miles—outwrestle currents, graze islands, watch volcanoes split the ocean's rim on one side and then days later see them silently sink behind its opposite lip—and still, if your goal is the horizon, you will end no closer, no matter how long or hard you pull. For more people than admit it, for many who labor not to notice it, satisfaction is a false summit. As soon as you get there, it isn't there. But, you learn with relief, it's just over the next ridge. The last day of school; summer; winning the division; finally, a date; admission and just enough financial aid; the right major; graduation; the job you hoped for; the apartment at the upper limit of your salary; engagement, the date set. Did any of these satisfy? What about the next one? The poet Christian Wiman says, "We are driven ceaselessly onward in this life and are certain of our desires only until we realize them, at which point they seem to dissolve and shimmer farther off, like a heat mirage on a road down which we can't stop racing."

At each summit, happiness flickers. The view dims. We crave satisfaction that will stay put, but it doesn't. This leaves two options: keep looking or try to silence the craving. The poet Wallace Stevens seemed to try the second door in his breakthrough 1915 poem "Sunday Morning." Observing a woman's lightly indulgent, churchless languor, the poem's narrator denies God's monopoly on devotion. "Divinity must live within herself," so within herself is where she must find fullness. Can she?

> She says, "But in contentment I still feel
> The need of some imperishable bliss."
> Death is the mother of beauty; hence from her,
> Alone, shall come fulfilment to our dreams
> And our desires.

Though full for now, she wants satisfaction that will stay put. She wants gain safe from death's canceling reach. But the best the narrator can offer her is death. The mother of beauty, he calls it, because death sharpens sight and taste while we have them. But if death alone can fulfill dream and desire, both return empty. The poem's answer to the desire for gain that outstrips death is not a refutation but a dodge. If you want happiness that death can't crush, think of death differently. Mind over matter—until something sinks both.

What Stevens's poem "Sunday Morning" obliquely commends, many openly embrace. Call it a Stoic option or nirvana plan. If life won't measure up to your longings, sand down your longings till they either fit your life or disappear. There is some wisdom here. Often, we want the wrong thing, or the wrong amount, at the wrong time, in the wrong way, or for the wrong reason. Many longings call for sanding or for more drastic change: sawing, chopping, burning. For instance, if you are obsessed with making as much money as possible, you'll never be happy until you find a way to want it less.

But our problem runs deeper than longings. Dig down far enough and eventually the pains of the plural yield the far hotter problem of a singular molten core: longing. Our surface longings turn at a different rate than the core longing, so that many never infer core from crust. Yet underneath the drastically different surface desires lies a singular desire for something all out of proportion with anything that sticks to earth's spinning skin. Beneath your longings for things you know you want lies a longing for something you want but don't know. If you pull up a weed from your garden every day, and the next day always reveals another weed, would you conclude that tomorrow you will no longer have to weed? Or that something in this ground will cause it to keep sprouting shoots that seek the sun?

What unsatisfied longing stings you most sharply? What are you looking for in the thing you're longing for?

You might tailor or trim longings, but what about longing itself? Can you switch it off? If your heart sprouts longings quicker than you can weed them, maybe the solution isn't to weed faster but to find the sun and eat it.

▪ ▪ ▪

Who can eat the sun? Plants. The chlorophyll in their leaves absorbs energy from the sun's light waves. A plant puts the sun's energy to work on the water and carbon dioxide that it draws from air and soil, turning sunlight into sugars. By eating sunlight, the plant feeds itself and becomes food for others.

Plants don't have to gain the sun; it always already gives its light. Plants don't earn or achieve sunlight; they receive it as a gift. Before the plant does any work, the sun is already up and at it, pouring out light and heat like a faucet in the sky with no off switch. Sure, the planet spins and clouds cut in. But the sun is still there, throwing out its life-giving gifts regardless of whether anything or anyone is there to catch them.

Let's say that yesterday was an unseasonably warm fall day. In the afternoon you sat in your front yard reading. The sun shining onto your face warmed your skin just enough to melt away some stress. You didn't and couldn't do anything to earn, achieve, or gain that sunlight. It chased you down from 93 million miles away at 186,000 miles per second, every wave-particle of it a gift. Happiness is not striving for gain from life but receiving life itself as a gift.

■ ■ ■

Leave hard-earned savings in an account for a year. Take the money out, and it's worth maybe a tenth less than when you put it in. You've done nothing to deserve loss—this is no fine for a moral or legal offense—yet forces ungraspable as wind have scooped the top off your small pile of gain. Leave your money alone, and some of it walks away.

Leave your job, and your employability will walk away even faster. I recently spoke on the phone with a friend who worked for ten years as a software engineer at a company whose name is ubiquitous as both noun and verb. Two years ago, he quit his high-status, well-paying job to begin a doctorate in history in the hope of teaching, which is his passion. He's a gifted, lively teacher and a serious scholar. He hopes his hope isn't a pipe dream, but the academic hiring market is bleak. I suggested that if no good teaching job is waiting for him at the end of his doctorate, he could stay in the game by applying for a postdoctoral research position, revising his thesis for publication, and starting his next book. He hesitated, saying he would rather make a move while he's still employable. I didn't get it. Wouldn't a postdoc and publications make him more employable? No, his point was that his life raft is steadily deflating.

His backup plan's expiration date is both uncertain and uncomfortably near. Every month he spends not employed by a tech company, he grows less employable by a tech company.

Air escaping from hard-earned gain is not just a feature of the rarefied world of big tech or times of atypical inflation. The treadmill feeling of running to stay in place is a systematic feature of the late modern world. Hartmut Rosa's term for this condition is "social acceleration," and he likens it to walking up a down escalator. The shape of late modern life is like a triangle in which technological acceleration speeds up social change, which accelerates the pace of life, which in turn catalyzes further technological acceleration, and so the race keeps speeding up. Consider the potent pairing of email and smartphones. Email and a platoon of instant messaging systems allow anyone anywhere to stake a claim on your attention and action, and the smartphone in your pocket ensures that you will never be unreachable. This technological cocktail lubricates social change by radically shrinking expected response times. The changed social norms that follow leave many feeling short on time: time-poor, even time-bankrupt.

And, even when you are blessed with a modest time surplus, how often do you spend it in ways you soon regret, like mindlessly scrolling through social media? Your feeds demand that you feed them attention, otherwise you'll miss out on even more and fall even further behind.

Under conditions of social acceleration, we all must run as hard as we can to stay in the same place. Like computer software, every dimension of our lives requires constant updating. Rosa states, "If you do not constantly strive to stay up to date, your language, your clothing, your address book, your knowledge of the world and of society, your skills, your recreational gear, your retirement fund and investments . . . will become anachronistic." Keep swimming upstream or get flushed out to sea.

This walking-up-a-down-escalator existence causes predictable psychological injuries, including a constant fear of falling behind. Rosa summarizes, "Instead of moving forward, modern subjects feel they must run faster and faster just to stay on pace; they are not running towards a goal, but fleeing from an abyss. Fear, not promise, is the dominant dynamising force on the cultural plane." If you are not presently employed, your work experience is devaluing by the minute. If you are not continually adding to it, your CV is growing obsolete. If you are not gaining social status, you are, however slowly or silently, losing it. The steps beneath your feet do not hold still but steadily sink.

Late modern structures of production and reproduction, patterns of competition and consumption, render Qohelet's complaint that there is no gain no less true, only more obvious. If you retreat from the bombardment of electronic communication long enough to hold still a moment, the benefit is, you can watch your professional, economic, and social capital turn to vapor. Nothing stays put. Vapor of vapors, says Qohelet. Everything is vapor.

3

Work

No matter how much you love your job, it doesn't love you back. Schools and television shows, mentors and bus stop ads, politicians and celebrities all proclaim that we should do the work we love and love the work we do. And we don't just love our work; we devote ourselves to it, build our lives around it, give up more and more for it. As Derek Thompson of *The Atlantic* puts it,

> The economists of the early 20th century did not foresee that work might evolve from a means of material production to a means of identity production. They failed to anticipate that, for the poor and middle class, work would remain a necessity; but for the college-educated elite, it would morph into a kind of religion, promising identity, transcendence, and community. Call it workism.

Thompson defines workism as "the belief that work is not only necessary to economic production, but also the centerpiece of one's identity and life's purpose." A member of my church recently said to me, "At the consulting firm where I work, there's a sense of 'What else are you going to give your life to?' "

As it has been for so many religious movements, America is the hotbed of workism. Among large nations with comparable levels of productivity, none averages as many hours of work per year as America, and the gap is growing. Samuel Huntington summarizes: Americans "work longer hours, have shorter vacations, get less in unemployment, . . . and retire later, than people in comparable societies." By 2005, the wealthiest 10 percent of married men in America worked the longest average workweek. And a 2018 research article found that, compared to women who graduated from lower-ranked schools, women who attended elite, selective universities do not, on average, earn more per hour, but they do work more. For women, it seems, the benefits of an elite diploma are more time at work and lower chances of marrying and having children.

Derek Thompson again: "In the past century, the American conception of work has shifted from *jobs* to *careers* to *callings*—from necessity to status to meaning." Drawing a longer arc, the historian Mary Hartman has observed that in the modern era, work has become "the chief repository of male identity." And not just male. Camille Paglia pronounces a Qohelet-like verdict on a substantial swathe of contemporary feminism:

> In my opinion, second-wave feminism, for all its professed concern for mainstream, working-class, or disenfranchised women, has drifted toward privileging the concerns and complaints of upper-middle-class career women, who seek the lofty status and material rewards of an economic system built by and for men.

In America today, men and women alike adhere with growing devotion to what Scott Yenor calls "the career mystique—a set of ideas that tries to convince men and women that changing the world through their careers is the paramount path to fulfillment, growth, and happiness." What happens when work becomes the chief repository of identity, the prime source of status and reward, the paramount path to fulfillment? What happens is failure that we are poorly equipped to acknowledge, much less respond to fruitfully. What happens is "collective anxiety, mass disappointment, and inevitable burnout." What happens is our worship of work is shown and seen to be hevel, absurd.

▪ ▪ ▪

"What does man gain by all the toil at which he toils under the sun?" The question opens Qohelet's investigation into all of life. Toil is the engine of expected gain. And the negative answer Qohelet returns—no gain—proves that since toil is hevel, all is hevel.

By "toil" (Hebrew *'amal*), Qohelet means roughly what we mean by "work," typically with a negative tint. Elsewhere in the Old Testament, the word can mean "distress" or "anguish," even "misfortune" or "disaster." In Ecclesiastes, *'amal* typically means labor tainted by frustration or futility. But it also names the fruits of labor: not just the money made from selling milk but the whole thriving farm that has taken decades of work to cultivate.

What does a person gain from all this work, and even from its fruits and profits?

We have considered already, and will consider again, Qohelet's systematic exploration of potential sources of pleasure and profit.

In his experiment that encompasses all of life, work features prominently.

> I made great works. I built houses and planted vineyards for myself. I made myself gardens and parks, and planted in them all kinds of fruit trees. I made myself pools from which to water the forest of growing trees. . . . I had also great possessions of herds and flocks, more than any who had been before me in Jerusalem.

Here Qohelet displays his résumé. He describes the work of establishing a business and a household, from which and in which he could live in luxury. We should picture an ample, carefully conceived, skillfully developed estate. Qohelet's accomplishments were built to last. As Old Testament scholar Stuart Weeks comments, "Qohelet's business is not ephemeral, and he makes his wealth not from, say, buying low and selling high or from providing services, but from vineyards, orchards, timber and livestock." In fact, his operation is in some measure self-sustaining: pools water orchards and timber groves; timber furnishes building material. Neither the orchards and irrigation, nor the flocks and herds nourished by them, nor the grand dwelling at the center were apt suddenly to vanish. All would likely outlast him.

So far, so exceptionally successful. But, after cataloguing his enjoyment of other pleasures his wealth could purchase and his leisure permit, Qohelet declares, "Then I considered all that my hands had done and the toil I had expended in doing it, and behold, all was absurd and a striving after wind, and there was nothing to be gained under the sun." Qohelet here appraises not just his labor but its outcomes. He assesses not just his wealth but the infrastructure of his fortune, which will generate more fortune. What did his work and his work's outputs do to deserve this derogatory label of "absurd"? At the very least, their problem is not so much them as him, not that they will disappear but that he will. They'll last a while yet; he won't much longer. The problem with even lasting success is that it can't last long because its agent and beneficiary won't. Yet, as far as we can discern, Qohelet denounces his work's harvest with plenty of breath left in him. This seems to suggest a deeper contradiction.

By calling his life's work hevel, Qohelet asserts that there is a rupture in the chain that joins desire, effort, and outcome. He calls work absurd because of the disparity he discerns between what he put in and what he got out. But surely his work went as well as he could reasonably have hoped. Whence then comes the divorce between what he wanted and what he got? Somehow even striking success left him wanting something more.

Shortly after this judgment, Qohelet gives two more reasons why work is absurd:

> I hated all my toil in which I toil under the sun, seeing that I must leave it to the man who will come after me, and who knows whether he will be wise or a fool? Yet he will be master of all for which I toiled and used my wisdom under the sun. This also is absurd. So I turned about and gave my heart up to despair over all the toil of my labors under the sun, because sometimes a person who has toiled with wisdom and knowledge and skill must leave everything to be enjoyed by someone who did not toil for it. This also is absurd and a great evil. What has a man from all the toil and striving of heart with which he toils beneath the sun? For all his days are full of sor-

> row, and his work is a vexation. Even in the night his heart does not rest. This also is absurd.

By definition, the person to whom Qohelet will leave the legacy of his labor did not work for it. Worse, Qohelet can't guarantee a fitting successor. The more successful you are, the more you will leave in the hands of a successor of uncertain character and competence. Both toil and wisdom are irrelevant to inheritance. Even if you're an executive who can select your own replacement, you can't control what they do with your enterprise when you're gone. Time alone will tell you whether you chose wisely—only you won't be around to hear. Death stops ambition short. What's beyond your time is beyond your control.

Qohelet's second reason is that work is full of pains. He piles up those pains like stacks of unread emails and unanswered voicemails: toil, yearning, sadness, anxiety, sleepless nights. He bemoans hardships that are not physical but psychological. Nothing human was foreign to him; long before our age of anxiety, he knew and named the malady.

In another passage on work, Qohelet stirs some proverbial wisdom into his empirical observations.

> Then I saw that all toil and all skill in work come from a man's envy of his neighbor. This also is absurd and a striving after wind.
>
> The fool folds his hands and eats his own flesh.
>
> Better is a handful of quietness than two hands full of toil and a striving after wind.
>
> Again, I saw an absurdity under the sun: one person who has no other, either son or brother, yet there is no end to all his toil, and his eyes are never satisfied with riches, so that he

> never asks, "For whom am I toiling and depriving myself of pleasure?" This also is absurd and an unhappy business.

The Hebrew at the start of this passage is difficult. Most translations and commentators take it to say that all effort and achievement arise from envy, but a good case can be made that the verse instead ascribes ambitious work to a passion that draws one person away from another. If you stumble at the "all," remember that it's hyperbole. Like a stand-up comic, Qohelet knowingly keeps qualifications and counterarguments out of the frame, and then he squints at the resulting picture to bring one aspect into sharp focus. Whichever translation we opt for, Qohelet's point is that work is a fertile field for self-destructive desires to take root, go to ground, and spread wide.

Whether fueled by envy or self-isolating obsession, if work is the consuming passion in your life, what will it consume? What will be left after the fire cools?

When Qohelet commends a little quietness over a lot of striving, he is saying that there are limits to what work will give you, so there should be limits to what you give work. If you try to grasp gain with two hands, both will come up empty. There is no contentment without knowing and submitting to limits.

Speaking of limits, the last part of the passage profiles someone who, like many modern workers boast, doesn't have any. He has no one else to work for—no partner, no heir—yet he never stops working. Sounds like so many single city dwellers for whom work is life and life is work. Not only does he never stop working, but he also never asks, "Who am I working for?" He never asks who gains from his giving up everything to give it all to his work.

Who does the religion of workism benefit? If you have no dependents or heirs, then it can't help them. Your workism may benefit your boss. It might especially benefit your boss's boss's boss and their shareholders. But does it benefit your neighbor? Does it benefit you?

■ ■ ■

My wife, Kristin, is both a foodie and a homebody. She enjoys good food and is happy to cook it, but she doesn't much like going out for dinner. So, in the past few years we've settled into a relaxing, rewarding Friday night ritual. We get the kids fed and in bed (or at least in their rooms) early, then cook together. Dinner, dessert, decaf espresso, conversation throughout—Friday night helps us stitch back together what the week has tugged apart.

I'm a pastor, and some of my hardest and happiest work is preaching. I spend fifteen to twenty hours preparing every new sermon. In weeks when I'm preaching, I do all I can to have my sermon manuscript written, practiced, and revised by Friday evening at five-thirty. The deadline motivates and liberates. I don't want to mess up date night or mangle the weekend. All week, the weight of the sermon sits on me as I prepare it amid counseling appointments and phone calls and other teaching and last-minute needs and neglecting my inbox.

Once the sermon is ready on Friday at closing time, my shoulders relax in response to the lifted-off load. I feel like I just woke up from a full night's sleep. I'm suddenly more talkative than I've been all week. And Kristin gets to enjoy (what I hope is) the benefit of (what should be) my undistracted attention.

On Sunday I have serious work to do. But from Friday at five-thirty through Saturday night, I do my best to rest with my family. That rest can involve a daunting amount of chores and cleaning and laundry, but it also makes room for hikes and playground time and leisurely library visits.

If you want to keep work from ruling your life, set limits to its domain. Confining work keeps it from strangling and devouring everything else that gives life meaning. Commenting on the Jewish practice of Sabbath, Abraham Joshua Heschel reflects, "There is a realm of time where the goal is not to have but to be, not to own but to give, not to control but to share, not to subdue but to be in accord." Happiness comes not from working yourself raw but from knowing when and how to rest.

▪ ▪ ▪

"What has a man from all the toil and striving of heart with which he toils beneath the sun? For all his days are full of sorrow, and his work is a vexation. Even in the night his heart does not rest. This also is absurd."

What swords swing over modern workers' heads? Uncertainty, instability, and unpredictability all loom larger than they used to. For a while in the middle of the twentieth century, for better or for worse, many workers' employment was virtually a marriage. They and Ford were equally stuck with each other. But economic upheavals of the past forty years have rendered such marriages vanishingly rare. The Sorbonne economist Daniel Cohen observes, "Whoever begins a career at Microsoft has not the slightest idea where it will end. Whoever started it at Ford or Renault, could be well-nigh certain that it will finish in the same place." What we regard as a traditional career was a short-lived pattern. Today, very few workers will be employed by only one or two companies in their working life. Equally few will deploy a single set of skills. According to

Richard Sennett, "Today, a young American with at least two years of college can expect to change jobs at least eleven times in the course of working, and change his or her skill base at least three times during those forty years of labor."

Today's economy compels workers to constantly absorb risk, develop new skills, and change jobs regardless of how well they like their current work. Sennett explains, "Immense social and economic forces shape the insistence on departure: the disordering of institutions, the system of flexible production—material realities themselves setting out to sea. To stay put is to be left out." In many industries, from technology to marketing, youth is a prime asset and age a liability. "For older workers, the prejudices against age send a powerful message: as a person's experience accumulates, it loses value." Nothing stays put.

This uncertainty fertilizes anxiety. When past experience is no guide to the present, much less the future, how can you not worry? Days of sorrow, work a vexation, night no rest. With reason: "To be a workist is to worship a god with firing power."

4

Knowledge

Knowledge is not always power. Perhaps what you don't know can't hurt you; certainly what you do know can. In London, on July 9, 1955, two of the twentieth century's most renowned thinkers, philosopher Bertrand Russell and physicist Albert Einstein (who died a few months before the text was released) issued a manifesto. Their purpose was to warn the world of the grave results of nuclear war.

> Many warnings have been uttered by eminent men of science and by authorities in military strategy. None of them will say that the worst results are certain. What they do say is that these results are possible, and no one can be sure that they will not be realized. We have not yet found that the views of experts on this question depend in any degree upon their politics or prejudices. They depend only, so far as our researches have revealed, upon the extent of the particular expert's knowledge. We have found that the men who know most are the most gloomy.

More knowledge does not always mean more control. If the object of knowledge is fearful or foreboding or futile, more knowledge means more pain.

But today in the West, particularly in America, a certain kind of knowledge, or at least supposed proof of knowledge, is an increasingly crucial path to power. If you want more control over your life's path, your future earnings, your status, your options, and your choices, then you need knowledge—rather, education. Education unlocks achievement like nothing else. To those near the bottom of the ladder, education is held out as the only sure way to climb. Why should you get a college degree? To secure a better future. Or, if the status you were born into is good enough, to keep from sinking. While many students and teachers profess to love learning for its own sake, the constantly swelling ranks of college applicants suggest the prevalence of more primal motives. Over the past few decades, a common wisdom has congealed: A college degree is the primary path to a respectable job and a decent life. The dark underside of this consensus is that, as Michael Sandel puts it, credentialism has become the last acceptable prejudice.

A credential is a token of merit, signifying knowledge that deserves pay. A credential promises status, security, and control. The college degree has become a charm to wield against poverty. We gain knowledge to prove we have it: A diploma is a lever that pries open the future.

▪ ▪ ▪

> And I applied my heart to seek and to search out by wisdom all that is done under heaven. It is an unhappy business that God has given to the children of man to be busy with. I have

seen everything that is done under the sun, and behold, all is absurd and a striving after wind.

What is crooked cannot be made straight,
  and what is lacking cannot be counted.

I said in my heart, "I have acquired great wisdom, surpassing all who were over Jerusalem before me, and my heart has had great experience of wisdom and knowledge." And I applied my heart to know wisdom and to know madness and folly. I perceived that this also is but a striving after wind.

For in much wisdom is much vexation,
  and he who increases knowledge increases sorrow.

Qohelet wields "wisdom" as a searchlight to assess all human pursuits and pleasures. He starts with wisdom and amasses more along the way. By "wisdom," English speakers typically mean accumulated insight that helps one live a good life. And other biblical authors generally mean something similar, with the added nuance that wisdom arises from the fear of God and enables one to live with the grain of God's design. But Qohelet does not exactly mean either of those things. At the opening of this passage, which frames his quest, when Qohelet says "wisdom," he basically means his independent rational intellect.

Qohelet does not merely examine all else by means of his wisdom; he also examines wisdom itself. He sets the life of the mind on the scale. He applies his heart to know wisdom and—to understand wisdom better by contrast—to know madness and folly. And he finds this assiduous effort to acquire and evaluate knowledge to be, like so much else, absurd. He tells us why in the last part of the passage: Those who know most are gloomiest. What could warrant such a dim view of knowledge? For one, death.

> So I turned to consider wisdom and madness and folly. For what can the man do who comes after the king? Only what has already been done. Then I saw that there is more gain in wisdom than in folly, as there is more gain in light than in darkness. The wise person has his eyes in his head, but the fool walks in darkness. And yet I perceived that the same event happens to all of them. Then I said in my heart, "What happens to the fool will happen to me also. Why then have I been so very wise?" And I said in my heart that this also is absurd. For of the wise as of the fool there is no enduring remembrance, seeing that in the days to come all will have been long forgotten. How the wise dies just like the fool! So I hated life, because what is done under the sun was grievous to me, for all is absurd and a striving after wind.

Qohelet allows that wisdom offers relative but not absolute gain. To walk a lit path is better than to grope in darkness and risk forehead meeting tree. But a path is only as good as its destination, and both paths, wisdom and folly, converge in death. What good is light if it illumines only a walk to the gallows? Wisdom won't defend against death or defer death. Wisdom won't make death any more doable or grant any predictive foreknowledge of death. Least of all will wisdom defeat death.

Too often, the more you learn about life, the more reasons you have to hate it. How many young girls are trafficked into sexual horrors every year? How many children die of easily preventable diseases? The more you learn, the more you discover problems that dwarf anything you could possibly do about them.

Near the beginning of his book, Qohelet previews his quest. Just past the midpoint, he reviews it.

> All this I have tested by wisdom. I said, "I will be wise," but it was far from me. That which has been is far off, and deep, very deep; who can find it out?
>
> I turned my heart to know and to search out and to seek wisdom and the scheme of things, and to know the wickedness of folly and the foolishness that is madness. And I find something more bitter than death: the woman whose heart is snares and nets, and whose hands are fetters. He who pleases God escapes her, but the sinner is taken by her. Behold, this is what I found, says the Preacher, while adding one thing to another to find the scheme of things—which my soul has sought repeatedly, but I have not found. One man among a thousand I found, but a woman among all these I have not found. See, this alone I found, that God made man upright, but they have sought out many schemes.

Qohelet tested everything by his wisdom to seek some better wisdom, but he didn't find it. And he claims that if you replicated his quest you would do no better. Qohelet sought "that which has been," which is a clue to the shape and size of the wisdom he pursued. He was looking for the picture on the puzzle box: "wisdom and the scheme of things." He hunted the plan that would make sense of life's bizarre shapes and groped for the lens that would turn the senseless scatterplot into a portrait. He concludes, "I said, 'I will be wise,' but it was far from me. That which has been is far off, and deep, very deep; who can find it out?"

No master of what he surveys, Qohelet instead finds himself a stranger to it, alienated from it. The longer he watches the world, the less he feels he belongs to it or it belongs to him. The closer he looks, the further meaning retreats. Camus's account of the absurd captures Qohelet's experience:

> A world that can be explained even with bad reasons is a familiar world. But, on the other hand, in a universe suddenly divested of illusions and lights, man feels an alien, a stranger. His exile is without remedy since he is deprived of the memory of a lost home or the hope of a promised land.

Why did Qohelet fail? Another clue: "While adding one thing to another to find the scheme of things—which my soul has sought repeatedly, but I have not found." Qohelet here reminds us of his method. He sought the big picture by adding up all the little pictures he could perceive and analyze. He took in all he could and took it all as far as he could. Each time, as the intercom crackled the announcement that the train of thought had reached its destination, he stepped out and greeted vanishing vapor. The judgment Qohelet renders here is not that all things are senseless but that his method is futile. The light from his headlamp of autonomous reason could not discover any far-off framing peaks of coherence. For all he knew, no answers towered in the distance; there was just a desert plain of frustration stretching farther than any eye can see.

Qohelet's confession that his autonomous quest for wisdom is a failure sheds needed light on this passage's two statements about a woman. Qohelet tells us that he sought both wisdom and folly. And what did he find? We know he didn't find wisdom. Instead, he found "something more bitter than death: the woman whose heart is snares and nets." And then he tells us he found one man among a thousand, but not one woman. Rather than betraying naked misogyny or alluding to sexual misconduct, as some suggest, both statements evoke the literary trope, evident in the biblical book of Proverbs, of folly and wisdom personified as women who beckon suitors. The woman Qohelet failed to find is Lady Wisdom; the one he did find, Dame Folly. Qohelet didn't find the answers he wanted, but he did find that all people are fundamentally flawed: "God made man upright, but they have sought out many schemes."

A little later, Qohelet again reflects on his quest's findings:

> When I applied my heart to know wisdom, and to see the business that is done on earth, how neither day nor night do one's eyes see sleep, then I saw all the work of God, that man cannot find out the work that is done under the sun. However much man may toil in seeking, he will not find it out. Even though a wise man claims to know, he cannot find it out.

It isn't that we can know nothing but that we can't know what we most want to know. We can't know that key or lens or code that would make sense of everything. What knowledge can guarantee that I'll succeed or that my life will make sense or that I'll be happy? What insight can reveal how everything in this world and in my life fits together to make some kind of sensible picture? The world-elephant is too vast and coy for any of us to infer tusk from trunk or ear from tail. Anyone who says they can is lying.

Still, wisdom is better than folly. In a nontrivial sense, wisdom makes its bearer better. Wisdom prepares persuasive rebukes, protects its agent from self-sabotage, and infuses strength greater than that of weapons. Yet wisdom is vulnerable, even weak. Wisdom is exposed to the bad bounces of fate: "Again I saw that under the sun the race is not to the swift, nor the battle to the strong, nor bread to the wise, nor riches to the intelligent, nor favor to those with knowledge, but time and chance happen to them all." Wisdom is also powerless before the fickle and forgetful court of public opinion.

> I have also seen this example of wisdom under the sun, and it seemed great to me. There was a little city with few men in it, and a great king came against it and besieged it, building great siegeworks against it. But there was found in it a poor, wise man, and he by his wisdom delivered the city. Yet no one remembered that poor man. But I say that wisdom is better than might, though the poor man's wisdom is despised and his words are not heard.

This obscure wise man averted disaster. His wisdom saved lives. So did he get a nice reward? A free house, a fat pension? No: He was forgotten. No degree, no patent, no knowledge-powered contribution to the common good can guarantee that you'll be recognized, rewarded, or remembered.

Wisdom is also liable to be outweighed by even the smallest quantity of sin and folly: "Wisdom is better than weapons of war, but one sinner destroys much good. . . . Dead flies make the perfumer's ointment give off a stench; so a little folly outweighs wisdom and honor." It takes only one hair in the salad to ruin your appetite, one sharp word to ruin a friendship, and one sold secret to ruin years of work. Wisdom is mightier than weapons, but stupidity is mightier still. It doesn't deserve to, but wisdom loses. No heap of knowledge or stack of degrees can guarantee that you will win life.

▪ ▪ ▪

Hardly a weekday goes by that one of my kids doesn't say something like, "Why do I have to learn all this stuff at school? It's never gonna be useful." Just this morning, while my wife and I were trying to usher him out the door at 7:48 A.M., our eight-year-old son reiterated the verdict, then added, "The only stuff I like learning about is in science. Or at recess."

Teachers often mark and mourn the difference between extrinsic and intrinsic motivation. Many students seem to respond only to the stick of bad grades (if that) or the carrot of college prospects. But sometimes, on rare, redeeming occasions, a student will simply incandesce. The subject or skill under study ignites a light within, and the student glows with energy, attention, creativity, joy, confidence. Something deep in the subject speaks to something deep in the student. What they want is not to get something for themselves out of the class but to keep digging themselves deeper into the subject.

What knowledge lights and warms you? Knowledge of what person or place, what subject or skill or way of life? Happiness comes not from using knowledge as a crowbar to pry open the future but from devoting yourself to the knowledge that is inherently worth knowing.

▪ ▪ ▪

What edge do you want knowledge to give you? It might not be more money you want but less illness, not more status but less suffering. What kind of knowledge can help?

People don't always want what they should want. Certainly people don't always want what we want them to want. Impersonal forces—market trends, stomach cells—obey us even less. Whatever edge knowledge promises it can't guarantee. At best it can help your odds.

Qohelet would endorse the judgment of political philosopher Jason Blakely: "No predictive science of human behavior is possible." The skill of living is not a natural science: Antecedent conditions do not predict consequent conditions. Human creative faculties intervene in an infinite variety of prediction-fouling ways. Yet still we strain for any fingerhold on the smooth face of chance, trusting most those strategies that come clothed in science. Blakely states, "What methods hold out is the promise of forcing people and circumstances into predictable outcomes. In the self-help literature and popular press this is expressed in endless lists of scientifically validated 'steps' necessary for achieving a vast variety of life goals." Neither the wisdom of a sage nor an Ivy League diploma can channel life's chaos into a series of predictable preferred outcomes. No knowledge can turn your life into a machine for delivering desired returns.

5

Pleasure

Much of life is lived in the gap between yearning and satisfaction. You want something but don't have it. Not yet anyway. But then you get it, and it turns out you want something else.

Simone Weil saw this: "Man's great affliction, which begins with infancy and accompanies him till death, is that looking and eating are two different operations." To see is not to be satisfied. Between longing and enjoyment lie long miles and many exits. When you arrive at enjoyment, whether after minutes or years, the desired destination often fails to deliver. Weil states, "That which we look at here below is not real, it is a mere setting. That which we eat is destroyed, it is no longer real." The eaten cake may no longer be had. Consumed, the desired good turns out to be not substance but a shadow thrown by a source you can't see.

■ ■ ■

One way to measure pleasure's depth is to dive in and hit bottom. Another is to listen to the diver tell his tale as he drips dry and tapes gauze to his forehead. Qohelet found pleasure's floor the hard way. Here's his tale.

"I said in my heart, 'Come now, I will test you with pleasure; enjoy yourself.' But behold, this also was absurd. I said of laughter, 'It is mad,' and of pleasure, 'What use is it?'" This stage of Qohelet's quest follows his discovery that wisdom produces pain. Perhaps the pursuit of pleasure will turn up some more obvious good. The directive guiding Qohelet's inquiry is "enjoy yourself," or, to render the Hebrew idiom more literally, "see good." By "see," he means what Weil means by "eating": to know the good not from without but by filling oneself with it. Just after announcing his plan, he offers an executive summary of its key finding: "This also was absurd." He finds laughter and pleasure equally senseless and useless.

Having published the headline, Qohelet provides the details, first in general: "I searched with my heart how to cheer my body with wine—my heart still guiding me with wisdom—and how to lay hold on folly, till I might see what was good for the children of man to do under heaven during the few days of their life." In his inquiry into pleasure's value, Qohelet used wine not for drunkenness but sustenance. Qohelet sought to answer this question: Can pleasure grant the good life?

Thus provisioned, Qohelet launches his investigation of the possibilities of pleasure:

> I made great works. I built houses and planted vineyards for myself. I made myself gardens and parks, and planted in them all kinds of fruit trees. I made myself pools from which to water the forest of growing trees. I bought male and female slaves, and had slaves who were born in my house. I had also

> great possessions of herds and flocks, more than any who had been before me in Jerusalem. I also gathered for myself silver and gold and the treasure of kings and provinces. I gathered singers, both men and women, and those human luxuries, a fine wine-table and settings.
>
> So I became great and surpassed all who were before me in Jerusalem. Also my wisdom remained with me.

Qohelet's prior declaration of purpose shows that this whole vast project falls under the master category of pleasure. His architectural feats and agricultural achievements, his thriving businesses and the fruits they bore, literal and metaphorical, are entrées heading a long menu of pleasures. Other delicacies he savored include unprecedented wealth, exotic possessions, and skilled musicians on retainer.

Qohelet had increased his share of the world beyond anyone else's mark. He had all he could want, all you could want, all anyone could want. He denied himself no satisfaction he could obtain from any of it: "And whatever my eyes desired I did not keep from them. I kept my heart from no pleasure, for my heart found pleasure in all my toil, and this was my reward for all my toil." In Weil's terms, Qohelet made every effort to turn seeing into eating. He did not postpone pleasure for far-off retirement. Instead, he consumed enjoyments as soon as they drew within reach, scarfing each prize fresh from the oven of his work.

But after each course Qohelet's stomach growled again. Eventually the growling grew so loud it was all he could hear. "Then I considered all that my hands had done and the toil I had expended in doing it, and behold, all was absurd and a striving after wind, and there was nothing to be gained under the sun." Why did all this eating leave him empty? Shouldn't achievement plus acquisition plus enjoyment equal a good life?

Pleasure's goalposts always move. You think that this relationship or that new food or this much more money will finally make you happy, but then you get it, and it doesn't. In a recent survey, Americans across a vast range of income brackets consistently reported that they would need to earn between 30 percent and 50 percent more to feel happy. The person who earns $50,000 says he'd be happy with $75,000. The person who earns $75,000 says he'd be happy with $100,000. And on and up it goes.

As we've seen, another reason Qohelet finds pleasure insufficient is that even if it lasts, he won't. The wind will blow away; the vapor will dissolve. Yet the lack of leftover gain can't be all that troubles Qohelet. Otherwise, why declare defeat amid such victory? Why not give himself fully to pleasure as long as pleasure will give itself to him?

Further, death doesn't answer the question Qohelet asks. His radar is set to detect "what was good for the children of man to do under heaven during the few days of their life." Even on those terms, pleasure does not qualify. There is something Qohelet finds culpably absent in each pleasure and in his whole project of maximizing pleasure. Something isn't there that would have to be there for pleasure to count as the good we should embrace and imbibe. Pleasure won't fill you; it always needs to be refilled.

Elsewhere Qohelet gives more reasons why pleasure is an insufficient plot in which to grow a good life. "There is an evil that I have seen under the sun, and it lies heavy on mankind: a man to whom God gives wealth, possessions, and honor, so that he lacks nothing of all that he desires, yet God does not give him power to enjoy them, but a stranger enjoys them. This is absurd; it is a grievous evil." Qohelet is not speaking of situations where untimely death keeps someone from enjoying what they've worked for. His point is wider and scarier: Possessing all that should produce pleasure does not guarantee pleasure. Having everything you could possibly enjoy does not mean you will enjoy any of it. Like having pine needles, twigs, and crisp logs but nothing to light them, you could have a perfect house, piles of money, and impeccable prestige but get no warmth from any of it. What good is a Michelin-starred meal if you have no taste buds? Some who get one lack the other.

Here Qohelet speaks the very words of Weil: The phrase translated "power to enjoy" is literally "authority to eat." More strictly, then: "But God does not allow him to eat of it." Looking—acquiring, amassing, possessing, protecting—is not eating.

Qohelet then works a variation on this scenario, extending and intensifying it:

> If a man fathers a hundred children and lives many years, so that the days of his years are many, but his soul is not satisfied with life's good things, and he also has no burial, I say that a stillborn child is better off than he. For, though it comes in absurdity and goes in darkness, and in darkness its name is covered, and though it has not seen the sun or known anything, yet it finds rest rather than he. Even though he should live a thousand years twice over, yet enjoy no good—do not all go to the one place?

Qohelet paints a picture of a man who embodies the ancient Near Eastern ideal of a good life, at least in terms of objective, external goods—long life and a staggeringly large number of offspring. Yet with these abundant goods "his soul is not satisfied." He looks but cannot eat. The huge quantities in the plus column are all canceled by this single subjective lack. By contrast, the stillborn child is introduced with a stark sequence of privations whose oppressive weight is suddenly lifted by the surprising conclusion that "it finds rest rather than he." The patriarch full of days has everything but rest; the stillborn child has nothing yet has rest. Clearly this man is an exceptional case. But Qohelet claims that the exceptional is unnervingly possible.

Desire can always outrun fulfillment. Desire can also detach from its object when you are on the brink of obtaining it, like a plane that nearly grazes the runway but then suddenly pulls up. You can always want something more or something else.

> All the toil of man is for his mouth, yet his appetite is not satisfied. For what advantage has the wise man over the fool? And what does the poor man have who knows how to conduct himself before the living? Better is the sight of the eyes than the wandering of the appetite: this also is absurd and a striving after wind.

Appetites are like cats who know when you've refilled their bowl; they always come back. But what comes back is lack. What returns is demand holding up a badge emblazoned with gold-lettered "need." To satisfy an appetite does not satisfy it. It returns with strength undiminished, its rap on the door just as loud.

Like mind and heart, the appetite is prone to wander. Biblical scholar Michael Fox distills the contrast:

> If we are enjoying a good meal with friends, this is a "sight of the eyes," and it is good. But if we start to think of other things we crave—a better cuisine, perhaps, or prestige, or success, or sex—we lose contact with the actual place and moment, and our soul departs, as it were, and wanders off to another, non-

existent place. Then the moment is depleted of meaning, and we have nothing.

Even with a meal set before you, looking can keep you from eating. There's always something else to look at. There's always something in you that wants something else.

■ ■ ■

All pleasures are not created equal. Some pleasures free; others enslave. Some pleasures dignify; others degrade. Do you know the difference? Does your life display the difference?

Some pleasures are like fire: In the right setting they are equally safe and satisfying, but outside their proper place and limit they devastate. Our culture has enthroned sex as master pleasure, but any pleasure elevated to monarch turns tyrannical. In the eyes of many, the only thing that counts as "sex positivity" is letting the fire have free run of the house.

Happiness comes not from being pleasure's servant but from making it yours.

6

Money

Stefan Thomas, a computer programmer who lives in San Francisco, has two guesses left to recall a password that, at the moment, is worth roughly $394 million. If he can remember it, the password will unlock a small hard drive called an IronKey. This hard drive contains private keys to a digital wallet holding 7,002 Bitcoins. Years ago, Thomas lost the paper on which he wrote the password to his IronKey. No IronKey, no access to Bitcoin wallet. No access to Bitcoin wallet, no $394 million. IronKey allows its users only ten password attempts before it seizes up and encrypts its contents forever. Thomas has tried eight of his most common passwords. None has worked. He said, "I would just lay in bed and think about it. Then I would go to the computer with some new strategy, and it wouldn't work, and I would be desperate again."

■ ■ ■

Qohelet had no such problem accessing the fortune he amassed. "I also gathered for myself silver and gold and the treasure of kings and provinces." He got as much money as he could want, and his money could get him anything he wanted. Qohelet is "*the* accumulator of all things in his society." Yet, as we've seen, having all he wanted left him wanting.

He was disgusted with the fact that he would have to hand the whole heap to an heir of uncertain merit. "I hated all my toil in which I toil under the sun, seeing that I must leave it to the man who will come after me, and who knows whether he will be wise or a fool? Yet he will be master of all for which I toiled and used my wisdom under the sun. This also is absurd."

In others' endless labor, Qohelet saw the insatiability of the love of money:

> Again, I saw an absurdity under the sun: one person who has no other, either son or brother, yet there is no end to all his toil, and his eyes are never satisfied with riches, so that he never asks, "For whom am I toiling and depriving myself of pleasure?" This also is absurd and an unhappy business.

The workaholic can never get enough work or money. No matter how big a pile he sees before him, it never looks big enough. No matter how great the sacrifices he makes in service of wealth, he never asks whether they're worth it.

What's true of the unsleeping workaholic is true, Qohelet says, of everyone who loves money. "He who loves money will not be satisfied with money, nor he who loves wealth with his income; this also is absurd." One reason money doesn't satisfy is that the bigger your pie, the more of it you see eaten away by retainers and taxes and repairs and inflation. "When goods increase, they increase who eat them, and what advantage has their owner but to see them with his eyes?" The more that is gained, the more people materialize who want some. Money multiplies false friends. The more wealth, the more likely its owner is to find him or herself watching it, and watching it diminish, rather than enjoying it. The more wealth you have, the less it seems you control. Instead, your wealth starts to control you, which brings in another reason why money doesn't satisfy.

More money is notorious for making more problems. "Sweet is the sleep of a laborer, whether he consumes little or much, but the surfeit of the rich will not let him sleep." The rich person is too full—whether his stomach with food or his mind with worries—to sleep. The more economically productive you are, the more others depend on you. If you employ ten people, that's good for you and them, until cash flow dries up and you have to make impossible choices. If you have an empire to maintain, someone can always break off a piece, and few empires are designed to survive dismemberment.

The more money and investments and property you have, the more they clamor for your attention and affection. Riches promise blessing but deliver burden. The more you have, the more you have to worry about. And the more you have to lose:

> There is a grievous evil that I have seen under the sun: riches were kept by their owner to his hurt, and those riches were lost in a bad venture. And he is father of a son, but he has nothing in his hand. As he came from his mother's womb he shall go again, naked as he came, and shall take nothing for his toil that he may carry away in his hand. This also is a grievous evil: just as he came, so shall he go, and what gain is there to him who toils for the wind?

There is no guarantee that you will keep all you earn. Markets crash; currencies deflate; goods depreciate; thieves plunder. And even if you keep it all, death ends all keeping.

Wealth is only good if you can enjoy it, and not everyone who has it can:

> There is an evil that I have seen under the sun, and it lies heavy on mankind: a man to whom God gives wealth, possessions, and honor, so that he lacks nothing of all that he desires, yet God does not give him power to enjoy them, but a stranger enjoys them. This is absurd; it is a grievous evil.

The lack here is not money or goods but enjoyment. Why? Qohelet doesn't say. There's simply a crucial component missing. Some part of the personal machinery that turns possession into pleasure is absent. Without it, no quantity of hoarded wealth can produce a single volt of joy.

"He who loves money will not be satisfied with money, nor he who loves wealth with his income; this also is absurd." Many bathtubs have a small hole two-thirds of the way up their faucet side. If you fill the tub too high, water will drain automatically. The tub won't let you overfill it and flood your house. Money is not like that tub. It has no built-in shut-off switch, no set stopping point. You can always get more, so you can always want more. The love of money is a treadmill and a trap. If your desired destination is more money, it will lie just beyond an ever-receding horizon.

■ ■ ■

Picture a savings account with your name on it. Pick a number between one and nine, then add as many zeroes pushing rightward as you wish. Is this number wealth? That depends on what you can do with it. The money is only a counter, a token, a ticket. You can't wear it, live in it, or eat it.

Money is a means, not an end. Since it is a medium of exchange, money is only as good as what it can get you. But in a modern market society, money can get you more and more, to the point where money can buy almost anything. The more money can buy, the more tempting it is to treat money as end rather than means. As Georg Simmel, a founding father of sociology and one of history's greatest theorists of money, put it over a hundred years ago,

> Thus—and this is very important—money becomes that absolute goal which it is possible in principle to strive for at any moment, in contrast to the constant goals, not all of which may be wanted or can be aspired to all the time. This provides the modern person with a continuing spur to activity; he now has a goal which appears as the *pièce de résistance* as soon as other goals give it space; it is potentially always there. That is the reason for the restlessness, feverishness, the unrelenting character of modern life, which is provided by money with the unremovable wheel that makes the machine of life a *perpetuum mobile.*

Money can always get you more, and you can always get more money. This world-encompassing hamster wheel is excruciatingly difficult to escape. Because so many people must devote so much of their lives to the immediate goal of acquiring money, "the notion arises that all happiness and all definitive satisfaction in life is firmly connected to the possession of a certain sum of money." Money thereby "grows inwardly from a mere means and a presupposition to an ultimate purpose." Almost inevitably, often imperceptibly, the means becomes the end.

In a modern market society, money is power. Money promises security and calm. The more money you have, the more problems you can either prevent or purchase your way out of. Money is an all-purpose rescue dog, the most versatile Swiss Army knife. As Hartmut Rosa observes, money "serves secularized capitalist society as a replacement for religion by taking the place of God as a *master of contingency.*" Money promises control, freedom from disaster, and freedom from worry. Money thus displaces God not only as highest good but as refuge in time of need.

This cosmic substitution follows from the prior exchange of means for end. Over two thousand years ago, Aristotle distinguished between an object's use value and its exchange value. A leather chair that you bought used for seventy-five dollars and could sell for even less means far more to you than the money you spent for it, or the money you could get for it, because of how comfortable it is to read in and how perfectly it fits in your living room. The chair's use value far exceeds its exchange value. Qohelet anticipates this distinction when he plows a wedge between having it all and enjoying any of it. Money's problem is that it is all exchange value and no use value. Yet, because it can be exchanged for almost anything, we are tempted to assign more value to money than to anything else, buyable or unbuyable. Money tricks us into treating it not as the means it can only ever be, but as an end—even the greatest end.

Simmel spotted this a hundred years ago: "This colonization of ends by means is one of the major features and main problems of any higher culture." As soon as someone invests money with ultimate value, money loses its only true, modest value. Money "is only the bridge to definitive values, and one cannot live on a bridge." A system in which you can purchase virtually anything from anyone anywhere wants to keep you wanting. As William Cavanaugh has put it, "In globalized capitalism, exchange value has overcome use value, and what is desired is desire itself."

One of money's cleverest tricks and most dangerous traps is that it masquerades as wealth. The two are so linked in modern minds that we often use one word to mean the other. If you think money is wealth, what do you think that wealth will do for you? What do you think it will do to you?

Money promises to bring more of the world within reach. Money offers to turn more of this world's treasures and joys into things you can treasure and enjoy. As Rosa observes, "The richer we are . . . the more the world is made available, attainable, and accessible to us." But the power of money that brings objects near also pushes people away. Byung-Chul Han sees this clearly: "Money, by itself, has an individualizing and isolating effect. It increases my freedom by liberating me from any personal bond with others." To hire someone to perform a task for you is to vacuum seal the relationship: Thus far shall you come, and no farther. The more your needs can be met by paying people to meet them, the less you have to need people. The more your money can command other people's time, the less liable you are to the unpredictable demands of reciprocity. The more money you have, the fewer friends you need—and, as Qohelet warns, the harder it is to tell who your friends are. Andy Crouch describes what life feels like when countless interactions are greased and buffered by money: "My life is full of convenience. It is full of transaction, at its best a mutually beneficial exchange of value, a kind of arm's-length benign use of one another for our own ends. But it is not full of contemplation. It is often efficient. But it is lonely." Money delivers lonely efficiency because wherever it governs, it replaces and prevents durable dependence on other persons. Crouch observes, "The distinctive thing that money allows us—its most seductive promise—is abundance without dependence."

■ ■ ■

Our four-year-old daughter, Margaret, has a bad cough. Thankfully, her symptoms signal nothing worse. Last night at 9:40, my wife texted our friend Rebekah to see if she had some medicine for the cough that we didn't have. We live in a church-owned house across from the church's building on the same city block; Rebekah lives with her husband, Josh, and their three school-aged children in a third-story apartment across the street. At 9:45, I met Rebekah on the steps of her apartment building to get the medicine. Not long after, Margaret was breathing better and cracking jokes.

Josh and Rebekah have not pursued a money-delivered life of lonely efficiency. They have built their life together neither around making as much money as possible nor on gaining all that money can get them. They have three kids and no yard. They live across the street from our church so that they can do things like share medicine with church members in need on short notice at night. Their lives, and ours, and those of dozens of others, are richer for it. Their goal is not abundance without dependence but a better abundance that comes through interdependence.

Happiness comes not from building a contingency-proof co-

coon of money around your life but from seeking and sharing what money can't secure. As Qohelet says, shortly after lamenting the plight of the lonely workaholic,

> Two are better than one, because they have a good reward for their toil. For if they fall, one will lift up his fellow. But woe to him who is alone when he falls and has not another to lift him up! Again, if two lie together, they keep warm, but how can one keep warm alone? And though a man might prevail against one who is alone, two will withstand him—a threefold cord is not quickly broken.

▪ ▪ ▪

Money and wealth are two, not one. Few have seen this as clearly as John Ruskin, the late nineteenth-century English art critic and philosopher. Ruskin distinguished between "wealth radiant and wealth reflective": True wealth is like the sun, having its own energy and vitality; money is, at best, a moon that reflects its source. Money can reflect much light of real wealth or none.

> Any given accumulation of commercial wealth may be indicative, on the one hand, of faithful industries, progressive energies, and productive ingenuities: or, on the other, it may be indicative of mortal luxury, merciless tyranny, ruinous chicane. Some treasures are heavy with human tears, as an ill-stored harvest with untimely rain; and some gold is brighter in sunshine than it is in substance.

For Ruskin, "money-gain" is "only the shadow of the true gain, which is humanity." True wealth is enjoyment, flourishing, the flowering of human abilities. You can have that wealth without much money, and you can have much money but not that wealth. You could possess everything yet have nothing worth the name "wealth."

> THERE IS NO WEALTH BUT LIFE. Life, including all its powers of love, of joy, and of admiration. That country is the richest which nourishes the greatest number of noble and happy human beings; that man is richest who, having perfected the functions of his own life to the utmost, has also the widest helpful influence, both personal, and by means of his possessions, over the lives of others.

Will your life spell out the conviction that the only life is wealth, or that the only wealth is life?

7

Time

Time flows in only one direction. Try to push time back up the hill, and it will surge around you, future ceaselessly churning into past. This river obeys not tides but gravity.

Time only flows. The purer the pain or pleasure, the closer time comes to standing still. But the eddy is only as wide as the feeling, and it soon lets out into the surge.

Time, like a river parched by drought, never seems full enough to do all you need, much less want. If time is a resource, it's scarce, far from renewable.

Time runs out. It takes a droplet of water three months to journey the length of the Mississippi from its source in Lake Itasca in northwestern Minnesota to its mouth in the Gulf. In just ninety days, the river runs out. The stream that drains half a continent keeps coursing, but the drop is done.

Are time's riverine traits a problem? That depends. It depends on whether you have ever wanted to redo a mistake or undo a tragedy. Whether you have ever longed to hold something precious longer than time's clawing hands will let you. Whether you have ever wanted more time—more now or more between now and the inevitable, final then.

Time is our native habitat. It's not like you can opt out. Time is as much a part of you as are hydrogen, oxygen, carbon, and nitrogen. Not only are you in time, but time is in you, from your heart's percussion to gray hairs that arrive like poverty—slowly, then all at once.

If we are creatures of time, why are we so ill at ease with time? Why are time's limits an insult? Why do we so seldom feel at home in the present? A child chafes all week at the confines of school and homework, straining for the weekend, then says at ten o'clock on Saturday morning, "I'm bored. There's nothing to do." You spend years training to attain some goal or get some job, and all you can think about once you get there is, *What's next?*

Four hundred years ago, Blaise Pascal diagnosed the disorder that detaches us from the present, divorcing us from the only time we have:

> Let each of us examine his thoughts; he will find them wholly concerned with the past or the future. We almost never think of the present, and if we do think of it, it is only to see what light it throws on our plans for the future. The present is never our end. The past and the present are our means, the future alone our end. Thus we never actually live, but hope to live, and since we are always planning how to be happy, it is inevitable that we should never be so.

■ ■ ■

> For everything there is a season, and a time for every matter under heaven:
>
> a time to be born, and a time to die;
> a time to plant, and a time to pluck up what is planted;
> a time to kill, and a time to heal;
> a time to break down, and a time to build up;
> a time to weep, and a time to laugh;
> a time to mourn, and a time to dance;
> a time to cast away stones, and a time to gather stones together;
> a time to embrace, and a time to refrain from embracing;
> a time to seek, and a time to lose;
> a time to keep, and a time to cast away;
> a time to tear, and a time to sew;
> a time to keep silence, and a time to speak;
> a time to love, and a time to hate;
> a time for war, and a time for peace.

Qohelet's poem of times has typically been interpreted in one of two ways. Neither quite captures the sense of the whole. One common reading is that the poem names the appropriate or opportune times at which to act. On this view, part of what makes an action right is proper timing, which wisdom teaches one to discern. One serious problem with this view is that in the first pair, the first item is an action over which we have no control, and the second is one which we should not seek to control. A second common interpretation is that the poem does not prescribe human action but describes divine action. God has ordained that, and when, each of these events will occur. This view fits snugly with Qohelet's comment a few verses later: "I perceived that whatever God does endures forever; nothing can be added to it, nor anything taken from it. God has done it, so that people fear before him." But this view does not go far enough. Qohelet has arranged this tapestry of human actions and passions into a carefully patterned picture. The pattern is the point.

What pattern? Given enough time, time will take back all it gives. Given enough line, time will reel back all it cast your way. Every blessing time brings will eventually make way for a burden. Time runs in only one direction, but it gives and takes equally. All its gifts are loans. Each of time's goods gets shoved off the shelf by its opposite. In all time's changes, the constant is the balance sheet's relentless homing in on zero. No profit stays put for long. Every action will sometime meet its equal and opposite. Once time finishes you, your final balance will perfectly match the zero you started with.

Sometimes time's substitutions are more welcome than any swap from the sidelines, as when peace succeeds war or dance dawns after mourning. There is beauty here, blessing and bounty. This ledger of time's loans marks many joys. The list is not all bad, but only half good.

However welcome one of time's guests may be, no stay is permanent. Each will leave and give their room to one whose very presence is an overstayed welcome. Whatever fullness time brings, time will empty out. And eventually, time will leave your house to you desolate. All time's forces converge and collapse on the same point: the null point, the point where it started, the point where it ends.

Why can't you keep to the present? Because time keeps taking away the time you love long before you're willing to let it go.

Why do you try to hurry up the future? Because you've had enough of being broken down and want to build.

Why do you try to stay the past's too-rapid flight? Because you miss its now-refraining embrace.

Why does the present usually hurt? Because time is killing you, and you yearn to heal.

■ ■ ■

In June of 2017, my family moved from Cambridge, England, where we had lived for nearly three years, back to Washington, D.C., which is a city we love. *Love* seems too weak a word for the feelings Cambridge sometimes slips under the skin of those who, for a time, live under its spell.

I don't collect many souvenirs, but I did bring back one from Cambridge. It's a white ceramic coffee mug that lives on the desk in my office, a few inches back from the rear left corner of my laptop. The side facing me bears a two-tone print, black and aqua, of an artist's rendering of the glowing storefront of Fitzbillies, a central Cambridge bakery and café famous for its cinnamon-butter-filled Chelsea buns. The first time I used the mug, I placed a tea bag inside, filled it with near-boiling water, and then placed the mug on my desk. A pool of hot water slowly spread, seeping out from below. A crack had sliced clear across its base, rounded the corner, and spread from bottom to rim.

A few months after that mug cracked, we took a road trip to visit my in-laws for Thanksgiving. I packed our full complement of coffee gear, including a mug I had recently retrieved from storage. This mug wore the logo of Peregrine, our superb local coffee shop. It had a wide, insulated base, perfect for steady desktop fueling. After a thirteen-hour drive from D.C. to Murfreesboro, Tennessee, I opened our minivan's liftgate. From its hidden, and now shifted, perch atop a mound of suitcases and supplies, the Peregrine mug tumbled at me and past me, landing lip-down on the rough cement driveway. Too many breaks to mend; pieces too small and scattered. After our trip, I asked Peregrine's staff about that model of mug. None of them recognized my description. They don't make it anymore. Haven't for years.

A time to keep, a time to lose, and a time to lose even the memento that tied you to the memory of what you lost. Eventually, a time to lose even the memory. Time equally takes and gives, and time never promises to give back anything it takes.

▪ ▪ ▪

After hanging his time tapestry on the wall, Qohelet steps back, eyes the whole, and asks a question that naggingly, necessarily follows. "What gain has the worker from his toil?" Qohelet seems to ask this not for his sake but for ours, since he already knows the answer. Every line's sum is zero, so the whole thing can only total nothing. This is no snap judgment or partial reckoning; Qohelet has watched the whole show clear to the end of the credits. "I have seen the business that God has given to the children of man to be busy with." However busily you go about your business, no dividend will follow you out of this life.

Yet, within the frame that time fixes, each plus and minus has its assemblage of graces, its properties that please. "He has made everything beautiful in its time." Every time bears some trace of God's beauty. But none of the glory we glimpse through time's latticework of giving and taking delivers anything like the big picture we crave. "Also, he has put eternity into man's heart, yet so that he cannot find out what God has done from the beginning to the end." God has made us cosmic misfits. He has put something in us that is bigger than anything around us. No polar bear wakes up in the morning and asks, "Why am I here?" No bottlenose dolphin weighs whether to prefer non-existence.

God has planted in us a vastness that spawns yearning, seeking, searching. The eternity within renders us not serene but restless. It is not fullness but a void more immense than our still-expanding cosmos. This inner chasm leaves us longing for an understanding as big as our desire, but our sight lines stop at the edges of time's frame. God's work starts long before and ends long after the snippet that time lets us glimpse.

Your life is a tapestry, but you get to see only the reverse side. You find frayed ends of threads and glimpse muffled blurs. Only the Weaver sees the picture. With eternity gnawing at us from the inside, we yearn to have more, hold more, see more, and know more than time will allow. As Annie Dillard sees,

> Time is the continuous loop, the snakeskin with scales endlessly overlapping without beginning or end, or time is an ascending spiral if you will, like a child's toy Slinky. Of course we have no idea which arc on the loop is our time, let alone where the loop itself is, so to speak, or down whose lofty flight of stairs the Slinky so uncannily walks.

Qohelet knows whose stairs the Slinky cartwheels down, but he remains as bereft as Dillard of the view he seeks. When he pulls back to take in as much as he can, all he sees is more of the same: "I perceived that whatever God does endures forever; nothing can be added to it, nor anything taken from it. God has done it, so that people fear before him. That which is, already has been; that which is to be, already has been; and God seeks what has been driven away." God writes time in permanent marker, leaving us no chance to erase or revise. Why? So that we will come to discern the infinite difference between author and characters. So that we will come to consider history not a tale told by an idiot but the steady, inscrutable handwriting of the living God.

Next Qohelet returns to the theme of return; he repeats repetition. He tells us nothing new by telling us there's nothing new. What has "been driven away"? That which time's latest offering shoves off its seat. Time is a perpetual game of musical chairs with only two participants: Whoever lost their seat last gets it back next. Mourn, dance; keep silence, speak; love, hate; war, peace. God propels time's cycles, ceaselessly pushing the merry-go-round around again.

▪ ▪ ▪

Time crunches and crushes; time flees; time spreads and stretches like dough rolled too thin. Neither a middle-aged, working-class single mother nor a glamorous young management consultant has anything like "enough time," but for starkly different reasons.

One of the cleanest ways to slice modernity open is to ask what we have done to time and what time does to us. In the times (and places) we call modern, the object that most defines our relationship to time is the clock. Not the sun or moon, not the earth itself in its yearly seasonal spin, but a device that divides days into equal hours, hours into equal minutes, minutes into equal seconds, and, if desired, seconds into equal infinitely divisible segments. The farther you go and the faster you move, the more crucial it is to move in measurable sync with whoever is wherever you're going. In the late nineteenth century, more and quicker and farther travel, especially by rail, created pressure to globally standardize timekeeping, culminating in the International Meridian Conference in 1884, which established the Greenwich meridian as a common zero of longitude and a worldwide standard of time reckoning. Since then, the clock's domain has only grown.

The clock catechizes us to manage time, like money, as a scarce resource. Under the clock's reign, time must be tracked, monitored, regulated, organized, and saved. Time is a commodity; in the right conditions, time and money are convertible. As Hartmut Rosa observes, in our modern market society, time, like money, is always scarce. Just like money, you can lose time, waste it, save it, and spend it. If you have time but lack money, you can spend time to get money. If you have money but lack time, you can spend money to buy time, like by ordering takeout or hiring cleaners. But there are limits to how money and time can be exchanged: If you're unemployed, your time's supply painfully exceeds demand. And there's no way to bank time and make it pay interest in the future. Ultimately, you can't save time; you can only choose how you spend it. Rosa's point was anticipated by the eminent senior sociologist Jerry Seinfeld:

> We all try and save time.
> All our little shortcuts.
> But no matter how much time you save,
> at the end of your life, there's no extra time saved up.
> You'll be going,
> "What do you mean I'm out of time?
> I had a no-iron shirt,
> Velcro sneakers,
> clip-on tie:
> Where is that time?"

It's not there.

Because when you waste time in life, they subtract it.

The modern world has not only clocked time but contracted it. Moral norms and values, romantic relationships, jobs, technologies, household goods, means of production—these all change quicker than they used to, and many change at rates that continually speed up. The present isn't what it used to be.

Modernity is subject to what philosopher Hermann Lübbe has called "the contraction of the present." The more quickly shared practices and values change, the shorter the time "over which we can look back without seeing a world alien to our trusted present-day lifeworld." The quicker the present changes, the sooner the past looks unrecognizably strange. The quicker the present changes, the sooner you will no longer be at home in it. The more the present contracts, the sooner your skills and values and you yourself become obsolete.

In lives molded by modernity, our tools, skills, possessions, and promises have increasingly short shelf lives. All that is present decays ever more rapidly into the unfertile compost of the past.

What does this clocked, contracted time do to us? It tricks us and traps us. The more you try to master time, the more time masters you. In the modern West, time feels like an unstoppable conveyor belt, bringing you new tasks as fast as you finish the old ones. Speed up your pace, and the belt speeds up too. Respond to that email, and three more appear in reply. Try to detach from your phone, and when you pick it up you have twelve texts to answer. Hand in that assignment on time, and the next time around your boss gives you two to do in the time you took for one.

Productivity is a trap. The more efficient you become, the faster tasks fly at you and the more rushed and anxious you feel. (In the words of Lucy to Ethel, as the conveyor belt slings chocolates at them: "I think we're fighting a losing game!") This clocked, contracted time constantly presses us, leaving even the most successful feeling time-poor. Many surveys indicate that present-day Americans, for instance, feel more harried, anxious, and time squeezed than they used to. On average, Americans have at least as much leisure time as ever, yet feel more harried than ever. Some scholars call this contradiction the "time-pressure paradox." Rosa's description of it shows a Qohelet-and-Seinfeld-like eye for irony:

> One very curious but consistent fact about late modern life is that almost irrespective of their values, status and moral commitments, subjects feel notoriously short on time and tirelessly pressed to hurry. . . . Individuals from Rio to New York, from Los Angeles to Moscow and Tokio feel caught in a rat-race of daily routines. No matter how fast they run, they close their day as *subjects of guilt:* they almost never succeed in working off their *to-do lists.* Thus, even and especially if they have enough money and wealth, they are indebted temporally. This is what perhaps characterizes the everyday predicament of the overwhelming majority of subjects in Westernised capitalist societies most aptly: amidst monetary and technological affluence, they are close to temporal insolvency.

A time to work, and a time to rest, but even at rest, work's demands crowd in and claw away. A time to work, but never enough. A time to rest, but you have to keep telling work to be quiet and go away.

■ ■ ■

Happiness comes not from trying to freeze time's flow but from receiving its limits. Say you have a young daughter. You feel buried under tedium and drained by demand. This evening, when you lie on the floor next to her bed to help her fall asleep, say to yourself, "She'll never be this young again."

■ ■ ■

Qohelet often treats time as the medium in which everything happens, the paper on which your whole life is printed. He also uses *time* to mean something we know will happen but we know not when. Sometimes, though, by *time* he means the last page, the edge where life runs out. "Be not overly wicked, neither be a fool. Why should you die before your time? . . . For man does not know his time. Like fish that are taken in an evil net, and like birds that are caught in a snare, so the children of man are snared at an evil time, when it suddenly falls upon them." If time will run out, so that *time* names both whole and end, then time is also a series of ends before the end, each end a preview.

In her poem "Lost and Found," A. E. Stallings sends the protagonist on a dreaming search through the moon's mythical valley of lost things. Her guide, the goddess of memory, points to a roomful of items in the valley's permanent collection:

> "Look there," she said, and gestured to the keys,
> "Those are the halls to which we can't return—
> The rooms where we once sat on others' knees,
> Grandparents' houses, loving, spare, and stern,
> Tree houses where we whispered to the trees

> Gauche secrets, virgin bedrooms where we'd burn,
> Love's first apartments. As we shut each door,
> It locks: we cannot enter anymore."

A time to open and a time to shut. You won't always know when it happens, but, sooner or later, every door shuts for good. In the end, all doors prove self-locking.

In the end, every paradise gets lost. If doors can lock themselves, hills can rearrange themselves and rivers drain through unfamiliar folds. The ancient Chinese poet Wang Wei tells a tale of some who discover a hidden paradise, the source of a stream that flowed with peach blossoms. They find peaceful people, a fertile valley: "To live here would be fulfillment." So they return home in order to bring their families back to settle there. Again they leave home behind, setting off "with packs on our backs" to seek "the place where the peach blossoms fell." But,

> We could not find it. Somehow the hills were
> Not the same. No such river where we thought.
> Back and forth we made a search, back and forth
> But nothing. Different streams, different lands.
> That place in space was a moment in time:
> You can never find your way back.

8

Enough

Between roughly 2007 and today, hundreds of millions of people have developed habits that, by widely accepted measures, qualify as addictions. The addictive substance is not OxyContin or fentanyl but a small rectangular glass screen. Such screens have become portals not only to all the music ever recorded and every book ever printed, not only to practically infinite streams of news and entertainment, but, most crucially, to games and hits of social stimulation engineered to keep us craving more.

Some software designers openly acknowledge that they aim to addict. Nir Eyal, an expert in "behavioral engineering," has advocated the development of programs that aim to turn customers into addicts via a hook model: a looping cycle of trigger, action, variable reward, and continued investment. Unlike a garden-variety feedback loop, the hook model can create a craving. Once an app creates a craving through repeatedly exposing its user to some pleasure, what draws a user back is, as Eyal says, "not the sensation we receive from the reward itself, but the need to alleviate the craving for that reward." One software design company that employs Eyal's methods promises the power to predictably change users' behaviors. The company recently changed their name to Boundless Mind. Matt Feeney reports, "Its original name was the majestically cynical 'Dopamine Labs,' after the brain chemical that drives compulsive and addictive behavior cycles." If you want to create an addictive product, what matters more than satisfaction is craving. The key to a supercharged feedback loop is not pleasure but desire.

▪ ▪ ▪

"All things are full of weariness; a man cannot utter it; the eye is not satisfied with seeing, nor the ear filled with hearing." Qohelet is saying that, for our sensory organs, everything is never enough. Neither eye nor ear—nor hand touching, nose scenting, or tongue tasting—can be satisfied.

Why not describe our senses as neutral instruments of detection, ready when needed but making no demands? Qohelet attributes to the body's receptive faculties insatiable desire. Why? To answer, we need to retread ground Qohelet has led us through and refresh our memory of characters we have already met.

> Again, I saw an absurdity under the sun: one person who has no other, either son or brother, yet there is no end to all his toil, and his eyes are never satisfied with riches, so that he never asks, "For whom am I toiling and depriving myself of pleasure?" This also is absurd and an unhappy business.

This person has no one to work for, yet he never stops working. He doesn't even slow down enough to ask why he willingly enslaves himself to his work. What keeps him spinning his hamster wheel? "His eyes are never satisfied with riches." He is insatiable. His gains will never match his desires. "He who loves money will not be satisfied with money, nor he who loves wealth with his income; this also is absurd." The problem with money isn't money but the heart that wants it. If you want money for money's sake, you'll always keep wanting.

Remember Qohelet's man who had everything he could desire? Objectively, he had it all: "wealth, possessions, and honor." He fathered a hundred children and lived many decades. Subjectively, he suffered from a fatal lack. God did not "give him power to enjoy" what he had, so "his soul is not satisfied with life's good things." This man's only possible source of dissatisfaction lies within. Everything outside is perfect; his only lack is his innate insatiability. In one crucial respect, a stillborn child is better off than him, since the stillborn has rest. Rest is the one thing this fabulously fortunate man lacks. Not rest from hard labor or grating conflicts but psychological rest. Rest where the heart says "enough" and means it. The kind of rest Augustine said we all lack, when he confessed in prayer: "You have made us for yourself, and our hearts are restless until they rest in you." Our innate insatiability commits a compound fraud: It keeps us restlessly striving and blocks pleasure in what's present. If you always want more, you never enjoy what you have.

These two characters are certainly exceptional. Qohelet does not mean that every human being is a workaholic or is fabulously wealthy yet miserable. Instead, he introduces these exceptional characters to caricature the universal. Innate insatiability is not unique to them but belongs to all who have eyes and ears. Every human being has appetites that outstrip the world's ability to fulfill. As Benjamin Storey and Jenna Silber Storey observe, "No psychic equilibrium is possible for a being whose desires so radically outstrip his possibilities. Misery follows ineluctably from an honest estimate of the gap between what we want and what we are."

"All the toil of man is for his mouth, yet his appetite is not satisfied. . . . Better is the sight of the eyes than the wandering of the appetite: this also is absurd and a striving after wind." Here Qohelet treats hunger as a paradigm for humanity's innate insatiability. One could almost say that humans don't have appetites; we are appetite. Our appetite is like an industrial garbage disposal that's always running: No matter what you throw into it, after absurdly quick digestion, its gullet will gape, empty as ever.

Maybe you'll be different. Maybe the problem with your appetite isn't innate, you just haven't yet found the right fruit to bite. Maybe your heart isn't insatiable but has simply not yet discovered the thing that will satisfy with no disappointment. If you knock on enough doors, eventually one will open that will leave you lacking nothing. Pascal says the evidence on that hypothesis has already come in, namely, the experience of everyone else who has ever lived.

> A test which has gone on so long, without pause or change, really ought to convince us that we are incapable of attaining the good by our own efforts. But example teaches us very little. No two examples are so exactly alike that there is not some subtle difference, and that is what makes us expect that our expectations will not be disappointed this time as they were last time. So, while the present never satisfies us, experience deceives us, and leads us on from one misfortune to another until death comes as the ultimate and eternal climax.

▪ ▪ ▪

"He has made everything beautiful in its time. Also, he has put eternity into man's heart, yet so that he cannot find out what God has done from the beginning to the end." The problem with stuffing the vastness of eternity into the cramped compartment of the human heart is that it doesn't fit. What God has put inside us guarantees an enduring mismatch between what we want and what this world can give.

The eternity within does not satisfy but renders us innately insatiable. Old Testament scholar Eric Ortlund observes that this innate insatiability explains why Qohelet fruitlessly strives for gain that time won't obliterate: "If there were no echo in the human heart of some transcendent reality, why would it occur to Qohelet to strive after some enduring memorial which time and death cannot touch?" The human heart is pierced with a hole that lets in the infinite. That is why all the finite goods that our toil gains fail to satisfy.

But you don't experience this infinite gap between what you want and what you have merely as an always-failing aspiration, something just out of reach ahead of you. Instead, it sneaks up behind you. It haunts you like the ghost of a lost bliss. It scars your heart's landscape like the ruins of a vanished kingdom. It harasses you like a benchmark you can't help but evaluate your happiness by. The eternity that gapes within is like a memory of something that never happened but that you still can't forget.

Many astute students of the heart, including secularists, Jewish thinkers, and Christians, have described this innate insatiability as a species of nostalgia. What we yearn for, somehow, is not just a satisfaction we've never yet had but a fullness we've irrecoverably lost. Giorgio de Chirico titled a painting, "The Nostalgia of the Infinite." The philosopher Jeffrey Gordon identifies the absurd disconnect between what we yearn for and what the world provides:

> Capable of feelings that embrace all mankind, the world, all the Cosmos, we crave contact with the Whole, with all the time unfurling before us, with all the space of the galaxies; and though this is not a constant craving, the most profoundly moving moments of our lives—whatever their earthly occasion—are marked by this nostalgia for the infinite.

From this infinite gap between what we crave and what the world yields, Pascal infers, "What else does this craving, and this helplessness, proclaim but that there was once in man a true happiness, of which all that now remains is the empty print and trace?" C. S. Lewis describes the helpless craving: "The sense that in this universe we are treated as strangers, the longing to be acknowledged, to meet with some response, to bridge some chasm that yawns between us and reality, is part of our inconsolable secret." And he names a "lifelong nostalgia, our longing to be reunited with something in the universe from which we now feel cut off." As we have heard Michael Chabon say, in the excerpt that opened the body of the book, this huge world is so stuffed with marvels that it takes years for most people to discover that "it is, also, irretrievably broken." "Broken" implies original wholeness. Chabon's inquirer discovers that "the world has been broken for as long as anyone can remember, and struggles to reconcile this fact with the ache of cosmic nostalgia that arises, from time to time, in the researcher's heart: an intimation of vanished glory, of lost wholeness, a memory of the world unbroken."

Any of Chabon's painfully poignant phrases could serve as a poetic gloss on Ecclesiastes 3:11. What has God put into the human heart? An ache of cosmic nostalgia, an intimation of vanished glory, a memory of the world unbroken. Pascal, Lewis, and Chabon all concur with Qohelet: This feeling haunts people all their lives.

■ ■ ■

Happiness comes not from trying to make this world satisfy all your desires but from realizing that it never will. Happiness begins to glimpse new dimensions when you discover that everything is never enough.

9

Power

In October 2004, political philosopher Michael Ignatieff was happily teaching at Harvard. Then one night, three men in black suits arrived from Toronto to take Ignatieff and his wife out to dinner. The three "men in black"—two lawyers and a filmmaker who was the son of a Liberal Party campaign manager—asked Ignatieff if he would consider returning to his native Canada and running for a seat in Parliament.

The Liberal Party was then in power, so Ignatieff asked if the prime minister, Paul Martin, had sent them. Not exactly. They were acting on their own initiative, proposing a "run from outside." The men in black were dissatisfied with the party's direction and leader. They would find Ignatieff a seat to run for and help him win it. Not only that, but they hoped eventually to make him prime minister. At the end of the evening, Ignatieff told them only that he would think about it. But within a few months, he bit.

In January 2006, Ignatieff won his seat but the Liberal Party lost their majority. After a failed bid that year, in 2009 Ignatieff was endorsed as party leader. In 2011 he introduced a motion of nonconfidence against the current government in an effort to force a federal election. The motion narrowly passed, and Ignatieff hit the campaign trail. Though he didn't realize it until far too late, and the experts didn't see it coming, from the start the Conservative Party outmaneuvered him. Ignatieff and his party didn't just lose; they lost spectacularly. The Liberal Party lost forty-three seats, their worst defeat ever and the worst result in Canadian history for an incumbent Official Opposition party. Ignatieff lost his own seat to a Conservative challenger. He announced his resignation from party leadership the next day. In just five years, Ignatieff's political career lit, blazed, and turned to ash. How did that feel?

> There were times when I felt I was shaping and moulding events, other times when I watched helplessly as events slipped out of my control; I knew moments of exaltation when I thought I might be able to do great things for the people, and now I live with the regret that I will never be able to do anything at all.

▪ ▪ ▪

Michael Ignatieff is a theorist, and was a practitioner, of political power. Qohelet, too, was both. He was "king over Israel in Jerusalem," and he often cast a critical gaze on power's pincers. When Qohelet considers political power's operations and effects, he often sees its gears squeezing those it should've served. "Moreover, I saw under the sun that in the place of justice, even there was wickedness, and in the place of righteousness, even there was wickedness. I said in my heart, God will judge the righteous and the wicked, for there is a time for every matter and for every work." Here Qohelet watches the courts in which disputes are judged. In the place where justice should hold court, injustice sits instead. The place you go to get a wrong righted deals out more wrong. Qohelet confesses that injustice will not speak last, but for now it shouts down the rights of the downtrodden.

> Again I saw all the oppressions that are done under the sun. And behold, the tears of the oppressed, and they had no one to comfort them! On the side of their oppressors there was power, and there was no one to comfort them. And I thought the dead who are already dead more fortunate than the living who are still alive. But better than both is he who has not yet been and has not seen the evil deeds that are done under the sun.

As so often in Ecclesiastes, Qohelet merely observes. He does not justify or defend oppression. Neither does he say, "Therefore, go save the world." Unlike many of us who are fortunate to enjoy large measures of freedom and prosperity, Qohelet refuses to ignore oppression. Whether or not Qohelet could have ignored injustice if he chose, many have no choice. Qohelet's "better than both" might sound extreme to you, but it wouldn't have to the Congolese refugee who once said to a friend of mine, in view of the atrocities flaying his homeland, "It would be better not to be alive."

What's wrong with power? Too often it's in the hands of the wrong people who use it only to extract. And too often when power gets into others' hands, it turns them into the wrong people. Speaking of power changing hands, Qohelet also tells a story of succession, success, and what succeeds both.

> Better was a poor and wise youth than an old and foolish king who no longer knew how to take advice. For he went from prison to the throne, though in his own kingdom he had been born poor. I saw all the living who move about under the sun, along with that youth who was to stand in the king's place. There was no end of all the people, all of whom he led. Yet those who come later will not rejoice in him. Surely this also is absurd and a striving after wind.

The incumbent outlived his usefulness, like the men in black thought their prime minister had. Advice is tough for a king. If bad advice makes him look good, he might be only too eager to hear and heed. But if good advice makes him look bad, his advisor might pay dearly.

We are not told how, but somehow, the old king's young successor rose from poverty and prison to the land's highest office. Once in power, the young successor is universally loved. For the hour he struts and frets upon the stage, he spellbinds the body politic. But both old king and young successor learn that no one is strong forever. Impermanence wrecks every pretense of omnipotence. As Richard Sennett has said:

> No one is strong forever; parents die, children take their place; . . . authority is not a state of being but an event in time governed by the rhythm of growing and dying. To be conscious of the link between strength and time is to know that no authority is omnipotent.

The old foolish king starts in power but loses it. The young successor seizes not only the throne but the people's hearts. Yet their hearts don't stay seized; few ever do. Those who came later did not rejoice in him. Even getting your name on a building doesn't mean it will stay there.

Qohelet doesn't tell us whether the fall in popularity brought the young ruler's reign down with it or whether it was his postmortem reputation that met mud. Either way, at one time, the young ruler had both power and love; later, he had neither. After his electoral shellacking, Michael Ignatieff could relate: "In the weeks afterward, the solitary reality of defeat began to sink in. It turns out that there is nothing so ex as an ex-politician, especially a defeated one. Your phone goes dead."

But losing an election isn't the only way to find yourself on the wrong side of power.

> I say: Keep the king's command, because of God's oath to him. Be not hasty to go from his presence. Do not take your stand in an evil cause, for he does whatever he pleases. For the word of the king is supreme, and who may say to him, "What are you doing?" . . . No man has power to retain the spirit, or power over the day of death. There is no discharge from war, nor will wickedness deliver those who are given to it. All this I observed while applying my heart to all that is done under the sun, when man had power over man to his hurt.

Here Qohelet speaks not to those who wield authority but to those it is wielded on or against. His main point is that you can bend an authority to your will only so far. Sometimes not at all. If you serve as a king's minister or, say, senior advisor to a company's CEO, it is not your word that is law but the boss's. If the boss doesn't approve your latest proposal, it will do you no good to become the patron saint of lost causes. If the person in charge has already nixed your latest great idea, continuing to pound on it is a great way to get fired.

What do you own? A car, a house, a record collection? Ownership grounds authority. Without just cause, no one can take your car, expel you from your house, or liquidate your shelves of vinyl. But no one is proprietor of life's most fundamental good: namely, life itself. "No man has power to retain the spirit, or power over the day of death." Qohelet's Hebrew word for "power" has the flavor of mastery, rule, and proprietorship. No one is the owner or even the manager of their own life-breath. Life-breath is a gift; more precisely, a loan. All your breaths are leased, and one day the lease will expire. You can't know the term of the loan in advance. All you know is that it will end. When the loan comes due, you will have no chance to request an extension.

Later, Qohelet tells another story of faithfully exercised authority that was unfaithfully forgotten:

> I have also seen this example of wisdom under the sun, and it seemed great to me. There was a little city with few men in it, and a great king came against it and besieged it, building great siegeworks against it. But there was found in it a poor, wise man, and he by his wisdom delivered the city. Yet no one remembered that poor man. But I say that wisdom is better than might, though the poor man's wisdom is despised and his words are not heard.

For once, wisdom triumphed over muscle. One threadbare sage saved a city. Yet, while his wisdom did many good, it didn't do him any. Crowds forget, and sometimes that forgetting is so swift as to be absurd. Better to be wise than strong, sure. Just don't expect your wisdom to win you an election, even if it just won a battle.

■ ■ ■

Most people today know the wheel of fortune only as a device on a long-running game show that sets the prize value of the next consonant to be guessed. But the phrase has a classical pedigree. The wheel belongs to the goddess Fortuna, who spins it at whim. People are strapped to the wheel. With every turn, some rise and others fall. No one stays up for long.

This classical commonplace passed into the medieval and modern worlds through Boethius, who was a Christian theologian and philosopher in sixth-century Rome and a prominent public servant under Theodoric, king of the Ostrogoths. Boethius had a richly successful career in politics until the king developed a distaste for him, accused him of conspiracy, imprisoned him, and, in A.D. 524, executed him. From fire to ashes. Boethius was around forty-four when he was killed.

While in prison awaiting execution, Boethius wrote *The Consolation of Philosophy,* which became one of the most widely read books in Europe for the next thousand years. In it, he imagines the goddess Fortuna appearing to him, saying,

> You imagine that fortune's attitude to you has changed; you are wrong. Such was always her way, such is her nature. Instead . . . she was just the same when she was smiling, when she deluded you with the allurements of her false happiness. You have merely discovered the changing face of that blind power: she who still conceals herself from others has completely revealed herself to you. . . . For this is my nature, this

is my continual game: turning my wheel swiftly I delight to bring low what is on high, to raise high what is down.

■ ■ ■

Who will love you when you're nobody? A former U. S. president isn't exactly nobody, but the recent passing of Rosalynn Carter, Jimmy Carter's wife of seventy-seven years, brought to my notice the thirty-ninth president's eloquent testimony to a love that did not rise or fall with power or fortune. "For me, as Rosalynn and I approach our 75th wedding anniversary coming up in July, my home is wherever she is, whether in South Georgia or South Sudan. Holding her hand, reading our Bible together each night, falling asleep next to her, that is my home." Happiness comes not from making it to the top but from love that won't rise on the way up, fall on the way down, or desert you at the bottom.

I recently saw my daughter Margaret carrying Opal across the playground on the church parking lot behind our house. Opal, a large orange tabby cat, is our block's at-large pest control officer. I was surprised that Opal consented so calmly to Margaret's embrace. As cats go, Opal is remarkably pleasant. But she's still a cat. She could slip your grasp whenever she wanted. If she wanted to hide, you'd never find her. Chasing power is like chasing Opal. If you want to be happy, don't give your heart to something that can spring away in an instant.

10

Death

Obviously, I have not yet died. As far as I know, I haven't even come close. But my wife once narrowly scraped past death. My oldest daughter, too, in the act of being born.

When Rose was born, Kristin was twenty-four and I was twenty-three. Kristin's pregnancy had been tiring but uncomplicated. Three days after her due date, she went into labor, we drove to the hospital, and she labored through the night. Slow progress is not unusual for a first birth, but around the twelve-hour mark, Rose's vitals took a concerningly sharp downward turn. Change of plans: immediate C-section. A now-larger team of doctors and nurses wheeled Kristin into the operating room and began to surgically open her abdomen. One obstetrician asked another, "Have you ever seen so much blood in a uterus?" I was ushered to the hallway so the doctors would have one less worry.

Minutes later, Rose was born, but she almost wasn't. Kristin had suffered a placental abruption, in which the placenta detaches from the uterine wall, but neither she nor any doctor had known. The condition is often fatal for both mother and child. If Rose had remained in the womb even a few minutes longer, she would not have survived.

Newborn Rose was sent to the NICU. After a frightening few hours, she began recovering steadily. She came home a week later. But Kristin did not recover on schedule. Instead of regaining appetite and strength and mobility, she felt worse by the hour. Her stomach swelled. She hurt everywhere. She could barely move. Day after day, doctor after doctor tried and failed to diagnose her. Finally, on day six, I narrated Kristin's symptoms to my aunt, who is an accomplished ob-gyn and researcher of maternal and fetal health. My aunt called our lead doctor, confidently identified Kristin's problem, and urged her team to schedule an immediate laparoscopic surgery. They did, that day. The surgeon found Kristin's abdominal cavity flooded with infected fluid. He had to wash her intestine handful by handful.

Kristin had peritonitis, an infection of the abdominal cavity. Most likely, during the C-section, an imperfectly sanitized hand had planted germs that caused the infection. Kristin's condition was nothing her doctors expected from a healthy twenty-four-year-old. Given another day or two, it would have killed her.

After the surgery, Kristin's body was doubly wrecked, first by the placental abruption and C-section, then by the week of peritonitis punctuated by a second surgery. It took her days to walk—at first, tiny, tentative steps. Meanwhile, Rose was already at home, being bottle-fed by me, and my mom, between my trips to see Kristin in the hospital. After her surgery, Kristin didn't come home for another week.

When a couple conceives, they enter the ring with death. For those with access, modern medicine drastically reduces death's chances of victory. Still, it's a face-off, one that you or the baby could always lose.

■ ■ ■

Some people seem to think they live beyond death's shadow. But touch it once, and it sticks, like bike-chain grease on skin.

■ ■ ■

Death's shadow chills Qohelet's whole treatise. Qohelet is not a person who fancies himself, or anyone else, immune from death. He draws the conclusions he does about wisdom and work and wealth because he views them through the dark rays that death shoots backward across our allotted span. Qohelet's biggest problem with life is death.

Death practices an unjust equity. Wisdom usefully lights the path before you, but how does the path end?

> The wise person has his eyes in his head, but the fool walks in darkness. And yet I perceived that the same event happens to all of them. Then I said in my heart, "What happens to the fool will happen to me also. Why then have I been so very wise?" And I said in my heart that this also is absurd. . . . How the wise dies just like the fool!

Wisdom does not guarantee living longer or dying better than a fool. Death treats the wise person exactly as it treats the fool, as if they were the same. To death, they are. Qohelet takes this as an insult not only to the wise but to justice. The wise deserve better, but death denies them justice.

As far as death is concerned, deserving doesn't enter the picture. Death doesn't care whether you're virtuous or immoral, how good or how bad you are. Death inflicts the same penalty on good and evil alike.

> It is the same for all, since the same event happens to the righteous and the wicked, to the good and the evil, to the clean and the unclean, to him who sacrifices and him who does not sacrifice. As the good one is, so is the sinner, and he who swears is as he who shuns an oath. This is an evil in all that is done under the sun, that the same event happens to all. Also, the hearts of the children of man are full of evil, and madness is in their hearts while they live, and after that they go to the dead.

"This is an evil": Death uncaringly inflicts itself on all alike, however unlike they are. Qohelet reckons death's blindness to humans' different degrees of deserving as a radical injustice. Justice professes blindness to everything that should not influence the outcome, but death is blind to what actually should.

Qohelet is also incensed that death equalizes all differences between humans and nonhuman animals. This too he judges unjust. "What happens to the children of man and what happens to the beasts is the same; as one dies, so dies the other. They all have the same breath, and man has no advantage over the beasts, for all is absurd. All go to one place. All are from the dust, and to dust all return." You are made from earth dust, and one day the dust that used to be you will disperse into the earth. The dead skin cells that your body sheds become a small portion of the dust that settles on every surface of your home. Next time you spray a shelf and wipe it down, consider it a preview. That's a very little bit of you; soon it will be all of you.

Death tramples all our dignity into dust. With smug finality, death declares that man is no better than beast. Qohelet cries foul, but who can argue with death?

Not only does death disregard deserving in dealing itself out; it also disregards deserving in dealing out your stuff. You're not around to control who gets what. And even if you dictate airtight terms in your will, you're not around to ensure that your heirs make wise use of what your death bequeaths them.

> I hated all my toil in which I toil under the sun, seeing that I must leave it to the man who will come after me, and who knows whether he will be wise or a fool? Yet he will be master of all for which I toiled and used my wisdom under the sun. This also is absurd. So I turned about and gave my heart up to despair over all the toil of my labors under the sun, because sometimes a person who has toiled with wisdom and knowledge and skill must leave everything to be enjoyed by someone who did not toil for it. This also is absurd and a great evil. What has a man from all the toil and striving of heart with which he toils beneath the sun?

Work yourself to the bone to build a company; who knows how your successor will run it? Or where? Perhaps into the ground, where you are already. Deprive yourself to amass an inheritance for your children; at some point, you can no longer say what they can spend it on.

Death eventually erases every mark you leave on the world. "For of the wise as of the fool there is no enduring remembrance, seeing that in the days to come all will have been long forgotten." The poet Donald Hall has said that people deeply settled in a place will know the maiden names of their great-grandmothers. I don't know those of mine. Never have. I bet you don't either. Even if you do, will your children, if you have any? "There is no remembrance of former things, nor will there be any remembrance of later things yet to be among those who come after."

Unpredictably and permanently, death disrupts every goal, all aims, each cherished project.

> Again I saw that under the sun the race is not to the swift, nor the battle to the strong, nor bread to the wise, nor riches to the intelligent, nor favor to those with knowledge, but time and chance happen to them all. For man does not know his time. Like fish that are taken in an evil net, and like birds that are caught in a snare, so the children of man are snared at an evil time, when it suddenly falls upon them.

You don't and can't know when death will come. All you can know is that when death comes, it will carry off all. Often death's timing leaves everything to be desired. Its unannounced advent mocks our presumed dignity. Death doesn't ask whether you're busy, whether you'd prefer to be called back later. Instead, death sets a trap and waits in a blind. Or death tracks you, snapping no twigs.

The worst part of death—what makes death death and what makes death Qohelet's biggest problem with life—is its total deprivation. All other losses are partial; only death completes loss.

> But he who is joined with all the living has hope, for a living dog is better than a dead lion. For the living know that they will die, but the dead know nothing, and they have no more reward, for the memory of them is forgotten. Their love and their hate and their envy have already perished, and forever they have no more share in all that is done under the sun. . . .

> Whatever your hand finds to do, do it with your might, for there is no work or thought or knowledge or wisdom in Sheol, to which you are going.

Death annihilates all actual earthly enjoyments and all potential to enjoy them. Death removes not only food but palate and appetite. Death leaves you no work and no hands to work with, no thought and no mind to think with.

Death sometimes shows up unannounced. But, to many, death sends out troops of losses as advance teams. Donald Hall calls old age a ceremony of losses and a carnival of losses. He reflects, "You are old when someone mentions an event two years in the future and looks embarrassed. . . . You are old when mashed potatoes are difficult to chew, or when you guess it's Sunday because the mail doesn't come." In the last section of the body of Qohelet's book, he personifies the losses that prefigure death as a town fading to black as its life drains out. Not only does the town go dark, but even the sky over it dims.

> Remember also your Creator in the days of your youth, before the evil days come and the years draw near of which you will say, "I have no pleasure in them"; before the sun and the light and the moon and the stars are darkened and the clouds return after the rain, in the day when the keepers of the house tremble, and the strong men are bent, and the grinders cease because they are few, and those who look through the windows are dimmed, and the doors on the street are shut—when the sound of the grinding is low, and one rises up at the sound of a bird, and all the daughters of song are brought low—they are afraid also of what is high, and terrors are in the way; the almond tree blossoms, the grasshopper drags itself along, and desire fails, because man is going to his eternal home, and

> the mourners go about the streets—before the silver cord is snapped, or the golden bowl is broken, or the pitcher is shattered at the fountain, or the wheel broken at the cistern, and the dust returns to the earth as it was, and the spirit returns to God who gave it.

Scholars haggle endlessly over the details, but I think it's best to see Qohelet poetically portraying aging all the way up to the mourners going about the streets, at which point the series of sharp verbs snaps death into focus. The coming days of which you will say, "I have no pleasure in them," are the days in which death's advance teams of losses will do their dreary work: days when death's approach makes loss the loudest sound you hear, until your hearing itself goes. Hall says, "In your eighties it gets hard to walk. Nearing ninety it's exhausting to pull your nightshirt on." The weakening people and animals and forces that populate Qohelet's poem may refer to body parts that gradually give out, or more broadly to aging's deprivations: loss of courage, range, agency, dignity, strength. "In your eighties you are invisible. Nearing ninety you hope nobody sees you."

Aging steadily steals all that makes life life, and then comes death, total and final. When Qohelet's poem arrives at death, several striking verbs of undoing stab our pretensions of immortality. Your life, Qohelet says, will one day end like a snapped cord, a broken bowl, a shattered pitcher, a trashed wheel. Death is a brute, and it will brutalize you. As Pascal says, "The last act is bloody, however fine the rest of the play. They throw earth over your head and it is finished for ever." The life that kept your body moving will quit, and nothing will hold you together. God will recall the life-breath he loaned you, and your physical elements will disassemble. The dust that composed you will decompose into its status quo ante.

At the start of his poem, Qohelet evokes death's total deprivation by depicting the sky itself shutting off: "before the sun and the light and the moon and the stars are darkened." How can an individual death cause such cosmic consequences? Because for the one who dies, death is the end of the world.

"The mourners go about the streets." Qohelet's tableau pictures not just a death but a funeral. Whose? Yours. Biblical scholar Michael Fox reflects,

> What do all these people see that terrifies and afflicts them so? For whom are they mourning so intensely? The answer is inevitable: they see your death and mourn for you, you to whom Qohelet addressed his advice and warnings, the "you" of v. 1. Qohelet wants you to look upon your death and funeral from the outside. It is your fate that appalls the village. Your death is eclipsing their world, and you are present at the terrible scene. The bell tolls for you, and for everyone.

▪ ▪ ▪

Men in my family don't grow much facial hair. On my dad's fortieth birthday, I went with him to the grocery store. The woman who checked us out asked to see his ID. "Lady, you just made my day!"

I have been told that my face ages slowly. "Ageless!" a friend's sweet wife said upon seeing a group photo. "What do you use on your face?" Just soap, I'm afraid. Sometimes when people ask me how old I am, I tell them, "Older than I look, but not as old as I feel."

While preaching the sermons that first enthralled me with Ecclesiastes, and then researching and planning and writing and revising this book, I have passed through, and now out of, my midthirties. My thirties approach their late stage. I hope they will produce their finest work yet in this advanced season.

In these past few years, my sense of the relationship between time and death has palpably shifted. I am steadily growing more aware of years behind me piling up and, one way or another, diminishing ahead. Instead of getting gloomier, I think I'm lightening up. Loosening up too. There's so much I can't do. So much I won't do. But a gradually growing sense of time's scarcity is making me a little more thankful for what I get to do. Happiness comes not from denying or defying death but from letting death teach you humility.

▪ ▪ ▪

While death betrays no intent to change, how we die has transformed. Before about a hundred years ago, most people died at home in the care of their families. Now, since the rise of the modern hospital, hardly anyone does. As Columbia University physician L. S. Dugdale observes, today our homes are generally free from "hideous sickness" and "indecent death," both now diverted to "sterile standardized institutions run by strangers." Death has been hidden from public view and banished from polite conversation. Death has come to "replace sex as the ultimate 'unmentionable.' "

Because this crew of cultural, economic, and technological forces has hung a cordon sanitaire around death and established both our homes and public spaces as death-free zones, today it is far easier to do to death what we innately want to do: deny it. Pascal says, "Being unable to cure death, wretchedness, and ignorance, men have decided, in order to be happy, not to think about such things." It's not that you think you will not die but that you do your best not to think of your death. So death comes to seem distant and uncertain. Albert Camus wrote, "One will never be sufficiently surprised that everyone lives as if no one 'knew.' . . . Here, it is barely possible to speak of the experience of others' deaths. It is a substitute, an illusion, and it never quite convinces us." Partly because you so seldom see them die or see them dead, others' deaths fail to convince you that yours is as real and certain as theirs. Echoing Ecclesiastes 1:4, Annie Dillard makes the same point: "Our generations rise and break like foam on shores. Yet death, at least in the West, apparently astonishes and blind-sides every man-bubble of us, every time." She cites Ernest Becker: "One of the main reasons that it is so easy to march men off to war is that deep down each of them feels sorry for the man next to him who will die."

Denying death is closing your eyes as a storm nears. Ignoring the storm will not delay or divert it, and the storm does not care whether your eyes are closed when it hits. But it's not just that denial doesn't work on death; denying death doesn't work for you. It's nearly impossible to keep death from seeping into your thoughts merely by sandbagging them with denial. That is why diversion is a vastly more popular strategy for keeping your mind death-free. We amuse ourselves to deflect death. We divert ourselves to divert death. Diversion works better than denial because it offers an endless series of objects to fill the space death keeps threatening to claim.

Modern life is like a designer home with a gaping hole in the living room floor. What do you do with this pit menacing your every move? Cover it with a loud rug. Or say you come home to find an elephant in your kitchen. (You must have a big kitchen.) The elephant politely declines your request to vacate the premises. How can you hide an elephant? Easy: Cover it with ten thousand Post-it notes.

Entertainment diverts; pleasures sedate. How can you stop

hearing the alarm in your head that beeps to tell you death is coming? The right pleasure promises to either play louder or dull your senses. For a time, you can ignore the alarm. Just don't look up or you'll see it blink.

Modernity's defining aspiration is that every individual should come to possess an ever-increasing share of the world, like a charmed colonizer who always finds a "virgin territory" around the next bend. Death blocks and mocks that aim. As Hartmut Rosa writes, "Processes of bodily decay, the finitude of life, represent the hardest limit to modernity's program of increasing our share of the world. . . . Death itself remains fundamentally, categorically, and existentially beyond our control." Suicide—including all its euphemistically named, medically abetted varieties—does not control death; it only succumbs to death's control. Surrender is not victory.

You cannot control death, so how will you confront it? What will you carry into a fight against an enemy who you know will win? What will you cling to in a flood that you know will drown you? Christian Wiman reflects,

> On the radio I hear a famous novelist praising his father for enduring a long, difficult dying without ever "seeking relief in religion." It is clear from the son's description that the father was in absolute despair, and that as those cold waters closed over him he could find nothing to hold on to but his pride, and drowned clutching that nothing. This is to be admired? That we carry our despair stoically into death, that even the utmost anguish of our lives does not change us? How astonishing it is, the fierceness with which we cling to beliefs that have made us miserable, or beliefs that prove to be so obviously inadequate when extreme suffering—or great joy—comes.

Death strips pride's pretenses and reveals pride as the nothing that it is. Survey your skills, strengths, achievements, comforts. Is there a single one that death does not expose as nothing or turn to nothing?

> What do you do, what do you say, what in the world are you going to *believe in* when you are dying? It is not enough to act *as if* when the wave is closing in over you, and that little whiff of the ineffable you get from meditation or mysticism is toxic to the dying man, who needs the rock of one real truth.

11

Hevel (II): Absurd

Have you ever hated life? Qohelet has. "So I hated life, because what is done under the sun was grievous to me, for all is absurd and a striving after wind."

Life is a strange thing to hate. One of my daughters hates yogurt, a distaste she likely inherited from me since my wife loves it. Among its fellow foods, two features set yogurt apart: taste and texture. To love yogurt, both must please. If either offends, hatred may follow. As complex and mysterious as yogurt may be, hating it is simple. What it offers and what you want don't match. For many, yogurt slides down smoothly, refreshes, and satisfies. Others choke on it.

Qohelet choked not on a food but on his life. He says a few sentences later, "So I turned about and gave my heart up to despair over all the toil of my labors under the sun." The taste and texture of his life made him want nothing to do with it.

What made Qohelet's life hateful? What it offered and what he wanted didn't match.

■ ■ ■

Mismatches between what a person desires and what the world affords range from trivial to tragic. Observers of American life note with alarm the growing number of "deaths of despair," especially of men, especially in Rust Belt cities and Appalachian towns that investment and industry have abandoned. These deaths include not only suicides but accidental overdoses, harms caused by opioid addiction and alcohol abuse, and other maladies of those who give up on life because they conclude that life has given up on them.

The mismatches that Qohelet wrestles with, like the causes contributing to "deaths of despair," are all on the tragic end of the spectrum. The causes of these clashes between the shape of the world and the striving of the human heart are deeply rooted in each. As we have seen, Qohelet witnesses collisions between our basic drives and the world's basic patterns in the realms of pleasure, work, wealth, relationships, politics, and justice. And he sticks onto all these clashes a one-word label, *hevel,* which is the heart of the thesis that frames the book and rings like church bells throughout.

As we've seen, *hevel* is hard to translate, but, conceptually speaking, the best English equivalent is "absurd." Not absurd in the sense of something obviously untrue ("Everybody knows the moon is made of cheese") or ridiculous (a pet dog helped build a rocket to get cheese from the moon). Instead, what Qohelet means by *hevel* is essentially what Albert Camus, along with some philosophers since, means by "absurd." What unites Qohelet's hevel and Camus's "absurd" is the judgment that an action or fact embodies an expectation that the world fails to meet. Hevel names something dissonant, incongruous, out of tune, a misfit between the world and our hearts and minds. It describes a state of affairs in which the world fails to heed our desires, expectations, or sense of justice. In Camus's words,

> I said that the world is absurd, but I was too hasty. This world in itself is not reasonable, that is all that can be said. But what is absurd is the confrontation of this irrational and the wild longing for clarity whose call echoes in the human heart. . . . At this point of his effort man stands face to face with the irrational. He feels within him his longing for happiness and for reason. The absurd is born of this confrontation between the human need and the unreasonable silence of the world.

In British sport and idiom, a star footballer has a "shocker" when he or she performs stunningly below expectations. For Qohelet, the whole world is a shocker. Hevel is the tragic divorce between act and result, yearning and outcome, deserving and fate. It is the world's failure to satisfy our demand.

▪ ▪ ▪

In the previous ten chapters, we have surveyed Qohelet's pile of evidence for his verdict that all is absurd. Now that his full picture has come into view, we will review his case in the form of three summary statements: We don't get what we want. When we do get what we want, it either doesn't satisfy or doesn't last. And we don't get what we deserve. Now, Qohelet is not saying that we never get what we want or deserve, only that we do not get either one predictably, consistently, or reliably. The only thing you can count on in this life—besides death—is that you will not get all you want or deserve.

We don't get what we want. Qohelet sought satisfaction in every conceivable source of pleasure but didn't find it. "I said in my heart, 'Come now, I will test you with pleasure; enjoy yourself.' But behold, this also was absurd." Qohelet gulped every pleasure he could want, but pleasure did not give him what he wanted. Even getting what he wanted didn't get him what he wanted. Whatever he wanted, pleasure said, "I'm not it."

Or consider yet again Qohelet's unsleeping workaholic:

> Again, I saw an absurdity under the sun: one person who has no other, either son or brother, yet there is no end to all his toil, and his eyes are never satisfied with riches, so that he never asks, "For whom am I toiling and depriving myself of pleasure?" This also is absurd and an unhappy business.

The work of the person who never stops working never gets him what he wants, so he never stops working. We don't get what we want, sometimes because the world doesn't give it to us, but more often because even when it does, we want something else or something more. "Better is the sight of the eyes than the wandering of the appetite: this also is absurd and a striving after wind."

When we do get what we want, it either doesn't satisfy or doesn't last. "He who loves money will not be satisfied with money, nor he who loves wealth with his income; this also is absurd." Money always has a new trick up its sleeve; it can always find another way to disappear. Even if it stays put awhile, money never gives you a reason not to want more of it. The more you love money, the more treacherous money proves. And Qohelet repeatedly laments those who toil long to amass a fortune but are prevented from enjoying any of it:

> There is an evil that I have seen under the sun, and it lies heavy on mankind: a man to whom God gives wealth, posses-

> sions, and honor, so that he lacks nothing of all that he desires, yet God does not give him power to enjoy them, but a stranger enjoys them. This is absurd; it is a grievous evil.

Such a fortune is like the football that Lucy is forever snatching away just before Charlie Brown can kick it. And even one who both builds a fortune and enjoys it will not do so for long: "As he came from his mother's womb he shall go again, naked as he came, and shall take nothing for his toil that he may carry away in his hand."

Like a tank of gas, every earthly good runs out, but our hearts never stop wanting. Christian Wiman asks, "What is it we want when we can't stop wanting?"

We don't get what we deserve. Qohelet sees this happen again and again.

> The wise person has his eyes in his head, but the fool walks in darkness. And yet I perceived that the same event happens to all of them. Then I said in my heart, "What happens to the fool will happen to me also. Why then have I been so very wise?" And I said in my heart that this also is absurd.

Death deletes the wise as easily as the fool. Wisdom is no shield against cancer. The wise die just as often as the foolish, and often sooner. "In my absurd life I have seen everything. There is a righteous man who perishes in his righteousness, and there is a wicked man who prolongs his life in his evildoing." Actions have consequences. Character matters. People get what's coming to them. If those three sentences were true without exception, then Qohelet would not see commendable people cut down young and crooked people collecting seashells, tanned and sleek in their seventies. The absurd is the gut punch of seeing someone get the opposite of what their character merits. "There is an absurdity that takes place on earth, that there are righteous people to whom it happens according to the deeds of the wicked, and there are wicked people to whom it happens according to the deeds of the righteous. I said that this also is absurd." It is as if someone switched the ledgers, as if some sick cosmic account swap occurred: The righteous receive what the wicked have stored up and vice versa.

I should handle my wife's china teacups and saucers more carefully than our IKEA glasses. I mean, I should handle those carefully too, but with four kids, we use so many of them so often that breaking and replacing are routine. Not so the decorated, gilt-edged fare we use to elevate date night. The china is worth more and gets treated better. That's what you expect: the more valuable, the better care. But Qohelet doesn't see that kind of distinguishing care reflected in how death indiscriminately drops human animal and nonhuman animal alike.

> I said in my heart with regard to the children of man that God is testing them that they may see that they themselves are but beasts. For what happens to the children of man and what happens to the beasts is the same; as one dies, so dies the other. They all have the same breath, and man has no advantage over the beasts, for all is absurd. All go to one place. All are from the dust, and to dust all return.

Death treats human and beast the same, which seems to say we are the same. Are you happy with that verdict? Qohelet calls it absurd. Does anything in you resist the judgment that you do not deserve to be treated any better than a rat?

For decades, centuries even, very many very smart people have worked very hard to try to show that humans do not differ from nonhuman animals in any fundamental way. Such scientists and philosophers have long tried to disprove Qohelet's stubborn intuition that something sets humans apart from and above our fellow creatures. As Walker Percy puts it, "The modern objective consciousness will go to any length to prove that it is not unique in the Cosmos, and by this very effort establishes its own uniqueness."

■ ■ ■

According to the World Health Organization, around the world today, depression and burnout are the fastest-growing health problems. These take their place alongside other increasingly widespread pathological reactions to stress, such as eating disorders, sleep disorders, and chronic anxiety. Depression has many causes and takes many forms; here I focus on what is unique to the experience of depression in modern achievement society.

Depression is an illness of responsibility; its dominant feeling is failure. As the French sociologist Alain Ehrenberg has said, "The depressed individual is unable to measure up; he is tired of having to become himself." Depression is not merely sadness but a crippling sense of inadequacy. Depression is the inevitable shadow side of a society in which every man and woman is his or her own sovereign. It is a consequence not of acting badly but of feeling unable to act at all. Depression forms not under the pressure of law but under the pressure of performance. Depression registers a deficiency not of moral fiber but of capacity. Someone who's depressed is out of gas.

Depression is an inevitable by-product of modern individualism. The modern world proclaims that anyone can be exceptional, and therefore everyone should be exceptional. This places a tremendous burden of responsibility and initiative on every individual. Drained empty, tired beyond hope of recharge, the depressed person is crushed by the weight of their own sovereignty.

Our whole existence has been rendered vulnerable, precarious, insecure. Change is a threat because it can always bring harm or failure. Depression is the price millions of people pay for the demand that you be more than human: that you create yourself, surpass yourself, act on your own marvelously malleable nature, and make yourself more than yourself. Depression is the shattering sense that you are only yourself, and yourself is not enough.

Burnout is a state of mental and physical exhaustion that drains joy from acts and relationships that would otherwise bring it. Depending on your vantage point, burnout could be a cause and precursor of depression, a synonym for it, or a consequence of it. In any case, the fit between depression and burnout is tight. Like depression, widespread burnout is the hallmark of a society structured not by discipline but by achievement. People in the modern West have become entrepreneurs of themselves. We live under relentless pressure to achieve and then market our achievements. In a late modern market society such as the United States, achievement is life's defining commandment: "Thou shalt make something of thyself." You are what you achieve. Achievement society turns us into performance machines; burnout happens when the machine-self breaks. Burnout hits when you optimize yourself to death.

Ehrenberg calls depression "the perfect disorder of the democratic human being." Rosa names it "the *pathology of late modernity* . . . because it seems to embody the temporal experience of a *frenetic standstill* in a pathologically pure form." And Byung-

Chul Han argues that burnout is modern society's signature affliction. But depression and burnout are by no means merely modern problems. This chapter began with Qohelet's confession: "So I hated life." Why did he hate life? Because of its absurdity. Because wisdom doesn't guarantee you a legacy, shield you from death, or even secure you a better or later death. Qohelet's experience is not much different from someone who optimizes their whole life for achievement but either fails to achieve or achieves and finds it empty. Qohelet hated life because none of the work he did or saw seemed worth it. He devoted himself fully to every conceivable employment and achievement and enjoyment, and at the end of it all, he hated it all. *Burnout* is a good word for that collapse.

And, as we've seen, just sentences later, Qohelet narrates a similar inward act of giving up on it all: "So I turned about and gave my heart up to despair over all the toil of my labors under the sun." Why? Because, in just a few insultingly short years, the one who gains it all will have to give it all up, and the heir might be a loser. As Qohelet walked it, the path to achievement became a treadmill. It didn't take him anywhere. All journey, no destination. All pain, no gain. Qohelet's negative verdict on achievement was not merely mental; the result of his experience and judgment was a heart drained of energy. He gave up. His drive to continue vanished. If Qohelet had consulted his physician or therapist, they would have called him depressed.

Depression and burnout descend when you don't want to, or can't, do what the world demands. Here we meet another form of the absurd, another tragic misfit—this time between what the world requires and what the human heart can supply. Depression and burnout are modern branches of an older and deeper double problem. This double problem is that, first, this world and the deepest longings of our being don't line up and, second, we are just as alienated from ourselves, just as divided within, as we are from the world without.

We are irreparably estranged from this world that, despite being our home, doesn't feel like much of a home, and we are equally estranged from ourselves. As Christian Wiman laments, "What is this world that we are so at odds with, this beauty by which we are so wounded, and into which God has so utterly gone?" In such a strange, estranged world, and with such strange, estranged selves, depression is not necessarily a sign that you are viewing your life wrongly. Instead, it could measure the suffocating weight of all that you rightly see is wrong with the world, and even some of what is wrong with yourself. Walker Percy says,

> You are depressed because you have every reason to be depressed. No member of the other two million species which inhabit the earth—and who are luckily exempt from depression—would fail to be depressed if it lived the life you lead. You live in a deranged age—more deranged than usual, because despite great scientific and technological advances, man has not the faintest idea of who he is or what he is doing.

Do you know who you are and what you are doing?

A useful modern name for this condition of being permanently estranged from the world and from oneself is "alienation." Alienation is the opposite of being at home in the world and at peace with yourself. In Rosa's words, "Alienation has come to serve as the keyword for a world which has become cold and grey, harsh and non-responding, experienced by a subject that inwardly feels deaf, mute, cold, and empty, too." Alienation is a state of not outward but inward poverty. It easily, frequently afflicts those who are popular, successful, and rich. As Rosa points out, drawing on the work of Rahel Jaeggi, alienation describes a state in which one has many relationships and activities that should provide meaning (family, work, political party membership, religious affiliation, hobbies) "yet deems them meaningless, having become indifferent to or even repulsed by them, despite having been highly successful in them in terms of accumulating resources." Rosa's description of alienation resembles nothing so much as Qohelet at the end of his sweeping quest for satisfaction. Alienation is a state in which the world itself appears indifferent or repulsive and does not yield to our effort or desire. Alienation is the state of being a stranger to, and estranged from, both yourself and the world.

What are you alienated from? Try these on, and see how many fit: yourself, your body, nature, your family, your friends, your work, your hometown, your country, your culture, people in general, the whole world.

Alienation depends on the intuition, even the conviction, that our relationship to the world and ourselves should not be strange or estranged. Imagine that Martians exist and you travel to Mars to meet them. You would expect Mars and Martians to be strange, opaque, and alien. You would not describe yourself as alienated from Mars and Martians, not unless you somehow expected to feel at home there, and why would you? But you do expect to feel at home here. You do expect to be at home in your own self. And yet you're not. This bewildering disconnect between our most basic expectations and our most pervasive experiences is why alienation is an umbrella that includes, and partially explains, the absurd.

Depression, burnout, alienation. Surely you've experienced at least one. Many, sadly, know them all. Each is an expression or consequence of, each a bleak witness to, life's fundamental absurdity. And, as philosopher Jeffrey Gordon puts it, "If human life is indeed absurd, it would be difficult to imagine a more important fact about it."

The question now is, Why is life absurd? Is life's absurdity yet another absurdity? Absurd turtles all the way down?

■ ■ ■

Qohelet has an answer to why life is absurd. Throughout his work, this answer is assumed rather than argued. The answer is simple. In theological circles it travels under the understated name "the fall." Walker Percy calls it "an aboriginal catastrophe." Qohelet believes that God created the universe and that its original state was goodness and integrity. To this good, whole world God added humanity, a man called Adam and a woman called Eve, who originally were good and whole. He installed these humans as gardeners of Eden and guardians of the earth. He gave them virtually free run of the place, on the sole condition that they obey the single prohibition not to eat of the tree of the knowledge of good and evil. Enticed by Satan, Adam and Eve discarded God's command and ingested the fruit. So, instead of knowing immersive communion with God and each other, they hid from God, passed blame, and covered their nakedness.

Every feature of the absurd, each aspect of our alienation, flows from this single fatal failure. In response to Adam and Eve's sin, God cursed them with death and consigned the world to futility. Now, instead of yielding only nourishing abundance, the ground will shoot up thorns and thistles. Now, instead of work being strictly pleasure, it will be riddled with pain. Now, life will count down numbered days, each haunted by the nearing end. Now, instead of being at peace with God, at home in the world, in love with each other, and at one within, Adam and Eve—and everyone after them—are alienated from God, the world, each other, and themselves. Exit original goodness and wholeness; enter alienation and the absurd.

Qohelet's assumption that the fall is the answer to why life is absurd surfaces in several statements. When he recapitulates his failed quest for wisdom two-thirds of the way through the book, he concludes: "See, this alone I found, that God made man upright, but they have sought out many schemes." Humanity as we encounter it does not reflect the factory settings. A radical rupture lies between God's original creative act and the people we encounter every day. What people now seek is not what God made us to seek. Our many schemes do not embody the uprightness God intended and still intends. What is normal in experience is abnormal according to our designer. We were not always selfish at others' expense. There was a time when no form of injustice yet existed.

Just before this conclusion, Qohelet asserts, "Surely there is not a righteous man on earth who does good and never sins." A consequence of the fall is original sin—not that people were originally sinful but that the sin committed at the headwaters of human history has bequeathed to all people a polluted moral constitution. Original sin teaches that we commit sinful acts because we have sinful hearts and minds. As Peter Kreeft has put it, "Actual sin is simple: it means the sins we commit. Original Sin is more problematic: it is the sin we are." If you are inclined to dismiss or despise the doctrine of original sin, how else could you account for just how awful the human race is? Read a newspaper; cross a street; raise a child; live with another responsible adult of seemingly sound mind for a few months.

How can you explain what you observe and how you respond without concluding, in Alan Jacobs's words, that "all of us arrive in this world already selfish, rebellious, and corrupt"?

In his lament over the shared end of human and beast, Qohelet sighs, "All go to one place. All are from the dust, and to dust all return." These words echo God's declaration to Adam and Eve, in his curse hot on the heels of the fall, "By the sweat of your face you shall eat bread, till you return to the ground, for out of it you were taken; for you are dust, and to dust you shall return." Decomposition was not our destiny until God's judgment, answering our sin, made it so.

Twice Qohelet taunts us with our inability to unbend all that is bent out of shape in our lives: "What is crooked cannot be made straight, and what is lacking cannot be counted." "Consider the work of God: who can make straight what he has made crooked?" What is God doing making life crooked? He is executing his own sentence against sinful humanity. This world will not be made right until we are. Qohelet confesses the unfixable: Our estrangement from God and world and self is beyond our ability to repair. Like Qohelet, sober-minded secular observers have long recognized that the factors that render life alienating and absurd are beyond our power to fix. Organized, power-backed, large-scale efforts to fix the world show a marked tendency to make it worse. The Soviet Union's Five-Year Plans led not to promised utopian bounty but to famines in which millions of people died. The roots of our problems are deeper than we can reach, finer than we can see, and stronger than we can pull.

Inward corruption, universal sin, destined dissolution, all of it unfixable, at least by us: This is the account of the human condition that Qohelet finds in Scripture's first few chapters. This is one of the key lenses through which he reads the world.

This account is also why Qohelet, unlike modern secular thinkers, not only describes life's alienation and absurdity but can explain why life itself is alienating and absurd. Why should life so dependably frustrate us? Why should our hearts so persistently yearn for what the world equally persistently refuses to give?

Can evolution explain such a perfect misfit between our expectations and our environment? That does not sound like an adaptive advantage.

▪ ▪ ▪

A secular person can say only that, not why, the conditions of alienation and absurdity are universal and impossible to eradicate. Qohelet can say why, and so can Pascal, since he read the world through the same lens of humanity's aboriginal catastrophe. Paradoxically, Pascal takes humanity's wretchedness as the proof and measure of our greatness—the greatness we had and lost and, despite losing, still can't fully shake off. "All these examples of wretchedness prove his greatness. It is the wretchedness of a great lord, the wretchedness of a dispossessed king." We are not merely poor but impoverished. Not merely lost but shipwrecked. As C. S. Lewis has put it, "Nature has all the air of a good thing spoiled." Pascal adds, "Who indeed would think himself unhappy not to be king except one who had been dispossessed? . . . Who would think himself unhappy if he had only one mouth and who would not if he had only one eye?"

We experience our alienated, absurd condition not as a given but as a loss, not as natural or fitting but as an insult. We experience happiness as amputees do a phantom limb, an absence that hurts. But how could we, unless we had some dim residual sense of a time when, however briefly, we were happy and whole? As Peter Kreeft puts it, "One who had never been a prince would not be unhappy to be a peasant. But a dispossessed prince would never be happy as a peasant." Whether we know it or not, we judge earth inadequate by the standard of Eden. Back to Pascal:

> Is it not clear as day that man's condition is dual? The point is that if man had never been corrupted, he would, in his innocence, confidently enjoy both truth and felicity, and, if man had never been anything but corrupt, he would have no idea either of truth or bliss. But unhappy as we are (and we should be less so if there were no element of greatness in our condition) we have an idea of happiness but we cannot attain it. We perceive an image of the truth and possess nothing but falsehood, being equally incapable of absolute ignorance and certain knowledge; so obvious is it that we once enjoyed a degree of perfection from which we have unhappily fallen.

Would you rather believe that humans arrive in this world naturally and perfectly innocent? Would you rather concede that this world as we have it is all we were ever meant to have? The doctrine of original sin is a shock—a shock that restores our senses and reveals the source and object of our inconsolable yearning. As Pascal recognizes,

> Certainly nothing jolts us more rudely than this doctrine, and yet, but for this mystery, the most incomprehensible of all, we remain incomprehensible to ourselves. The knot of our condition was twisted and turned in that abyss, so that it is harder to conceive of man without this mystery than for man to conceive of it himself.

■ ■ ■

What did Qohelet discover? The same thing as Michael Chabon's researcher, who finds "that the world has been broken for as long as anyone can remember, and struggles to reconcile this fact with the ache of cosmic nostalgia that arises, from time to time, in the researcher's heart: an intimation of vanished glory, of lost wholeness, a memory of the world unbroken."

Has been broken; vanished; lost; a memory. What came before? Does anything come after? If the world and the human self were once unbroken, their mending may not be impossible. It all hinges on finding the right repairman.

MIDDLE FLOOR

Gift

"The Present, at Last"

Annie Dillard, *Pilgrim at Tinker Creek*

I never merited this grace, that when I face upstream I scent the virgin breath of mountains, I feel a spray of mist on my cheeks and lips, I hear a ceaseless splash and susurrus, a sound of water not merely poured smoothly down air to fill a steady pool, but tumbling live about, over, under, around, between, through an intricate speckling of rock. It is sheer coincidence that upstream from me the creek's bed is ridged in horizontal croppings of sandstone. I never merited this grace, that when I face upstream I see the light on the water careening towards me, inevitably, freely, down a graded series of terraces like the balanced winged platforms on an infinite, inexhaustible font. "Ho, if you are thirsty, come down to the water; ho, if you are hungry, come and sit and eat." This is the present, at last. I can pat the puppy any time I want. This is the now, this flickering, broken light, this air that the wind of the future presses down my throat, pumping me buoyant and giddy with praise.

■ ■ ■

The present is the wave that explodes over my head, flinging the air with particles at the height of its breathless unroll; it is the live water and light that bears from undisclosed sources the freshest news, renewed and renewing, world without end.

12

Gift

I sometimes aggravate Kristin by how long I take to answer a question. Not on purpose. It's just that if I'm not otherwise occupied, I'm usually reading. If my eyes are on the page and a question comes at me from two rooms away, the effect is like trying to speak to someone who's underwater. It might take a second for them to surface. Kristin could say I was not very present. I could say that I was in fact very present, but it takes time and effort to travel from being present to the book to being present to my wife's query.

We appear to be living through an epidemic of distraction. Electronic portals to elsewhere make it easier than ever to be absent from your present space and time. What does it take to be present to the present?

In his work on craftsmanship, Richard Sennett relays a rule from the great violinist Isaac Stern: The better your technique, the longer you can practice without getting bored. Like Annie Dillard, Qohelet is a virtuoso of being present to the present. He knows what it takes to stay in the present and stay happy in the present. He can teach you how to receive the present as a gift rather than scorning it for whatever tastes better (or worse) in memory or whatever scent you're chasing from the future.

▪ ▪ ▪

"Everything is absurd" does not mean that everything is worthless and you had better find a way to die quicker. This is evident in Ecclesiastes' second main intellectual movement, which is a series of seven affirmations about what is good, stationed like road signs at the book's structural divisions. This second movement constructs what I'm calling the book's middle floor. After a long stay on the ground floor, we now climb a set of stairs and look with Qohelet out the second-story window.

The central theme of these seven statements is that the present, with its ceaseless splash and careening light, is a gift from God. Receiving it as a gift, rather than grasping for gain, makes the difference between misery and happiness. It's not gain, but it's still good. Why? Gift.

This chapter and the next seven will focus almost exclusively on these seven statements. In this chapter we will focus on five of the seven, since those five explicitly say that life is, or life's good things are, a gift from God.

> There is nothing better for a person than that he should eat and drink and find enjoyment in his toil. This also, I saw, is from the hand of God, for apart from him who can eat or who can have enjoyment? For to the one who pleases him God has given wisdom and knowledge and joy, but to the sinner he has given the business of gathering and collecting, only to give to one who pleases God. This also is absurd and a striving after wind.

I perceived that there is nothing better for them than to be joyful and to do good as long as they live; also that everyone should eat and drink and take pleasure in all his toil—this is God's gift to man.

Behold, what I have seen to be good and fitting is to eat and drink and find enjoyment in all the toil with which one toils under the sun the few days of his life that God has given him, for this is his lot. Everyone also to whom God has given wealth and possessions and power to enjoy them, and to accept his lot and rejoice in his toil—this is the gift of God. For he will not much remember the days of his life because God keeps him occupied with joy in his heart.

And I commend joy, for man has nothing better under the sun but to eat and drink and be joyful, for this will go with him in his toil through the days of his life that God has given him under the sun.

Go, eat your bread with joy, and drink your wine with a merry heart, for God has already approved what you do.

Let your garments be always white. Let not oil be lacking on your head.

Enjoy life with the wife whom you love, all the days of your absurd life that he has given you under the sun, because that is your portion in life and in your toil at which you toil under the sun. Whatever your hand finds to do, do it with your might, for there is no work or thought or knowledge or wisdom in Sheol, to which you are going.

In these five passages, Qohelet tells you how to view life itself, the present, and all the daily joys that are yours for the receiving. One word does the whole job: "gift." When he says repeatedly that there's nothing better, he's telling us what's good. What's good is to receive all of life as a gift—because it is a gift and is itself good—and to receive each day's heaping handfuls of blessings as gifts. As far down as absurdity reaches, gift runs deeper still.

When Qohelet calls life a gift, he speaks not metaphorically but literally. Life itself is a free donation conferred on a receiver by a giver. He identifies the span of life, limited though it is, as a gift from God. He says that enjoyment is "from the hand of God." Wealth and possessions as well as the inward ability to enjoy them are given by God and are therefore his gifts. Qohelet names each person's share of work and pleasure their "lot" or "portion," mindful that every lot is allotted, every portion apportioned by someone. As Qohelet says again and again, it is God who grants life, measures its span, and stuffs in goodies like mom and dad filling Christmas stockings.

How does Qohelet know this? Not the same way he discovered life's absurdity. Not by empirical investigation. Not by inference from observation. Instead, Qohelet is here telling us what he knows by faith. He is not investigating but confessing.

What if you don't believe in God? Then "life is a gift" shrivels into a mere metaphor. However grateful you may sometimes feel for life and all its most basic and abundant enjoyments, you have no one to thank. If it isn't given by someone, it isn't a gift.

That your life is a gift from God means that ultimate reality is not random or empty, not mute or malicious, but is personal, is loving, and intends good. In an impersonal, undesigned world, enjoyment can be at best a meaningless accident. But in God's world, enjoyment is a clue to reality's deepest, brightest secret: that the universe is the gleeful invention of an unassailably happy God.

How would your life be different if you believed that your existence is the good idea of an infinitely glad God? What would it look like to found your life on the conviction that a happy God made you because he was happy to?

If you heed Qohelet's command to be joyful, you aren't shoplifting from the universe but following its maker's instruction manual or, more to the point, your host's wishes. God devised the recipe, obtained the ingredients, cooked the meal, set the table, and handwrote your name on the little folded slip of paper. Every gift bears a trace of its giver. Enjoyment is fitting because joy beyond and behind the universe joyed you and all things into existence. To enjoy life as God's gift is not to pretend life is something it isn't but to receive life as what it is. To enjoy is not to act as if but to act because.

▪ ▪ ▪

If human life is indeed a gift, it would be difficult to imagine a more important fact about it. If life is a gift, its gift-ness should shape how you view all of it. Every gift both invites and demands a fitting response. If life is a gift, how should you live it?

Not striving but receiving. If life is a gift, it's already been given. You don't need to take the world by force; someone has already given you your share in it. Not only that, but if life is a gift, then the countless inflows of energy and support and nurture you receive from the world and the people around you are so many streams of gifts. Beneath anything you want and don't have and might strive for lies life itself, given before you could ask for it or strive for it or deserve it or achieve it or do anything else for it (since you didn't exist). You can neither give yourself life nor secure your own life. You are in no way self-sufficient. Your being is neither self-grounding nor self-sustaining. Instead, you are a finite, vulnerable creature, defined by your needs for nurture, shelter, and company. As obvious as it is that you exist, it's equally clear that your life is not your own but comes from elsewhere. If life is a gift, then life is a grace and a miracle. Grace because you didn't deserve it; miracle because you can't explain it. What you can and must do is receive it. What does that receiving look like?

Not grasping but opening and loosening. Grasping seeks to keep whatever you receive and conform it to your will. But receiving with loose, open hands allows you to let everything you receive be itself and come and go as its nature impels and its giver intends. Grasping is the way to break something, especially something fragile; holding gently and loosely is the way to enjoy it. Health, a house, a holiday, a job, a child—each is a gift, and each has its arc. Each not only comes but soon goes, or you go from it.

What does opening and loosening allow you to do with the gift? Not keep but give. Open hands allow you not only to receive gifts but to give them. One of the truest signs that you do not take your life for granted but receive it as given is that you give generously. To give a gift is to declare the goodness of the object and your delight in its recipient. Generosity is the mark of a person who knows that receiving lies deeper than earning or achieving because life is gift all the way down. As the apostle Paul asks, "What do you have that you did not receive?"

And generosity is only possible if your basic stance toward your life, its goods, and their sources is not control but trust. As Norman Wirzba says, "To receive is to trust that what the giver gives is good." You cannot control what gift someone gives you or when they give it. But if life is a gift, every moment announces the giver's generosity and love. If your life is a gift, then every beat of your heart thumps out evidence of God's generosity and love. The Jewish philosopher Abraham Joshua Heschel saw this:

> In receiving a gift the recipient obtains, besides the present, also the love of the giver. A gift is thus the vessel that contains the affection, which is destroyed as soon as the recipient begins to look on it as a possession. The pious man avers that he has a perpetual gift from God, for in all that comes to him he feels the love of God. In all the thousand and one experiences that make up a day, he is conscious of that love intervening in his life.

A gift is not only itself but more than itself: Every gift that deserves the name is wrapped in love. Your life is not only itself but is a beat-by-beat transcription of God's love for you. You can't control God's gifts, but, if you trust God's goodness, you don't need to.

Trading control for trust also allows you to not dominate but submit. One of our stubbornest illusions is that we own the world and can therefore do what we want with it. If your basic stance toward your life is ownership, if you think you possess your life and the goods that fill it, then it will be hard not to assume that everything in your life, from traffic to the weather, should conform to your wishes. But other creatures are not here to do your bidding. To realize that other creatures, too, are gifts is to respect their givens. A child will only walk so fast. A day will only last so long. All gifts weigh something; some are heavy. Marriage is a gift so heavy that fear keeps many away. To receive a gift is to submit to its weight, to bear it up and bear up under it.

But whatever their weight and however much work it takes to submit to their demands and refusals, recognizing all of life's goods as gifts sustains an attitude not of entitlement but gratitude. Not dissatisfied demand but the joy of giving thanks. To receive life as a gift is to recognize that this universe has a moral center and you aren't it. When life's gift-ness sneaks up on you, gratitude jumps up in you. But it catches in your throat, mute and sterile, and eventually dissolves, unless it can fly out as words addressed to someone.

But what words, and to whom? Who can you thank for air just warm enough for a T-shirt, the sun setting pink and orange through shredded clouds at the horizon, a breeze bearing hints of the ocean's living depths, and skin, eyes, and a nose to receive these gifts? Who can you thank for the softness of a newborn's cheek? Giving thanks to God for gifts he has given you is no mere formality or religious nicety but enjoyment's consummation and crown. Giving thanks seals and completes the happiness God means his gifts to bring you.

13

Enjoy

What are you supposed to do with a gift? Enjoy it. But enjoying a gift can be harder than it sounds.

There are numberless ways not to enjoy a gift. You could wish you didn't have it. Wish you had something else. Wish you were somewhere else. Wish the gift wouldn't go so soon, so that even when you have it you feel more like you don't.

We respond these ways all the time to all sorts of gifts. We are adept at failing to enjoy the gifts that crowd our days: breakfast, fresh spring air, walking the dog with your youngest, different flowers around the block opening daily.

■ ■ ■

In each of Qohelet's seven gift-manifesto passages, he commends joy. Sometimes he even commands it, as in another verse that resonates with those we're considering: "In the day of prosperity be joyful." In these seven passages, in a series of synonymous expressions, Qohelet celebrates joy, commends enjoyment, tells us what to enjoy, and explains—implicitly, but crucially—how to enjoy. To refresh our memories with a sampling:

> There is nothing better for a person than that he should eat and drink and find enjoyment in his toil.

> I perceived that there is nothing better for them than to be joyful and to do good as long as they live; also that everyone should eat and drink and take pleasure in all his toil—this is God's gift to man.

> And I commend joy, for man has nothing better under the sun but to eat and drink and be joyful.

How can you enjoy life as a gift, and enjoy life's gifts as gifts? Be present to the present's presents. Present your full self fully to what the present presents you, and you will receive its full helping of enjoyment. Enjoyment depends on the ability, even the discipline, to be fully attentive to the goodness on offer. *Enjoy* is a present-tense verb, and to do it you must be present and not tense.

Enjoyment is only a present experience, not an item you can stockpile for future use. In Qohelet's terms, enjoyment is gift, not gain. Take for instance his experience of work: "I kept my heart from no pleasure, for my heart found pleasure in all my toil, and this was my reward for all my toil." The reward of Qohelet's toil was not the money or goods he obtained from the work, to be enjoyed later, but the pleasure he experienced in the work, to be enjoyed only now. Enjoyment cannot be stored for winter; it must be eaten before it spoils. What Qohelet finds worthwhile in work is not a later reward that toil painfully extracts but the pleasurable exertion of effort and energy, despite its pains and frustrations, as long as the work lasts. That is why he instructs the worker to find enjoyment "in" toil, not "from" it. As Heschel puts it, "Not being a hibernating animal, man cannot live by what he stores away."

What brings you joy? A late three-hour conversation with a new friend on a warm weeknight. Cooking and eating Saturday dinner with your family, say homemade pasta with pesto made from homegrown basil and homemade custard-based chocolate ice cream for dessert. Playing hide-and-seek with a four-year-old. Joy in these activities is their proper immediate effect. The joy you experience in them is self-standing. It does not depend on some further, future condition coming true. The future cannot take this present joy hostage. Gift requires no gain to be good.

Qohelet's solution to being preoccupied with the future and with what's wrong with the present is being properly occupied with what's right about the present.

> Behold, what I have seen to be good and fitting is to eat and drink and find enjoyment in all the toil with which one toils under the sun the few days of his life that God has given him, for this is his lot. Everyone also to whom God has given wealth and possessions and power to enjoy them, and to accept his lot and rejoice in his toil—this is the gift of God. For he will not much remember the days of his life because God keeps him occupied with joy in his heart.

The sixteenth-century Reformer Martin Luther comments, "This statement is the interpreter of the entire book." Its goal is "to forbid vain anxieties, so that we may happily enjoy the things that are present and not care at all about the things that are in the future, lest we permit the present moment, our moment, to slip away." The only time you can ever enjoy is now, and in every now God gives you much to enjoy. You might preoccupy yourself with fearful thoughts of the future, bitter thoughts of the past, or bleak thoughts of the present, but if you receive the present as a gift from God, then God fills your heart with joy. The joy God gives now occupies your heart, leaving no room for regret or anxiety to crowd in.

Some winters Washington, D.C., receives just a couple paltry dustings of snow. A quarter inch one day, a half inch two weeks later. Melt, gone. Just enough to shoot young children's hopes way up before they realize the meager, short-lived "snow" is good for nothing. But at least once every two or three years, a generous helping of puffy powder buries backyard, church parking lot, front lawn, and tree limbs in muffling, glinting glory. Depending on their motivation or lack of it, my children can sometimes take so long to get out of bed and dress themselves that a nonparent would conclude that disaster had fallen. But the morning of a snow day, my children launch out of bed and apply four layers of clothing, plus hats, boots, and gloves, in fifteen seconds. They will not be detained by breakfast. Who cares about food when it's snowing? We live a few blocks from the U.S. Capitol building, where sledding down its west lawn is sometimes permitted. When that's not an option, we pack snow onto the left half of our front steps, turning our yard into a sledding course headed by a short, steep hill: shoot straight down, course correct with a small berm on the lawn, slide straight out the path through the front gate, and then land softly in the planter before the street. On a snow day, our kids stay outside about as long as the snow does, making snowmen and snow angels, crafting ice sculptures, staging snowball fights, and concocting snow ice cream. For a child who does not want to swim at the local pool in the summer, seventy-nine-degree water on an eighty-nine-degree day might be "too cold." That same child, blissfully lost in the work of making a snowman, will hardly notice lumps of snow breaching his waistband and icily trickling down his legs. He does not much remember the cold because God keeps him occupied with joy in his heart.

Learning to receive everything as a gift from God's hand turns life itself into a snow day. What can you do with a snow day? You can't control it. You can't schedule it. You can't order it for delivery. You can't will a forecast into a guarantee. You have no say over how much snow will fall or how long it will stay. All you can do is enjoy it.

▪ ▪ ▪

Our eight-year-old son William is the sometimes-reluctant swimmer. His four-year-old sister Margaret does not share his hesitation, though she can't actually swim yet. On summer Saturdays at the pool in a suburb next to D.C. or weekday evenings when we pack dinner and enjoy the slanting light and softer heat, she wants nonstop action, which means she needs nonstop assistance. All she wants, in her whole life it seems, is for me to catch her as she jumps off the edge of the pool, again. The whole time, she's gleeful and giggling, perma-smile radiant.

A couple Saturdays ago, after launching Margaret skyward and catching her upon splashdown for the 46th time, or fielding her leap from the side for the 233rd time, I felt my mind start floating into shadows. Desires started tugging me elsewhere and elsewhen. *A breather could be nice. When do the lifeguards break? I wouldn't mind swimming laps for fifteen minutes. It would be great to have an hour or two to write this afternoon, but I doubt that will work for the family.*

What beauties was my heart ignoring, what barricades of blessing was my mind scrambling over, in order to wander away from this "sight of the eyes"? Water just cool enough to render the too-hot, too-humid air a pleasing pairing. Steadfast sunlight softened by occasional cumulus clusters. A ring of tall maples and pines cupping the property. Time and place sealed off from my job such that I not only didn't have to work but couldn't if I wanted to. My wife, our four children, and me, all enjoying ourselves together at a place with something for everyone—a zero-entry section and a mushroom-shaped overhead waterfall for the youngest, an ample shallow end for a not-yet-proficient swimmer to play in, diving boards for the more adventurous preteen and teen—the whole ensemble making me feel lighter and looser and younger than I had since, well, probably the last time we were here. And then of course the beaming, insatiable four-year-old herself, her cheeks lightly freckled by this summer's sun, reveling in propulsion and flight and all manner of water landings, between every toss or jump clinging to my neck and pressing her face to mine.

How can you be content? How can you enjoy the good you have rather than being embittered by present suffering or absent good? One common paradigm, which both Christians and Stoics can claim, and which can do much good, suggests there are two paths to contentment: Either your circumstances can rise to the level of your desires, or your desires can fall to the level of your circumstances. Either goods go up or heart comes down. The latter, of course, is the only sure bet. But outside up and inside down are not the only two options: You can also go deeper in. You can also present yourself more fully to what the present is giving you. You can pay better attention. You can apply yourself not to improvement but to enjoyment. Apply your mind more unitedly to the present good so that you see and savor more of the good that your hurried, wandering desires are prone to miss.

Care creates contentment. Care for the right thing, at the right time, in the right way. Care more about what's in front of you than what's behind you or away from you. Enjoyment does not take something from the world or take you out of the world. Instead, in philosopher Charles Mathewes's words, "Joy plunges us into time and the world, without letting us think that the world can ever be an adequate locus of our delight."

Wendell Berry laments, "Perhaps our most serious cultural loss in recent centuries is the knowledge that some things, though limited, can be inexhaustible." There is a teeming world of good in an afternoon at the pool with a four-year-old. The better you see it, the more you will savor it. Life itself is unfathomable and inexhaustible. If you want to enjoy it more, quiet your heart, commit your mind, and open your hands and your eyes.

▪ ▪ ▪

How could this life, though so strictly limited, be inexhaustible? Because every gift bears a trace of its giver, and every day and breath and moment is given by the inexhaustible God. Qohelet commends joy, appending the reason that "this will go with him in his toil through the days of his life that God has given him under the sun." Though the days of your life are restricted, the depth of the good in them is not.

How can you enjoy whatever good things are in your life

when so many have so little, and when you could be doing so much more to help them? By recalling that enjoyment is not your idea, but God's, and that he has officially authorized your enjoyment in advance: "Go, eat your bread with joy, and drink your wine with a merry heart, for God has already approved what you do." As Berry says, "Because so many are hungry, should we weep as we eat? No child will grow fat on our tears."

For Qohelet, enjoyment is serious business. Enjoyment is not just a benefit but a test, a proof of whether you receive life as God's gift. "Rejoice, O young man, in your youth, and let your heart cheer you in the days of your youth. Walk in the ways of your heart and the sight of your eyes. But know that for all these things God will bring you into judgment." Because God commands enjoyment, he will hold us to account for the use we have made of all his gifts, including whether we have enjoyed them as we ought. As one passage in the Talmud has it, "Everyone must give an account before God of all good things one saw in life and did not enjoy."

▪ ▪ ▪

You've probably been thinking (and if you haven't, Qohelet has) that this account of enjoyment can't be the whole story. Bring your whole self, okay. Life's goods are deeper and richer than you know, sure. But only while they last. Eventually, they run out and so do you.

Qohelet's seven shining celebrations of life's delectability are dappled by shadows of death and the absurd. People should be joyful and savor good "as long as they live." Every person should labor with enjoyment in all "the few days of his life that God has given him"—literally, "the number of the days of his life." Number implies limit. The life God has given consists not of eons or millennia or centuries but "days." Qohelet commands you to enjoy life "all the days of your absurd life," and to work with your whole self, "for there is no work or thought or knowledge or wisdom in Sheol, to which you are going." The shadows lengthen in Qohelet's last and longest celebration of enjoyment:

> Light is sweet, and it is pleasant for the eyes to see the sun.
>
> So if a person lives many years, let him rejoice in them all; but let him remember that the days of darkness will be many. All that comes is absurd.
>
> Rejoice, O young man, in your youth, and let your heart cheer you in the days of your youth. Walk in the ways of your heart and the sight of your eyes. But know that for all these things God will bring you into judgment.
>
> Remove vexation from your heart, and put away pain from your body, for youth and the dawn of life are fleeting.

In reading these passages we must resist two temptations. The first temptation is to filter out these darker tones in order to maintain the thesis that Qohelet is fundamentally a preacher of joy. We must not ignore or downplay the fact that hevel's reach extends into enjoyment's territory. The gifts to be received are fleeting. The days to be delighted in are numbered. The life to be enjoyed is absurd. Enjoyment is not a solution to life's absurdity since the goods we enjoy remain absurd.

The second temptation is to let these darker notes drown out the bright music of Qohelet's emphatic refrain that life is a gift to be accepted with astonished delight. Delight has its own integrity and gravity in Qohelet's thought. Delight witnesses to the God-gifted character of all creation. Receiving gifts with delight provides a strikingly simple agenda for living a good life. The gifts are not free of hevel; neither does hevel negate the gifts.

Now we must ask the question, What are the character and limits of an enjoyment that fits life's twofold nature as gift and absurd? How do we enjoy life in such a way that we neither despise its gift-ness nor deny its absurdity?

Help comes, in the first instance, from within Ecclesiastes itself. As we saw in the whole first part of this book, one factor in life's absurdity is that we stubbornly long for the world to be something it is not. We yearn for the world to give us something it can't. Qohelet's main word for this is "gain." We long for permanence, but life proves fleeting; we desire wholeness, but the world stays broken; we crave satisfaction, but our appetites always rebound. This aspect of absurdity is a problem not only with the world but with us. Pascal describes this stance as seeking our ultimate happiness, which he calls our "sovereign good," in the goods of this world. Qohelet himself, in his existential quest for gain, embodies this futile search for the sovereign good in this world's goods. Pascal perceives the universal disappointment that follows from seeking ultimate good in any good in this world:

> Others again, who have indeed come closer to it, have found it impossible that this universal good, desired by all men, should lie in any of the particular objects which can only be possessed by one individual and which, once shared, cause their possessors more grief over the part they lack than satisfaction over the part they enjoy as their own. They have realized that the true good must be such that it may be possessed

> by all men at once without diminution or envy, and that no one should be able to lose it against his will. Their reason is that this desire is natural to man, since all men inevitably feel it, and man cannot be without it.

To enjoy any worldly good properly, you must not try to enjoy it ultimately. To rejoice rightly in any earthly pleasure, you must respect its limits. To delight in any finite good, you must not deify it.

Further help comes from the church father Augustine, who built an ethic on the distinction between the transient and the permanent. If you seek ultimate good in any of this world's goods, your self will scatter and dissipate among them. Not to mention you'll be perpetually disappointed. What then can be a fitting object for our ultimate desire? What object of desire can unite the self instead of scattering it? What can bear the full weight of our ceaseless yearning? Only God. Only God is all-satisfying. Accordingly, all created goods are to be treated as signs pointing to God as their source and goal. To capture this distinction, Augustine says that only God should be "enjoyed" in the sense of total affective investment, while created goods are to be "used," not in the sense of being manipulated or reduced to tools, but in that they point beyond themselves. The only right way to take pleasure in a creature is to receive it as a gift and sign of its creator; your desire should not end with the creature but be directed by the creature to God.

Augustine says Ecclesiastes exposes the whole transitory world as vain in order that we might long for eternal life with God. When the world is all that you love, your love sours and rots. But when you love the world for God's sake, your love breathes and flowers. To seek "gain" in this life is to seek what can only be found in God. But to treat creatures as signs announcing the generosity and abundance of their creator is at once to delight in them as goods and prevent them from becoming gods.

You can enjoy created goods most when you enjoy God infinitely more. You can love limited goods safely when you love the unlimited one supremely. You can only enjoy fleeting blessings as fully as you should when you seek fullness in the only unfleeting one.

14

Lot

If I could raise any periodical from the dead, it would be *Books & Culture.* That singular magazine ran from 1995 to 2016; it was something like a Christian *New York Review of Books.* John Wilson, who founded the magazine and edited it for its entire run, considers a magazine a microcosm, a tiny storehouse that proclaims the inexhaustible richness of the world. That richness was evident in the breadth of subjects that the reviewed books addressed, the fruitful diversity of authors, and the compelling craftsmanship of the prose. I started reading the magazine late in its run, in perhaps 2012. Every issue included pieces on books I had never heard of, written (both book and review) by authors I did not know, on topics I did not yet care about, but I would start reading, and by the second paragraph I'd be hooked.

In 2016, *Books & Culture* ceased. The magazine was not making financial ends meet. The publisher mounted a fundraising campaign, but it fell short. I was sorely disappointed, maybe even a little bitter. Why couldn't people with big money see the value here? But John Wilson, if disappointed, was certainly not bitter. He said, "When the magazine came to an end, I didn't think it meant somehow it had been a failure, and I didn't think it expressed some global truth about evangelicalism."

Early in the magazine's life, a well-meaning fundraiser would tell potential donors how *Books & Culture* was going to change the culture. Wilson recounts,

> I said, don't say that! Whatever "the culture" is, we're not going to change it.
>
> I had this phrase, *a small good thing*. You know, what we were doing was really good. We didn't have to make these sweeping claims for our work. It's just something worth doing and we should be glad that we can do it. I felt this way from the start to the end. I was very sad when we had to stop. But, you know, that's life.

▪ ▪ ▪

John Wilson's phrase, "a small good thing," closely fits Qohelet's Hebrew word that we translate as "lot" or "portion." When Qohelet says "lot," he means something good. He also means that good thing has limits. You can only receive the good by regarding the limits.

> So I saw that there is nothing better than that a man should rejoice in his work, for that is his lot.

> Behold, what I have seen to be good and fitting is to eat and drink and find enjoyment in all the toil with which one toils under the sun the few days of his life that God has given him, for this is his lot. Everyone also to whom God has given wealth

> and possessions and power to enjoy them, and to accept his lot and rejoice in his toil—this is the gift of God.

> Enjoy life with the wife whom you love, all the days of your vain life that he has given you under the sun, because that is your portion in life and in your toil at which you toil under the sun.

In ancient Israel, the Hebrew word for "lot" could refer to a share of something, such as spoil from war, distributed by lot—a device that randomizes decision-making, sort of like dice. It could also mean a plot of ground, as in a fixed place that one inhabits and stewards, or a share of money or property given by one to another. Qohelet uses the term "lot" as a capsule for all of life: work, opportunity, wealth, potential for enjoyment, the whole show. His use of "lot" implies not randomized distribution but the deliberate choice of an allotter. The property is God's. He distributes it as he wills. It's yours because it's first his.

Because God is the allotter, we human recipients have no say over the quality or quantity of our portion. A lot is something you are assigned and stuck with, regardless of whether you find it sufficient or think you deserve more. You have no say over its scope. You can edit the magazine, but who will fund it? You can write the book, but who will buy it? You can earn the degree, but who will hire you? Modernity is the illusion that you can always expand your share of the world; Qohelet's wisdom is that your life is enclosed by limits you do not set.

By definition, a portion is limited. Mom cooks a pound of pasta and then serves you a heap. Big or small, the portion is what you get. It is what it is. That's that.

"Lot" implies both responsibility and opportunity. The responsibility begins with accepting your lot, so receive it with thanks. But accepting your lot is the beginning of your responsibility for it, not the end. Like a plot of land, every person's lot calls for cultivation. Receiving your lot gratefully teaches you to care for the lot you have, not lust for one you don't. Unplanted crops will not grow. Untended relationships will not flourish. Undeveloped skills will not land a job or produce joy. To receive your lot rightly is to get to work planting, cultivating, tending, and harvesting. And your lot bears within itself the potential to yield joy: joy in the work, joy in its fruits, and joy in discovering the goodness and wholeness that come from adapting to your limits rather than trying, godlike, to bend the world to your will.

15

Eat and Drink

Among our four children, our pickiest eater, William, tends to eat quickest. His meals are spartan and offer little resistance. Plus, he is almost always eager to race back outside, or up the stairs, to whatever action our meal interrupted. But then his younger sister, who eats even more slowly than the adults, wants to follow him off into whatever he's doing or at least go play because he gets to. Sometimes dinner feels like forty minutes of work for four minutes of family time. At least dessert, when we have it, hauls them back.

Last night, during the window when the younger children had bounded off but the rest of us were still eating, our youngest daughter, Margaret, returned from the front yard. A bright, peppery scent billowed from her hands. The sweet, citrusy cloud thickened as she spoke.

"Hey, Meg," I said, "did you go pick some basil?"

"Yes," she said. Her gaze brightened, eyes gleaming: "I ate some!"

Basil is the only food that we are currently growing for ourselves. I would love to grow much more. Maybe soon we will. But, within a couple weeks, some of this lonely basil will be chopped and ground and mixed with olive oil and garlic and parmesan cheese and pine nuts, and then we will spread it over the homemade pasta we cook every other Saturday for dinner. The other Saturdays, we make homemade pizza: bread-machine dough topped with pepperoni, Italian sausage, and a simple homemade sauce. Lately we have added homemade ice cream, with a custard base and whatever flavors the kids choose, on rotation. I know this is a tall claim, it might sound self-serving, and you'll have to take my word for it, but the chocolate we just made was the best ice cream I've ever had, and I've had my share. It was creamier than the creamiest ice cream I have bought from any creamery. If you want a second opinion, ask my friend Michael Abraham. I am confident that, for me at least, it would pass any blindfold test you could set.

For many of its residents, Washington, D.C., is a city that lives and dies by the schedule. In my work as a pastor, my daily and weekly schedules are often full to bursting. To compensate, as a family, we try to keep Saturdays as unscheduled as possible. The two events that anchor our day are breakfast and dinner. For the past several years, virtually every Saturday that we're at home begins with me making a pancake breakfast for everyone, with bacon in the oven, scrambled eggs for protein, and usually Trader Joe's fresh-squeezed orange juice. Almost always, somewhere from one to four children pad downstairs and join the cooking. With a recipe as simple as pancakes, devising a job for each interested party requires careful division of tasks. Wet ingredients, dry ingredients, pouring, flipping. Recently, our two older girls, Rose and Lucy, have taken more active supervisory roles, and Kristin and I get to sit on the kitchen couch, watch, read, and drink coffee. Home never feels more like home than in those few minutes. Crafty preteen Lucy has taken over shaping specialty pancakes—dolphins, owls, otters, balloons—doing it far better than I ever did. Once the pancakes, bacon, eggs, and orange juice make it to the table, along with all six humans, we quickly consume the provisions. Bang—the kids shoot off to play and craft, and I get to wash the dishes. But the meal, both cooking and eating, brought us together.

▪ ▪ ▪

In all but two of his passages celebrating enjoyment, Qohelet lauds eating and drinking. He says there is nothing better for a person than to "eat and drink and find enjoyment in his toil," that every person should "eat and drink and take pleasure in all his toil," and that it is "good and fitting" to eat and drink. And he is so bold as to not only instruct us to eat and drink but to tell us how to feel while we do: "Go, eat your bread with joy, and drink your wine with a merry heart, for God has already approved what you do."

Why this focus on eating and drinking? As sources of enjoyment go, food's difficulty range starts at "almost effortless": picking fruit from a tree or berries from a bush. Food is necessary: To live well, we all need some every day. Beyond being necessary, eating is one of the most reliable, frequently repeated pleasures. Most of us eat multiple times a day, and most meals cast up at least some sparks of enjoyment. Eating is for everyone—young and old, poor and rich. Sometimes those who have less enjoy it more. "Sweet is the sleep of a laborer, whether he eats little or much, but the full stomach of the rich will not let him sleep." And eating is essentially a present-tense enjoyment. Sure, aroma-triggered anticipation is not all pain, and fullness after a meal is a kind of satisfaction, but most of the enjoyment comes in the eating itself—savoring the tastes, feeling the textures, sating the hunger, slaking the thirst—not before or after.

Seen in this light, eating is a paradigm of proper consumption. There is no "gain" to be had from food. Enough is as good as a feast; the cake cannot be both eaten and had. Unlike money, food has a built-in shut-off switch. Eat too much too fast, and bad things happen. Like heat from a burning log, food releases pleasure when it is consumed.

Our culture's distorted relationship to both food and drink can make it hard to see that, and how, both can be enjoyed. For many, especially many women, a desperate desire to be thin turns food into a nemesis to be kept at bay. For others, drinking is not a moderate, self-controlled way to enjoy company and savor rest but a self-destructive attempt to cope with or escape from burdens and ghosts. And some seek similarly empty solace in an excess of food. Food and drink can both be received with thanksgiving, but damaging cultural pressures and our own deceitful hearts turn them into dangers rather than gifts.

Why should you rejoice in eating and drinking? Because food is not merely necessary. Someone who loves you infinitely has ensured that required bodily maintenance has the potential to bring ever-new enjoyment. By God's design, the sustenance that keeps you from dying is not bitter or tasteless but endless varieties of delicious. The necessary is needlessly delightful.

This marriage of survival and delight is not a happy accident but a strategically planted clue to the secret of everything. This universe is the creation of a God so rich and full in himself that he needs nothing and no one else to be infinitely satisfied. This universe is not a symptom of need but a signature of generosity. God is so good that he created the universe, stuffed it with marvels, and made creatures in his image who can see and feel and touch and taste them. As Robert Farrar Capon says, "Food is the daily sacrament of unnecessary goodness, ordained for a continual remembrance that the world will always be more delicious than it is useful." Being itself is not only good but festive. We have taste buds to teach us that existence is delectable. Food's flavor reminds you that nothing had to exist. This universe's existence, and mine and yours, owes not to calculation but exuberance. It is God's untiring delight that powers the sun's fusion that heats the soil that sends the wheat skyward. The sun rises because, every morning, like a child who never tires of jumping off the side of the pool, God says to it, "Again!"

How can you rejoice in eating and drinking? Depending on your circumstances and means, all kinds of prudent practices might help you enjoy eating more. Slow down and savor. Eat regularly with your roommates or family, and regularly invite others to join you. Cook more from scratch. Eggs, flour, a fork to mix with, and hands to knead are all it takes to make pasta dough. Crushed tomatoes, butter, and an onion can make a delicious marinara sauce. To the extent that you can, buy food that was grown and raised near where you live, from the people who grew it. Grow some of your own, even if only basil.

Like all earthly gifts, food and drink are small good things. Like all earthly gifts, the better attention you pay to them, the bigger they grow.

Receive the gift of eating as a paradigm of a proper creaturely pleasure. Let the twice- or thrice-daily experience of taking nourishment remind you, or teach you for the first time, that you are dependent far more than you are autonomous. As Norman Wirzba observes, "Whenever people come to the table they demonstrate with the unmistakable evidence of their stomachs that they are not self-subsisting gods." Your life is not self-contained like a bubble but is a bundle of strands in an infinitely rich meshwork. Your life is a tissue of dependencies. Life is not a power or possession that you gave yourself or got for yourself. Even without intervening economies of processing, packaging, and transportation, your life continually depends on eating, which depends on many people's intelligent work of cultivating crops and raising animals, which depends on favorable weather and rain and healthy soil, which depend on healthy watersheds and viable ecosystems, which all depends, ultimately, on God's perpetual work of effortlessly upholding all things by his powerful word.

Who told you that you were autonomous? If you can't create yourself or sustain yourself, what makes you think you can decide right and wrong for yourself?

You depend on creation. And, along with all creation, you depend on God. Just as your body receives nourishment from outside to stay alive, so life itself, as it were, comes to you from outside. "Food is God's love made nutritious and delicious." Food is a daily reminder that life is God's gift, and it is good.

16

Toil

"First job, worst job?" My friend and fellow pastor Troy Maragos has a knack for keeping conversation flowing. Our pastoral staff was stuffed in our church van, driving back to the office after lunch. (Another time it was "First concert, best concert?")

My first job was unusual, my worst job unimpressive. Beginning in my early teens, I aspired to play professional jazz saxophone. My parents saw that I had talent and drive, and they are remarkably generous and supportive. During the summers of my middle school and high school years, they never required or even suggested that I get a summer job. Instead, they left me alone to practice in my room for six hours a day. Like I said: drive. In those years I started making small money performing music: restaurants, weddings, the occasional jazz club and concert venue. I also taught some lessons to younger students. So, my first job was as a jazz musician, I guess.

I went on to obtain an undergraduate degree in music performance. When I started the degree, I fully intended to spend my life eking out a living by my craft, though by the time I finished I was heading in a whole other direction. Most working jazz musicians scrape together their subsistence through varied, constantly changing portfolios: performing locally as a sideman; recording commercial music in studios; touring as part of a popular act's supporting ensemble; teaching private lessons or at high schools and colleges. Almost always absent from the list of what pays the biggest share of your bills is playing the music you most want to play. In taking the first steps into a career as a musician, I discovered that the more I liked the music I was playing, the less it paid, and the less I liked the music, the more it paid. But that's not why I changed paths.

By the time I finished the music degree in May 2008, I had a settled desire to serve as a pastor of a local church. At least I was already prepared for a job with a low financial ceiling. When I graduated, Kristin and I were newly married and needed short-term jobs to see us through the summer, at the end of which, we hoped, we'd be moving to Washington, D.C., so I could train for ministry at Capitol Hill Baptist Church. Kristin cleaned houses. I found a job as a driver for the Los Angeles Philharmonic, ferrying artists between LAX and the Hollywood Bowl and their hotels in a company-owned compact SUV. For a decade I had practiced and dreamed and practiced and networked and practiced and forsaken all other pursuits in order, in the not-too-distant future, to be one of those artists playing venues like the Hollywood Bowl. Now I was their driver. On top of the insult to my pride lay inconvenient hours, long evenings sitting around backstage, and plenty of predictably awful traffic. On my first day on the job, my passengers were a mid-level jam band whose party of the night before was nowhere near finished. Every job I've had since then has yielded more enjoyment and less hassle. For a "worst job" entry, though, this was pitifully mild and mercifully brief. Most people, in most places and times, had and have it harder.

■ ■ ■

In his passages that commend enjoying the good, Qohelet mentions work ten times. Three times he uses neutral Hebrew words for work, corresponding to our "work" and "do": "So I saw that there is nothing better than that a man should rejoice in his work." "Whatever your hand finds to do, do it with your might, for there is no work or thought or knowledge or wisdom in Sheol, to which you are going." The other seven speak of "toil": "There is nothing better for a person than that he should . . . find enjoyment in his toil." "Behold, what I have seen to be good and fitting is to . . . find enjoyment in all the toil with which one toils under the sun."

Qohelet says "toil" most of the time, even in passages urging enjoyment, to highlight work's defects. Toil is wearying and repetitive. Toil is hard on body, mind, or both. Toil is not a succession of peak moments but a slog that seems too long and too slow. Qohelet's talk of enjoying toil might seem defeatist and contradictory. How are you supposed to enjoy toil? Isn't toil unenjoyable by definition?

The elements of this riddle contain the seeds of its solution. It is precisely by treating work as toil that you can enjoy it rightly. If you expect work to be quick and easy, disappointment and disillusionment will team up against you. If you expect work to satisfy all your desires for novelty, variety, growth, recognition, status, significance, and glamour, you will crush enjoyment under the weight of your idolatries. Instead, expect frustration, delays, detours, breakdowns, roadblocks, conflicts, and all manner of interruption. Expect work to be hard. If you do, you may find enjoyment springing up when you least expect it.

But how? How can you find enjoyment in toil, as toil, despite all that makes work toil?

Respect limits. How much you can achieve, how long it will last, and how happy it will make you are all finite. If you haven't yet hit any of those walls, don't worry, it won't be long now. Respect the limits of those you work with: their abilities, responsibilities, strengths, and weaknesses. Respect the limits of those your work affects indirectly, like your family members. If you have a husband or wife, even more if you have children, how much of your absence can they bear and still flourish? Respect the limits of your own body and mind.

To enjoy toil, the first thing you have to learn is when to stop. Only finite toil gives enjoyment. Infinite toil is slavery, degrading and destructive. Unlike infinite toil, finite toil leaves time and strength to enjoy its fruits. If poverty is pressing you to work harder and longer than anyone should have to, just to survive, pray for strength and relief. In the too-rare times when you can rest, make sure you do rest. Resist temptations to blow off steam in ways that harm yourself and waste what God has given you to steward.

Rest does not exist for the sake of work but work for the sake of rest. That's what the Bible's Sabbath command teaches us. God did not create the world only to set it spinning into endless cycles of work. Instead, he worked, finished the job, and sanctified a day for enjoyment—both his and ours. You will enjoy toil when you leave yourself time to enjoy not toiling.

A second practical counsel: Cultivate craft. I don't primarily mean making things by hand, though that can certainly come into the picture. I mean, more broadly, cultivate the mindset and skilled practices of a craftsman. Approach all work—at home or out of it, paid or unpaid, professional or amateur—as a craft. One of the rewards of a craft is the practice of the craft: The better a craftsman you are, the more you enjoy the work. The essence of craftsmanship is to do a job well for its own sake. To enjoy toil, treat toil as something worth enjoying.

Work that respects the worth of toil is driven by quality. Prize quality over quantity, and you are on your way to becoming a craftsman. If you ask what it takes to do a job well, you will learn about it and grow through it. When you aim at quality, the small good thing grows bigger. As Richard Sennett observes, "The aspiration for quality will drive a craftsman to improve, to get better rather than get by."

What work in your life can you treat as a craft? If you're not much of a cook, maybe start by learning a recipe for a meal you love. If your job is tedious, find one skill (like writing!) that you can hone at work. When you approach work as a craft, difficulties are not a deterrent or defeat but a spur to growth.

Even a job as menial as driving can—or did—afford room for growth. Back in that summer of 2008, before ubiquitous GPS and real-time traffic data, more seasoned drivers told me which surface streets would flow faster than clogged freeways. That one tip left me not only one click more competent but three clicks more at home in Los Angeles, even though we left a few weeks later. Knowing that I could sometimes beat the traffic helped me find more to like in a city of asphalt as flat and sprawling as its sunshine. Toil endured patiently, gratefully, with respect for limits and an eye for craft, makes the world more of a home for you and those you love, and it makes you more at home in the world.

17

Wealth

One of the paradoxes of our consumer society is that we are not a consumer society. Instead, we are an acquirer society. We are a people devoted to endless acquisition, regardless of whether we ever get around to enjoying what we've acquired. When you buy something—say, a new shirt—it seems to expand your world and make it shimmer slightly. That buzz may last the first time or the first three times you wear the shirt, but you can feel it fade. The shirt buzzes less each wear. Eventually, forgotten on a hanger in the closet, it brings no buzz at all. Once you get the thing, it quickly turns to nothing.

So what do we do? Many keep purchasing goods without using them since each item just gets old anyway. Whether shirt or shoes or car or house, we keep buying to keep buzzing.

▪ ▪ ▪

If you calculate by simple number of mentions, Qohelet makes five negative statements about wealth and only one positive.

His ratio roughly matches that of the New Testament. Jesus warns that it is hard—humanly impossible, in fact—for the rich to enter the kingdom of God. He demands that a young rich man sell all he has in order to become his disciple. He warns of the folly of heaping up goods for projected future enjoyment when you could die any day. And the apostle Paul warns that those who desire to be rich pierce themselves with many pangs. But Paul also says to the rich:

> As for the rich in this present age, charge them not to be haughty, nor to set their hopes on the uncertainty of riches, but on God, who richly provides us with everything to enjoy. They are to do good, to be rich in good works, to be generous and ready to share, thus storing up treasure for themselves as a good foundation for the future, so that they may take hold of that which is truly life.

As we have seen in chapter 6, like Paul, Qohelet warns that wealth is deceptive and fleeting, and it often does its possessor more harm than good. Though not as full or theologically explicit, Qohelet's single affirmative statement about wealth chimes with Paul's in one crucial sense: "Everyone also to whom God has given wealth and possessions and power to enjoy them, and to accept his lot and rejoice in his toil—this is the gift of God."

Qohelet and Paul agree that wealth is a God-given gift to be enjoyed. But how? From a biblical point of view, asking how to enjoy wealth is like asking how to enjoy indoor fireworks. It's not impossible, but it's close. You had better heed the warnings and prepare safety measures. What can we learn from Qohelet about how to enjoy wealth without damaging your soul?

Make enjoying a higher priority than getting. Escape the cycle of getting without enjoying. Recognize that getting and enjoying can compete, such that the more you get the less you enjoy both what you get and what you already had. You may need to get less in order to enjoy what you already have. With enough money, your capacity to get far exceeds your capacity to enjoy. It's easier to buy a surfboard than learn to surf. As John Ruskin saw, "Wise consumption is a far more difficult art than wise production." We tend to think of wealth as a potentially limitless quantity, a figure to which another zero can always be added. Aristotle would have said that such astronomical accumulation is unnatural. By contrast, as he saw it and as we should too, natural accumulation of wealth aims at obtaining things useful for the household. In order to count as wealth, what money can get you has to be something your household can and will use.

Some of my kids' favorite summer weekdays and school-year Saturdays are what we call "library days." After breakfast, one or both of us parents will load all four kids into our minivan and drive to our favorite public library about twenty minutes away. Everyone then spends the rest of the morning browsing and accumulating books to borrow. We bring a collapsible wagon to haul off the morning's catch. If the weather is nice, we might pack a lunch and enjoy the nearby playground. After the drive home, an uncommon quiet gathers about the house. It lasts most of the afternoon. If money could buy that family-wide calm, I would pay dearly for a daily portion. But, in fourteen years and counting of parenting, so far such serenity has emerged only from the free pleasures of the library.

Of course, the books must eventually be returned. But then, the library is a renewable resource, not to mention a public good. You don't have to own the book to read it; you don't have to own the library to access it; you don't even have to pay the library to use it. They're just out there all day handing out stacks of books for free. Someone please put these people in charge of everything. We use the books, they come due, and we return them. The wealth belongs to the library. We may briefly withdraw as much of that wealth as we can reasonably enjoy.

And so the library teaches a second lesson about how to enjoy wealth. To enjoy what you have, remember that you do not really have it. As David Klemm observes, "Most people hold that owning property is an unqualified good, because property brings power, enjoyment, and prestige to its owner. They take delight in their possessions, become attached to the objects of their desire, and in this way are in fact possessed by them." If you inordinately desire material goods, they become your owner rather than you being theirs. And so disordered desire for wealth supplants love of God. You look to wealth to ensure your well-being and satisfy your longings, but ultimately only God himself can secure such ends, because he is the only all-sufficient security and satisfaction. Klemm continues, "From such attachment to goods, various forms of evil result: attitudes of envy, greed, and enmity lead to scheming, treachery, feuds, unfounded lawsuits, thefts, forceful expropriation, injury, murder, and even war."

In contrast to this epidemic of inordinate desire for wealth and the goods it promises, the only right and safe way to hold wealth's goods is loosely, with a protective detachment coating your hands that keeps you from grasping wealth's goods and hurting yourself. The key ingredient in that protective coating is gratitude. Every finite, fleeting possession is a leaflet dropped from heaven, proclaiming the God who alone is our infinite, permanent wealth. The way to enjoy wealth is to use it for the sake of enjoying God.

In what sense do you not really have what you have? Everything you have belonged to God before it belonged to you, and it still belongs to God though it also belongs to you. Everything you have, you one day will not have. You'd like to think you'll have a few more decades with it, but who knows? It could all be recalled tomorrow. Everything you have, you will answer to God for what you've done with it. You didn't make it but were given it. Even what you have earned is the result of deeper and more definitive giving. You worked for it? Who gave you hands and feet, eyes and mind, a heart pumping blood, and a brain astonishingly calibrated to attune you to reality?

Easy come, easy go. A right detachment allows you to enjoy wealth because you realize that, however easy or hard it came, it will go easier than you want. No matter how hard you worked for your wealth, the power that granted it was God's. No matter how carefully you plan and manage, very soon death will strip every item from your shelves.

All wealth is loaned from God's library. What should you do with it? Enjoy it. Share it. Remember that it's due soon.

18

Marriage

"That's why you're the happiest person I've ever met." That is one of the strangest things anyone has ever said to me. Certainly one of the oddest compliments, and hardest to respond to. It sounded like an accusation. Was I supposed to plead guilty? I think I just tried to laugh it off.

Before this exchange, my friend Matt and I had corresponded a bit and had a couple meals together. (Last name withheld to protect the eccentric.) In July of 2016, we were enjoying an idyllic English evening looking out over rolling, manicured garden and grounds after an academic conference had wound down for the day. Matt's comment came after the first time he computed my age, how long I had been married, and how many children I had. At the time, I was twenty-nine, had been married for eight years, and had three kids.

If you ask the next hundred people you see how you can become quickly, reliably, and lastingly happy, how many of them would tell you, "Get married and have kids as soon as you possibly can"? My guess is almost none. Plus one if your hundred happens to include my friend Matt.

Americans, Westerners, and people throughout the so-called developed world are marrying later and less. In 1970, among Americans ages twenty-five to fifty, only 9 percent had never married. In 2018, that figure was 35 percent. In America today, the median age at first marriage is twenty-eight for women and thirty for men, up from twenty for women and twenty-two for men in 1960. And children, like marriage, are coming fewer and later.

▪ ▪ ▪

If you were to ask Qohelet how to be happy, and of course that is the main thing we are doing in this book, his answer would include, "Enjoy life with the wife whom you love, all the days of your absurd life that he has given you under the sun, because that is your portion in life and in your toil at which you toil under the sun."

Why is marriage a staple in Qohelet's happiness program but disappearing from ours? You could point to structural, societal differences that separate us from his ancient, largely agrarian culture in which virtually everyone married as a matter of course. But then Qohelet does not have to mention marriage. If his society took marriage for granted, so could he. Instead, he praises it.

Throughout the modern era, beginning in about the sixteenth century, romantic love has undergone a series of radical transformations. Premodern love arose from and in turn fostered social order, virtues, and character. But in the modernizing West, love has been disentangled from traditional virtues, morals, and any widely held account of love's origins, limits, purposes, and duties. In brief, love has been set free from God and has become a god. Love has become a central drive requiring fine-tuned fulfillment. Love has given the self a narrative structure: I must quest for my true love and can only be happy if I find him or her. My desire, which demands satisfaction, has become the defining feature of love. Only if my desire can be lavishly satisfied does the relationship count as loving. And, as everyone knows, a person should only marry their true love. This redefined, romanticized, expressive-individualist love has become many people's first prerequisite for marriage.

Among many problems with modernity's transformation of love, two are especially pertinent to marriage. One is that it turns the beloved into an object to be consumed. In modern romances, lovers become extractive industrialists. If the goal of your quest is your own pleasure, you will try to get as much pleasure from the relationship at as little cost as possible—whether that cost is emotional investment, nurturing care, or the sacrifice of other aims. That cost-benefit analysis is no basis for a permanent pledge of exclusive mutual devotion. A second problem is that the quest to find one's true love, even if successful, does not equip one to skillfully sustain what comes next, which we might call the toil of nurture. The quest culminates, if it ever does, in a moment—a wedding, the altar, "I do," fade out, "and they lived happily ever after." But the quest does not train one for decades of toiling at nurture. That nearly half of all "first marriages" in America end in divorce attests to how difficult it is to cross the chasm from quest to nurture.

If you marry, there is no more quest for "the one." Now you are stuck with the one and have to figure out how to build a life with the one. Start by putting your spouse's happiness above yours and finding yours in theirs. Those are not two opposite or competing goals but two sides of the same goal. Happiness is always a by-product. You can only get happiness from marriage if you put into marriage the kind of thing that produces happiness, namely, what makes your spouse flourish. In short, practice continual self-giving love. Practice dying to your own desires. The only way to "get" from marriage is to constantly put giving ahead of getting.

Wedding vows are a blank check. In them you promise to give whatever needs giving, and give up whatever needs losing, in order to care comprehensively for the one you are covenanting with. You have no idea how much the vow will cost you or when the costs will come due.

If your love for your spouse is self-giving, then it will naturally extend in fitting ways to others, chiefly those others who are marriage's natural fruit and fulfillment. I mean children. If you desire sex but fear marriage, you don't know what sex is or what it is for. If you desire marriage but fear children, you don't yet know what marriage is or what it is for. Marriage is not for bottling love but making it flow.

Marriage is a soil that, when healthy, sustains both spouses. But, for the marriage to sustain husband and wife, each spouse must nurture the soil that nurtures them. Wendell Berry casts the vision: "It is possible to imagine marriage as a grievous, joyous human bond, endlessly renewable and renewing, again and again rejoining memory and passion and hope." The toil of nurture is the discipline by which husband and wife continually renew their marriage and find that it continually renews them. Practices that enact this discipline are endless and varied: gentle touch as a frequent token of affection; patient listening; providing for needs and wants before the other even asks; gladly surrendering minor preferences; jealously protecting time for unhurried lovemaking. The pleasures that grow from the toil of nurture differ in kind from those of the quest. They are richer, more complex, and more durable than the quest's fleeting highs. And, as with the taste of wines barreled in a cool cellar, passing years deepen them.

19

Resonance

In all seven gift-choruses, Qohelet commends enjoying what you have while you have it. The substance of his counsel is to find joy in present sources: work, food and drink, possessions, marriage, the shining sun itself. In the words of a song few readers will know, "But for now we are young, let us lay in the sun and count every beautiful thing we can see."

In order to enjoy these goods rather than scorn, ignore, or crush them, it is crucial to respect their limits and yours. These goods cannot be guaranteed or controlled. They cannot be perpetually protected from destruction or loss. They cannot be hoarded, preserved in vacuum-sealed bags until a future day of enjoyment finally arrives. There is no "future finally" about these small good things. They're here, they're yours, and the only time to enjoy them is now.

Equally crucial to enjoying these goods is recognizing that they are gifts in a literal, not metaphorical, sense. God gives life; God gives all the days that stretch life's span; God gives all the gifts that liven and lighten life's days. Because life is a gift, receiving with thanks is more basic to enjoying life than earning, and more decisive to finding happiness than achieving.

Though it is only a sketch in bold strokes, Qohelet's practical philosophy of the good life accounts for what your peak moments have in common with small joys amid daily grinds. From spectacular to so subtle it barely registers, each source of joy communicates good from the inexhaustible source of good who is himself infinite good. Every small good gift brings joy because it bears the fingerprints of joy himself.

■ ■ ■

Each of Qohelet's exhortations to delight commends or even commands enjoying *something.* He never treats happiness as a mere mood you can conjure at will. For Qohelet, happiness is not mind over matter or mind regardless of matter, but mind tuned to matter. Enjoyment is a matter of rightly relating yourself to all the world that lies within reach.

Think of a tuning fork. If you have never seen one, picture a long, thin, two-tined metal fork with a handle. If you strike one of the tines near its tip, the tines begin to vibrate and produce sound. If another tuning fork nearby is tuned to the same pitch, it will begin to sing the same note. Scientists call this sound transfer "resonance." For Qohelet, enjoyment is the music in you that the world's song calls forth when you are inwardly tuned to its frequency.

While their visions of the good life are not identical, in this critical respect Qohelet's philosophy of enjoyment and Hartmut Rosa's concept of resonance as a sociology of the good life strikingly coincide. Rosa develops his idea of resonance against the backdrop of what he calls "social acceleration": the modern condition of living in a hamster wheel in which the speed at which one has to live and work simply to stay in the race is constantly increasing. One feature of social acceleration is that basic structures and values change not over centuries or generations but in ever-shorter cycles within a single lifetime. For Rosa, social acceleration is the problem and resonance is the solution. Resonance is "not an emotional state, but a mode of relation." Resonance occurs when some aspect of the world moves you, reaches you, touches you, or calls to you. In resonance, the wire connecting you to the world starts to hum. Resonance also involves the response of "reaching out toward that which moves us": It happens when you are in some way able to move toward, reach in response, touch what touches you, and call back to what calls you. "To look into someone's eyes and feel them looking back is to resonate with them." Resonance never leaves you entirely unchanged. The mountain you have climbed looks different from the top than it did from afar. And at the peak, or back in the valley afterward, you have become a subtly different person than you were before. Further, "Resonance is inherently uncontrollable. Just as with falling asleep, the harder we try to make it happen, the less we succeed." Even if you try to engineer the perfect date—dinner at a quiet room in the back, a brilliant movie, gelato and a walk through a park afterward—the whole experience might leave you and the object of your affection cold, apathetic, and distant from each other. "It is a peculiar characteristic of resonance that it can be neither *forced* nor *prevented* with absolute certainty." Because resonance is uncontrollable, "it cannot be accumulated, saved, or instrumentally enhanced." To test this, try listening to your favorite song ten times in a row for ten days. No matter how many photos you take, you cannot bottle the moment. Resonance cannot be stockpiled.

Rosa regards modernity as both a catastrophe of resonance

and as providing conditions for great sensitivity to resonance. Yet, on balance, the relation of modernity to resonance is negative. "Resonance remains the promise of modernity, but alienation is its reality." In Rosa's view, common spheres of resonance in modern life include work, family, religion, nature, and art. Yet these spheres of resonance are constantly threatened by the competition and acceleration of modernity. The more you are in a hurry, the less likely you will resonate with the person in front of you or the task at hand. To be short on time is to be shut off from resonance. The more stress you're under, the less your work or spouse or children can call to you in a way that transforms you. The more you approach the world in a spirit of assertion, aggression, and competition, the more you dampen your resonance receptors. The promise of competition is always more, and such a mindset cares only for quantity of goods; resonance depends on quality of relationship.

Resonance does not come to those who grasp for it as gain. The more you try to control it, the more it slips away. Going into a vacation with a minute-by-minute plan for maximum enjoyment is one of the best ways to ruin it. You cannot chase down resonance or struggle successfully for it. Resonance can only be encountered, discovered, or, more precisely, received. "In sociological terms, this means that resonance always has the character of a *gift,* of something that is bestowed upon or befalls us. The inherent uncontrollability of resonance implies exactly this." Rosa's resonance, like Qohelet's enjoyment, is never gain, only gift.

As I hope my exposition of Rosa's views has shown, I regard his concept of resonance as a rich, insightful description of many aspects of a good life. Rosa's resonance is well worth reckoning with on its own terms and for its own sake. Still more, Rosa's resonance and Qohelet's practical philosophy of the good life sync in surprising ways. Throughout his corpus, Rosa's diagnoses of the modern conditions of acceleration, alienation, and the absurd chime in remarkable ways with Qohelet's judgments of hevel and his warnings against striving for gain. And Rosa's positive proposal bears striking similarities to Qohelet's enjoyment manifesto: Enjoyment (or resonance) is a mode of relating fittingly to the world. It cannot be grasped for, guaranteed, or controlled. It comes always and only as a gift.

Yet while Rosa sees far and digs deep, I would suggest that Qohelet sees farther and digs deeper. Here are three ways Ecclesiastes provides a deeper, more radical diagnosis of the ills of modern life and offers more compelling directions for finding and enjoying the good in this world of absurdity and alienation.

First, Rosa views resonance as a modern phenomenon relating to modern conditions. This reflects a conscious limit to the scope of his own project: He does not claim to speak about, much less speak for, times and places that are other than modern. This leaves one wondering whether people before modernity needed or experienced resonance, and, likewise, whether the rapidly shrinking remnant of people who still live traditional lifestyles relatively untouched by modernity need or experience resonance. Does this only apply to the subjects of "advanced" globalized capitalist societies? If those in traditional societies need and experience resonance, does their resonance differ from ours? By contrast, Qohelet diagnoses not the modern condition but the human condition. His diagnosis includes and accounts for Rosa's, but not vice versa. The particularly modern ways the world has gone wrong are branches of an older river called the fall or original sin. Rosa treats alienation as a crucial background condition of resonance, but why are we alienated in the first place?

Second, resonance is too fleeting and fragmentary an experience to form a stable basis for a good life. As Rosa says, "Now it is part of the nature of resonant experiences that they are always only temporary, short-lived, and inaccessible." And, "Resonance is the momentary appearance, the flash of a connection to a source of strong evaluations in a predominantly silent and often repulsive world." Temporary, short-lived, momentary, a flash. Qohelet also recognizes the transience of this life's goods, but his program for enjoyment features fare that offers up more reliable, if perhaps often more modest, delight. If you're supposed to rejoice daily in toil and eating and drinking, then, despite their overlap, Qohelet's enjoyment looks to be available to more of us more of the time than Rosa's resonance.

Third, in at least one fundamental sense, Rosa's account fails to explain why resonance works. Why should we resonate with the world at all? And why should that resonance count as a properly basic good? Rosa aptly names resonance a gift. But a gift from whom? Qohelet's view of life as a gift comes complete with a giver, without whom his account would make no sense. Rosa recognizes the problem but offers no solution: "And in fact, the idea of a responsive world ultimately cannot be defended from within the cognitive horizon of enlightened, rational modernity, according to which the universe presents only a silent drama performed under the direction of the laws of nature." Why does this not bother Rosa more? So far as I can tell, Rosa operates from within enlightened modernity's materialist worldview. How can he escape the silent drama? Is the world's apparent responsiveness an illusion?

Does this bother you? If this world is built to resonate with you and you're built to resonate with it, is that merely a happy accident? How could it be?

Why should the world-fork vibrate at all? Who struck it?

Does the note it rings in our hearts mean anything, or does it signify nothing? Despite the abundant insight and the illuminating power of Rosa's proposal, this is its weakest link. Whereas for Qohelet, gift explains why life is good and God explains why life is gift.

■ ■ ■

Today on a social media platform I read a historian's account of a frequently repeated conversation.

> YOU: You're a professor? What do you teach?
> ME: History.
> YOU: I hate history.
> ME: Well, history probably hates you, too.

Of course, history can't and doesn't hate you. But that also means history can't and doesn't love you. On any secular, materialist account, when you survey the pages of history, yours are the only eyes around. There is no face looking up at you, no gaze to answer your own, whether with affection or revulsion.

But forget history. What about the universe itself? When it feels for all the world like some pinpoint in the universe is charged with meaning, as if in its coded language the universe is calling to you, can that only ever be an illusion? The philosopher Jeffrey Gordon puts the question well:

> Man lives not only on this earth, but in the staggering Cosmos. And the question he must ask of this inevitable home he has in virtue of his power to conceive it is whether it is hospitable to him, whether it is infused with care for his anguish,

> or whether, like himself in his observation of the ant, it views him with dispassionate amusement, or worse, has no view of him at all.

For an atheist, the answer can only be that the universe has no view of you at all. It can't view you. An indifference infinitely vaster than anything a mere human could muster lies at the frozen base of all reality. For the universe to have a view of you—any view, from hostile to hilarious—there has to be someone doing the viewing. If God is exclusively responsible for the existence of the universe, then there is someone capable of viewing you, and of saying what he sees. If not, you're on your own. Meaning, enjoyment, consolation, resonance, happiness—it's up to you to make it all yourself, in the face of deafening cosmic indifference. How satisfying is that?

If you hold that the nature of ultimate reality is impersonal and purposeless, you work hard not to think of such things while you try to construct meaning for your life. If you believe that there is no ultimate purpose, you must keep that thought at a safe distance from all the smaller, fragile purposes you are trying to cultivate. If you want a meaningful life, you must not let the universe's meaninglessness ruin your party.

But if you believe that life is good because life is a gift, and life is a gift because God gives it, and life is full of good things because the creator is constantly flinging gifts at you faster than you can catch them, then any meaning you discover is catching up with the meaning that God has already built in. Any goodness you enjoy is scratching the surface of the goodness that life is. Any happiness you experience is a glimpse of the one who is happiness himself.

What gifts has God flung at you lately? What gifts is he

flinging at you right now? Have you been too busy chasing hevel to notice them or ask where they came from? The gift of resonance is a clue. Resonance is a signpost pointing the way up and out. This universe is one impossibly vast bell, struck by the hand that made it. The joy you feel in your best moments is a share of the joy of your maker.

TOP FLOOR

Beyond

"Through the Darkest of Crises"

Joseph Epstein, *Envy*

Apart from emulative envy, the only aspect of envy that does not seem to me pejorative is a form of envy I have myself felt, as I suspect have others who are reading this book: the envy that I think of as faith envy. This is the envy one feels for those who have the true and deep and intelligent religious faith that sees them through the darkest of crises, death among them. If one is oneself without faith and wishes to feel this emotion, I cannot recommend a better place to find it than in the letters of Flannery O'Connor. There one will discover a woman still in her thirties, who, after coming into her radiant talent, knows she is going to die well before her time and . . . faces her end without voicing complaint or fear.

20

Fear

The weather belonged to summer, the waves to winter. It was the tail end of September 2002. A day of cloudless sunshine with temperatures in the low seventies and no wind save a gentle breath of offshore breeze. The swell from the northwest that had just begun to collide with Northern California's coast measured seven to eight feet at twenty-second intervals. A swell that large, with peaks that far apart, moves quickly and carries surprising force.

I drove to the coast early from my home an hour away in "the valley." My destination was a little north of Santa Cruz. The surf spot is not exactly a secret, but I probably shouldn't name it. It's a fickle wave, far more often bad than good, accessible only by a long walk through farmland. That morning was the best I had ever seen it.

Heading north out of Santa Cruz, perhaps a mile before the small dirt pullout that serves, barely, as a parking lot for this spot, Highway 1 crests a small rise. From there, for only a few seconds at sixty miles an hour, the ocean view includes an area directly offshore from where the waves at this spot break. I had never glimpsed open-ocean swells from there. When I did now, their broad lines stacked and looming, a chill buzzed me and settled as a churn in my stomach. But I parked, grabbed my board and wetsuit, walked past the rows of strawberries and artichokes, suited up, and paddled out.

I was just barely brave enough, and just barely skilled enough, to scrape my way into set waves, link turns from bottom to top, and kick out before each wave collapsed onto a shoreline edged by jagged rocks. The waves approached what surfers call "double overhead": twelve or so feet from trough to peak. One of the few surfers in the lineup was an older, edgy local, a regular at this spot and its more reliable sibling to the north, who normally seemed on the verge of chewing someone out. Today he was ebullient. Once, he was paddling over the shoulder of a wave as I was carving a pivot off its top. He cheered me on afterward in standard surfing dialect: "Grom, you were flyin'!"

From paddling out through roiling white water and a sweeping current, to clawing into folding walls of water as tall and seemingly as heavy as small buildings, to triangulating swell and current and rocks in order to exit onto a narrow strip of steep sand, no surfer that day was ever far from harm. No aspect of the session was free of fear. That morning, fear was inseparable from joy.

The New Yorker staff writer William Finnegan, greatest of surf scribes, tells why waves hooked him in childhood: "Waves were better than anything in books, better than movies, better even than a ride at Disneyland, because with them the charge of danger was uncontrived." In surfing, the object of fear is not man-made but vast, wild, beyond human control. The pleasure in surfing cannot be disentangled from the terrifying encounter with an unreckonable power. Finnegan writes, "At thirteen, I had mostly stopped believing in God, but that was a new development, and it had left a hole in my world, a feeling that I'd been abandoned. The ocean was like an uncaring God, endlessly dangerous, power beyond measure."

■ ■ ■

Like the ocean that William Finnegan substituted for him, God is endlessly dangerous, power beyond measure. All natural forces owe their origin and continued existence to him, so all remain at his disposal. God is beyond our control; nothing is beyond God's control. Unlike the ocean, God cares for each tiny, drifting human, though that care is not always legible in the events of our lives.

What is legible, always, is God's infinite, transcendent power. Describing the whole vast assembly of natural and historical events, Qohelet observes, "I perceived that whatever God does endures forever; nothing can be added to it, nor anything taken from it. God has done it, so that people fear before him." What has Qohelet seen in this assembly? Toil, absurdity, unfulfilled yearning, a story neither he nor anyone else can make sense of. God not only superintends history but leaves signature traces of his power in its cracks, pitfalls, and paradoxes. God oversees history in the manner he does to teach us that we are not in control and to train us to fear him because he is. This fear arises from recognizing the infinite difference between his power and our weakness, his control and our impotence, his inscrutable wisdom and our ignorance.

A little later Qohelet warns about running your mouth off at God:

> Guard your steps when you go to the house of God. To draw near to listen is better than to offer the sacrifice of fools, for they do not know that they are doing evil. Be not rash with your mouth, nor let your heart be hasty to utter a word before God, for God is in heaven and you are on earth. Therefore let your words be few.

He follows these cautions with a warning about vows. If you promise God you will give him something, it would be far better if you had never promised than promised and not made good. What, you think he might forget?

Interwoven between these stern cautions are two admonitions about dreams. "For a dream comes with much business, and a fool's voice with many words. . . . For when dreams increase and words grow many, there is absurdity; but God is the one you must fear." I'm not entirely confident what he means by dreams or what his problem with them is. I think the basic point is that what pops out of our heads—especially unbidden, subconscious fancy—is no reliable guide to what this world is or how to live in it. Living by self-manufactured thoughts multiplies trouble for yourself and others. Qohelet's antidote is to fear God.

When you approach God, listen before and far more than you speak. If you make a commitment to him, treat it with the reverence you show your life itself. And instead of being guided by self-sourced supposed revelation, be grounded and guarded by what God says. To fear God is to let his voice speak louder than every inner voice. The fear of God deflates conceit and cements integrity.

In a passage we will revisit in the next chapter, Qohelet wrestles with the all-too-frequent disconnect between morality and prosperity: "Though a sinner does evil a hundred times and prolongs his life, yet I know that it will be well with those who fear God, because they fear before him. But it will not be well with the wicked, neither will he prolong his days like a shadow, because he does not fear before God." All we need to learn from this passage now is that the fear of God defines the difference between those who rightly relate to God and others and those who do not. The fear of God is a definitive distinguishing mark of life lived rightly.

In another passage we will treat more fully after a few more pages turn, the compiler or final editor of Qohelet's treatise sums up his life's work and adds a coda to close the book. The first part of that coda reads: "The end of the matter; all has been heard. Fear God and keep his commandments, for this is the whole duty of man."

Qohelet surveyed all of life under the sun and pronounced it all absurd. Now his editor reflects, perhaps with relief, that there is nothing left to say. Qohelet has seen it all and said all there is to say about it. When all is not only done but seen, and not only seen but said, what's left? "Fear God and keep his commandments, for this is the whole duty of man." The word "duty" is not in the original Hebrew, which is cryptically concise. We could translate more literally, "This is all the human" or, "This is the substance of every person." To fear God is to fulfill your humanity. This striking summary resonates with key questions and programmatic statements throughout the book. In the book's third verse Qohelet asks, "What does man gain by all the toil at which he toils under the sun?" And the scope of Qohelet's investigative program was "to seek and to search out by wisdom all that is done under heaven." So, when Qohelet's editor says that the final answer to everything is to fear God, he is not making up his own question or answering a question no one has asked but is distilling Qohelet's own final answer.

I mean "final" in both a logical and a literary sense. The last two sections of the body of the book are Qohelet's final enjoyment charge ("Light is sweet. . . . Rejoice, O young man") and his poem about aging and death ("the sun and the light and the moon and the stars are darkened . . . and the dust returns to the earth as it was"). The hinge between those two sections is Qohelet's final command, "Remember also your Creator in the days of your youth, before the evil days come and the years draw near of which you will say, 'I have no pleasure in them.'" What does it mean to remember your creator? It means remembering that you owe your life and everything in it to him. It means remembering that the maker gets to say what counts as proper use of what he made. It means remembering that you will one day answer to him for what you have made of what he made. It means fearing him. This kind of fear is reverent awe at God's power, humble trembling at his generosity, self-abasing confession before his holiness, stunned marveling at his grace, and self-rejecting dependence on his steadfast love.

Qohelet surveyed all and judged it all absurd: We can neither understand nor control it. But the creator of all, by definition, both understands and controls all. The verdict of absurdity teaches us not only that the world is not all we wish it were but that we are not all we think we are. Only God is the creator, sustainer, and judge of all. Only he sees the whole tapestry because, ultimately, he is the one weaving it. Only he understands the whole story because, ultimately, he is the one telling it. What should you do in the face of such a God? Revere him, respect him, worship him, and trust him. Fear him. Fearing

God is not an alternative to life's absurdity but a necessary response to life's absurdity.

Throughout Ecclesiastes, Qohelet takes the world in his hands, tosses it into a pan on medium-low heat, and lets it simmer. As the fire heats the pan, and the pan heats the world, and the world itself begins to melt, representatives from every realm of potential significance or satisfaction dissolve in the heat. Work, knowledge, pleasure, wealth, power—each reaches the boiling point, turns into vapor, and gets sucked into the exhaust fan. Through twelve tortuous chapters, Qohelet has subjected the world itself to a reductio ad absurdum. After all the hevel has steamed up before his eyes, what's left in the pan is a single solid: "Fear God and keep his commandments."

■ ■ ■

What do you fear? Failure? Missing out? Rejection?

Hartmut Rosa suggests that the structure of growth-oriented capitalist societies generates and compounds pathological fears. If life is a competition of everyone against everyone else, if you have to constantly gain ground just to stay put, if what you have worked hard to achieve can always evaporate before your eyes, then fear is inescapable. In Rosa's words, these societies "can be said to be driven by fear to the extent that every successive position a subject may occupy is subject to the erosive forces of the dynamics of competition, such that the fear of being left behind, out of date, or otherwise excluded becomes a mode of existence."

Targets of fear can be both external and internal. The world is a dangerous place. Pandemics erupt, fires spread, and cars crash. People inflict an unending, horrific parade of physical and emotional harms on one another. But you can also fear something within or fear how something about yourself that's beyond your control will play with your boss or friend or parents. You can fear losing your temper, gaining weight, or getting fired.

Fear and control usually sit on opposite ends of a seesaw. As L. S. Dugdale puts it, "All of us fear what we cannot control and aim to control what we fear." To this rule the fear of God is a massively significant exception. We do fear God because we cannot control him. Yet to fear God is to give up the need to be in control because you trust and submit to one who really is. With the fear of God, control does not eliminate fear; rather, this fundamental fear eliminates the need for control. The fear of God drives out fear of everything and everyone else.

To fear God is to no longer assert self. To fear God is to give up not only the need to master all threats but the drive to know all answers. To fear God is to trust that it is better to have him without answers than to have answers without him.

▪ ▪ ▪

What makes surfing different from other sports, says Finnegan, is "this horizon, this fear line" beyond which, in big waves that can harm you, you're on your own—or, rather, it's just you and the ocean.

> Everything out there was disturbingly interlaced with everything else. Waves were the playing field. They were the goal. They were the object of your deepest desire and adoration. At the same time, they were your adversary, your nemesis, even your mortal enemy. The surf was your refuge, your happy hiding place, but it was also a hostile wilderness—a dynamic, indifferent world.

In a life devoted to the one true God, fear is inseparable from joy and joy from fear. Joy in God is disturbingly interlaced with fear of God. God is the object of your deepest desire and adoration. He is your refuge, your happiest hiding place. And yet God stands over you, above you, often seemingly against you. As Job confessed, "Though he slay me, I will hope in him; yet I will argue my ways to his face." Taking refuge in God is intertwined with the knowledge that he who made you and sustains you and loves you can also undo you.

Like the ocean, God's ways are beyond our understanding and control. Surfers continually puzzle over the intricate intersections of forces and features that produce well-shaped waves, wondering about swell size and period and direction, wind and tide, drifting sand daily recontouring the ocean floor. But, per Finnegan, "When the surf is big, or in some other way humbling, even these questions tend to fall away. The heightened sense of a vast, unknowable design silences the effort to understand. You feel honored simply to be out there."

When you glimpse a humbling sight of God's hugeness or holiness, questions fall away. Though you cannot know his design, you do know it is vast. The more acutely you sense him, the more complete the silence that blankets your soul. You feel not merely honored but stunned to be loved and looked after by the same love that looks after a star twenty-eight billion light-years away.

21

Judgment

One night at eleven o'clock, Kristin and I were driving home from a concert—Iron & Wine at the Atlantis. There is a stretch of North Capitol Street NW, with no cross streets and no stoplights, that slopes down to dip under Rhode Island Avenue and elicits much reckless driving. About a hundred feet ahead of us, someone driving a white sedan in the right lane sped up and angled left to pass a motorcyclist in front of them. Their front right fender slammed the rear of the motorcycle and sent its rider skidding and tumbling across the right lane behind a spray of sparks as his bike slid ahead.

The white sedan barely slowed, then sped off. The motorcyclist got to his feet, stumbled to the curb, and sat against the cement wall of the overpass that angled down almost vertically from street level. After we passed him and his bike, I pulled into the right lane under the overpass, parked, put on our hazards, and called 911 while Kristin walked back to let the skinny young man know we were calling for help. He was already on the phone doing the same. His injuries seemed mercifully minor. He could walk and talk. He told us he was okay. Another driver stopped to help, and a woman who saw the accident from the overpass quickly walked down to the sunken semi-freeway. The rider's helmet had come off, presumably on impact with the asphalt, and lay on the far side of the other lane. The other motorist who had stopped retrieved it for him. Kristin set up a triangular reflector that she pulled out of a kit in our trunk, and the pedestrian waved her cellphone light to divert traffic into the left lane, away from the injured rider and his wrecked bike. Gasoline pooled on the street under the bike like blood from its heart. Firemen quickly arrived and took kind and competent command. We told one of them all that we saw—no, sorry, we didn't get the license plate—and resumed our trip home.

What do you want for that motorcyclist? At minimum, quick and skilled medical care, time to heal and recover, loving family members to help him however he needs. But what about his other losses? Who pays for repairs? What can you or I or anyone do about the fear that will stalk him the next time he travels by wheels on blacktop? What would it look like to make right the wrong that was done to him?

And what do you want for the driver of the white sedan? Of course, you and I wish he or she would have had the integrity, the basic bargain-barrel decency, to stop and care for a person whose life they had just endangered. But, given that they hit and ran, what now? What I want for him or her, and I trust you do too, is justice—specifically for the driver to be on justice's receiving end. Justice in this instance necessarily involves an element of judgment. They did something seriously wrong. If anyone deserves to pay for medical bills and bike repairs and any other losses, it is the driver who couldn't be bothered to keep a safe distance. And, in addition to being held responsible to right whichever wrongs they can, you want that driver to be told that what they did was wrong: both the hit and, especially, the run. You want them to be told that by someone whose speech binds. You want them to know they're wrong, to be seen to be in the wrong, and in some way to have to own the wrong and pay for it.

I have no idea whether any of that will happen to the driver of the white sedan. The District Department of Transportation site tells me that the nearest traffic camera on North Capitol Street NW is a mile south.

▪ ▪ ▪

Qohelet could have wished for more traffic cameras. They might have helped secure a greater number of just convictions, as well as properly dropped charges and righteous exonerations. As it was, and as we have seen, when and where he looked for justice, he found its opposite. "Moreover, I saw under the sun that in the place of justice, even there was wickedness, and in the place of righteousness, even there was wickedness. I said in my heart, God will judge the righteous and the wicked, for there is a time for every matter and for every work."

The most striking aspect of this passage is the contradiction between what Qohelet sees and what he tells himself. He sees widespread breakdown of the judicial system. The people authorized to administer justice are dishing out its opposite. In the courts Qohelet watches, if you have been wronged and appeal for redress, who knows what you'll get. If you've been falsely accused, it's anybody's guess whether you'll ever clear your name. Yet what Qohelet says opposes what he sees. At present, the human administration of justice allows rampant injustice. But, he tells himself, in the future, God will judge.

And he will not judge only some but all: righteous and wicked, every matter, every work. Unjust deeds don't have their "time" now. Their perpetrators walk free, and their victims bear the added indignity of trying and failing to get justice. But unjust deeds, along with all other deeds, will have their time. Justice will have its day in court.

As he so often does, Qohelet again addresses the mismatch between what people deserve and what they get. "Though a sinner does evil a hundred times and prolongs his life, yet I know that it will be well with those who fear God, because they fear before him. But it will not be well with the wicked, neither will he prolong his days like a shadow, because he does not fear before God." The problem Qohelet sees is that the wicked sin with impunity. Being immoral doesn't seem to harm their health or happiness. Very bad people live long lives, and apparently these lives are not full of suffering but pleasure. What Qohelet knows contradicts what he sees. Contrary to all appearances and an overwhelming pile of present evidence, the wicked will not receive good because they do not fear God, and the righteous will because they do.

An optimist is someone who asserts that things will go well, regardless of present evidence and even contrary to present evidence. Based on all we have seen of Qohelet, it would be difficult even for one of Qohelet's corrupt judges to convict him of optimism. It would therefore not be especially convincing to see Qohelet here applying lipstick to a pig. "Well, it sure looks like good folks get a bum deal and bad folks gobble up the pie, but I just know, bless their hearts, that it's going to go all right for the good guys." Rather, we should infer that Qohelet is confident of a coming change not of superficial circumstances but of the deep order of moral reward. Somehow (Qohelet doesn't tell us the means), sometime (he doesn't say when), Qohelet knows (he doesn't say how) that, unlike in the present order of this world, destiny and deserving will finally fit. Qohelet does not explicitly refer here to God's work of judging, but what else could achieve such a decisive reversal of the way the whole world works?

We begin to detect a pattern. Not only are this world's goods and pleasures fenced by limits, so are its injustices. Goods and pleasures are limited by injustice, by our divided selves that hinder us from receiving them, and ultimately by death. What is injustice limited by? Not the big crunch theory that says eventually the universe will collapse on itself, so there won't be any people to either commit or suffer injustice, and so injustice won't matter because there won't be anyone for it to matter to. According to what Qohelet knows, and what he tells himself in our hearing, injustice is limited by an act of God so vast and final that injustice will not only cease but be reversed.

Qohelet returns to the theme of judgment in discussing the motives and limits of enjoyment: "Rejoice, O young man, in your youth, and let your heart cheer you in the days of your youth. Walk in the ways of your heart and the sight of your eyes. But know that for all these things God will bring you into judgment." As Old Testament scholar Arthur Keefer observes, in this verse, "God's future judgment regulates the present pursuit of joy." How so? Again, Qohelet leaves much unsaid: when, how, with precisely what results for whom, and (perhaps most frustratingly for us) how he knows. And yet what Qohelet does say is enough to ground and guide all your present enjoyments, all pursuits, for all of life.

Again we meet the little word "all": "For all these things God will bring you into judgment." Qohelet's point is not that God will judge only your enjoyments but that, since he will judge all your deeds, every instance of pleasure taking fits within the all-encompassing "all." Qohelet presumably singles out experiences of enjoyment as actions to be judged because the line between licit enjoyment of God's gifts and illicit indulgence in sin is an easy one to transgress, and it's easy to convince ourselves that the latter is really the former.

Qohelet's teaching on judgment is not a personal strategy for sheltering from the absurd but the cosmic solution to the absurd. This is not a coping mechanism but hope in an all-transforming act. To confess that God will judge the earth is not to flee inward but to patiently wait for the day when everything that is wrong out there will be forever righted.

The contradiction we have observed between what Qohelet sees and what he says was not lost on Qohelet. He would not be surprised to hear that his claim that God will mete out justice contradicts the injustice running rampant all around him. The contradiction is the point. Qohelet is not indulging in wishful thinking. To oversimplify only slightly, we can distill Qohelet's thoughts on justice and judgment to two premises. The first premise is that injustice is rampant. The second premise is that God himself will ensure a global and final justice in which all get their due. At present, the second premise can only be believed, not proved. It can only be verified by a radical, fundamental, comprehensive change in the moral order of the universe. Nothing else will make true what Qohelet is claiming. So, yes, this is a contradiction—unless you believe, as Qohelet believed, that one day God will take the bench.

We have now considered all that Qohelet has to say about judgment. But Qohelet's editor, who adds a final summary to the book, ends his conclusion with a reference to judgment.

> Besides being wise, Qohelet also taught the people knowledge, weighing and studying and arranging many proverbs

> with great care. Qohelet sought to find words of delight, and uprightly he wrote words of truth.
>
> The words of the wise are like goads, and like nails firmly fixed are the collected sayings; they are given by one Shepherd. My son, beware of anything beyond these. Of making many books there is no end, and much study is a weariness of the flesh.
>
> The end of the matter; all has been heard. Fear God and keep his commandments, for this is the whole duty of man. For God will bring every deed into judgment, with every secret thing, whether good or evil.

I understand this editorial epitome to offer a fitting reflection on, and coda to, Qohelet's message in the book. This coda begins narrowly, reflecting on Qohelet's labors, but concludes broadly, with a command for everyone grounded in how God will one day deal with everyone. Fear God and obey him because one day you will answer to him.

Some scholars construe these concluding references to fear of God and final judgment as an orthodox bolt out of Qohelet's skeptical blue sky. But they can only do so by ignoring, downplaying, or explaining away Qohelet's repeated appeals to both the fear of God and God's judgment that we have considered in these last two chapters. Instead, while Qohelet's editor does not restate Qohelet's main point, he does offer a conclusion that follows, fittingly and necessarily, from Qohelet's whole argument. If all is absurd, and all is a gift, and God will evaluate all that you do with all that he gives you, what else should you do but fear and obey him? If everything in this life is radically fleeting and ungraspable, what gain can you grasp for besides living a life pleasing to God?

■ ■ ■

The ethicist Oliver O'Donovan defines judgment as "an act of moral discrimination that pronounces upon a preceding act or existing state of affairs to establish a new public context." His definition applies equally to judgment enacted by human government and judgment enacted by God as the supreme sovereign, and it aptly names the essence and consequences of Ecclesiastes' teaching on God's judgment. God will one day pronounce his verdict, in a decisive and discriminating fashion, upon all preceding acts and states of affairs. This comprehensive act of moral evaluation will necessarily establish a new public context. Otherwise, God's judgment would not solve the problem Qohelet says it does.

What happens when a society assumes this kind of judgment will never happen? As bloody as the seventeenth century's sectarian religious wars were, the massacres perpetrated in the twentieth century by secular, atheist, totalitarian governments were astronomically more atrocious. Lenin, Stalin, Mao, Pol Pot—not a believer in divine judgment among them. As the political philosopher Hannah Arendt once said, "I am perfectly sure that the whole totalitarian catastrophe would not have happened if people had still believed in God—or hell rather—that is, if there were still any ultimates."

What happens when an individual assumes this kind of judgment will never happen? Hope grows harder and harder to sustain. The bigger the problems that are beyond your control, and seemingly beyond anyone's control, the harder it gets to believe life is good, much less a gift.

Rightly understood, belief in God's judgment is the ultimate ground of hope. Every false charge will be dropped, every wrongful conviction overturned. The whole present corrupt order will be ended and reversed. Absurdity will vanish, not into nothingness but into a new public context that is healthy and whole. Qohelet's vision of divine judgment is good news for the world.

But is it good news for you? How could it be?

▪ ▪ ▪

That question launches us out of Ecclesiastes' orbit. Qohelet tells you that God's judgment is good news, but he doesn't tell you how. He tells you that God will one day set the world right, but he doesn't tell you how to get right with God, how to ensure your place in that right-set world. So, in the conclusion that follows, we leave the text of Ecclesiastes behind in order to answer this heavy, haunting question that Ecclesiastes asks and doesn't answer. Ecclesiastes' lack of answers doesn't mean there aren't answers. How can God's judgment be good news for you? The rest of the Bible answers Ecclesiastes' hanging question.

Throughout Ecclesiastes, Qohelet puts the world on trial. Can anything in this world fully and finally satisfy your heart? No: Everything is never enough. Now it's not the world on trial but you. How can you be enough to satisfy God? Not that God's heart is empty and yearns for fullness like ours; just the opposite. The question God's judgment asks is whether he is satisfied with the life you've lived. Can your life be good enough, whole enough, right enough, for God?

CONCLUSION

Pierced from Above

The end of the matter; all has been heard. We're done with Ecclesiastes. (Finally? Phew?) But not really. I hope you will never be done with Ecclesiastes. I hope Qohelet's words will haunt you and help you as long as you live, however much or little time you have left.

Here and now, we can't take our leave from Qohelet without first taking the photo negative of his whole book, placing it into a developing tank, and considering the picture that emerges. Ecclesiastes leaves us gasping for something—but what? If everything is never enough, what is? If God will one day judge the world, how can your life measure up in that final exam of all final exams?

Ecclesiastes is a quest that does not bring back all the quester hoped to find. Ecclesiastes is a question. Its pages do not return a full answer; many loose threads dangle. Qohelet, like a stand-up comic, squinted to bring truths into surprising focus, but what is the whole truth that he not only did not know but could not know? The philosopher at the party seems full of socially insensitive bad news. Sure, when you sit with him long enough, you hear some surprisingly good news too. But is Qohelet's good news the best we can hear? Qohelet the photographer captured and chronicled all that he saw, and he claimed to see it all. But has anything entered the picture since?

■ ■ ■

One reason for Qohelet's uncommon common sense is that he is painfully and persistently aware of his and everyone's limits. No one can tell the future. No one can guarantee success or secure gain. No one can turn away death at their door. There is nothing new under the sun.

To use the hackneyed current vocabulary, these are Qohelet's priors. Grant these premises—which are hard to deny—and Qohelet's conclusions follow with grim necessity. These premises draw the lines that have confined every human since Adam and Eve took their fatal bites.

Except one. Jesus of Nazareth is a human being. He is also, mysteriously, much more than a human being. He is not only a human being but the God who is the judge of humanity. He is not only a creature; he is also the creator who gives everyone every good gift they ever get. If you had met him in Judea two thousand years ago, what you would have seen was obviously and unimpressively human, but the one you were meeting is also the sole agent responsible for the existence of all things. As a man, he was subject to the natural limits of humanity, including, in our post-fall condition, mortality. As God the Son, he is subject to no limit, not confined by any finitude. Instead, he is himself full, free, unhindered, and unthreatenable life.

Is there anything new under the sun? Can any human being turn death away at their door? Can anyone secure gain or guarantee success? Who can tell the future? Jesus can and has and will do all this and more.

The incarnation of God the Son is a mystery and a marvel. To put it slightly playfully, one might even call it absurd. What is God doing here as a human? Isn't that a little, well, weird? Yes, it is cosmically weird. But absurd times call for absurd measures. An absurd disease requires an absurd remedy. Walker Percy discovers in Jesus's incarnate redeeming work a "new law in the Cosmos": "If you're a big enough fool to climb a tree and like a cat refuse to come down, then someone who loves you has to make as big a fool of himself to rescue you."

But for Jesus, the incarnation was only the beginning of the absurd. As one of his first followers said, Jesus went about doing good. Yet what he received in response was anything but good. He was mocked, opposed, persecuted, and rejected. He was brought to trial, declared innocent, and then condemned and crucified anyway. Never was the disconnect between deserving and receiving as extreme as it was in the life and death of Jesus of Nazareth.

Jesus was alienated. He was not alienated from himself but from just about everyone else. "He came to his own, and his own people did not receive him." Jesus was alienated from his family (who thought he was out of his mind), from his friends (who abandoned him in his most vulnerable hour), from his community's religious leaders (who envied him, schemed against him, and conspired to get him killed), and from political authorities (who spinelessly bowed to crowd pressure to execute him). Worst of all, more than all, while suffering on the cross, Jesus was alienated from God, crying out, "My God, my God, why have you forsaken me?"

Why was Jesus plunged into absurdity and alienation? Not because he deserved it but because we do. His incarnation was a rescue mission. He came to experience and exhaust and eradicate the forces of absurdity and alienation. How? By pulling them up by their roots. This world has been subjected to futility, against its will, as God's judgment on us for our sin. In his death Jesus endured the full measure of that judgment for all who will turn from sin and trust in him. Jesus suffered the most extreme absurdity and alienation, which we deserve, culminating in personally suffering God's wrath on the cross, so that we would receive the wholeness and fullness that only he deserves. In his death, Jesus became this world's futility and its absurdity. He became the waste of the world and so broke the circuit that continually turns the world into a wasteland.

Qohelet laments, "No man has power to retain the spirit, or power over the day of death. There is no discharge from war, nor will wickedness deliver those who are given to it." But Jesus declares, "For this reason the Father loves me, because I lay down my life that I may take it up again. No one takes it from me, but I lay it down of my own accord. I have authority to lay it down, and I have authority to take it up again. This charge I have received from my Father." No one has power to retain the spirit or power over the day of death—except Jesus.

Jesus was not taken by death but gave himself to death. Jesus was not seized by death but willingly committed himself to death. He gave himself into death's grasp, and then, on the third day, he delivered himself out of it. He rose from the dead, bodily, into a whole new mode of life—a life no longer tainted in any way by death, a life utterly free from death's chilling touch. Death is the hardest, firmest, coldest limit that holds us. Jesus freely entered death's prison in order not only to break himself out but to demolish the whole structure.

Qohelet's view from the ground floor is identical to what Charles Taylor calls "the immanent frame": life under the sun;

life lived solely within the bounds of what humans can learn and accomplish and create and discover; life without reference to any higher power or ultimate reality. In the immanent frame, death is final, meaning is fragile, and no one is coming to rescue us. The immanent frame is the default worldview of modern secular people, since they do not believe that there is anything beyond this life. The outer edge of the immanent frame is like a steel wall at the end of the universe: There's nothing beyond it, and even if there were, no one could get through it.

The immanent frame walls in our prospects for happiness. The only sources of and space for happiness must be found under the brass ceiling that makes this world and this life all there is. If you can't find happiness within the immanent frame, there's nowhere else to look.

But what if the immanent frame could be pierced from above? What if it already has been?

What if help has already come, and very many of us, for a very long time, have brushed off that help as ineffective or irrelevant? In the very last paragraph of Walker Percy's book *Lost in the Cosmos,* aliens offer to rescue self-destroying earthlings. Their appeal represents God's grace in the saving work of Christ and exposes our ignorance of our own condition.

> Repeat. Do you read? Do you read? Are you in trouble? How did you get in trouble? If you are in trouble, have you sought help? If you did, did help come? If it did, did you accept it? Are you out of trouble? What is the character of your consciousness? Are you conscious? Do you have a self? Do you know who you are? Do you know what you are doing? Do you love? Do you know how to love? Are you loved? Do you hate? Do you read me? Come back. Repeat. Come back. Come back. Come back.

■ ■ ■

The difference between Qohelet's immanent frame and the modern secular one is that his is permeable. Qohelet knows that this good but fallen world is not self-sustaining. He knows this world is not all there is. Qohelet's immanent frame is pierced by both his conviction that the whole world is a gift of the creator, who continually sustains it, and by his confidence that this same creator will one day judge the world. We've seen that the world's gift-ness is deliciously good news and that God's coming judgment also is good news for the world.

But how can judgment be good news for you? Isn't judgment only good news for the innocent? Are you innocent? Do you love? Do you hate? Do you only ever love and hate the right things, in the right way, at the right time, for the right reasons? Do you know who you are?

"For God will bring every deed into judgment, with every secret thing, whether good or evil." There's no way you pass that test. Every deed. Every secret thing. Not just public acts but private thoughts. Not just audible compliments but silent curses. God's judgment is not good news for you. It can't be. Not unless someone has been judged for you. Not unless someone else can guarantee your safe passage through judgment, based not on your merit but theirs.

That is the offer God holds out to you through the saving work of his Son. You can either face final judgment naked and alone, or you can face it clothed in the perfect righteousness of the only one who lived a perfect record and suffered the excruciating penalty due to those who haven't. As God, Jesus himself is the judge who will pronounce the final sentence upon all prior acts. As man, Jesus lived the only human life that could pass that test, and he endured the execution of God's verdict against our failures. Jesus is the judge judged in our place. Jesus is your only hope in the face of final judgment, and he is hope enough.

In this good news of what Jesus has achieved, God himself is calling to you. Do you read me? Come back. Repeat. Come back.

Jesus's incarnation is the rescue mission none of us thought possible. Jesus's death is the death of sin; Jesus's resurrection is the death of death. Together, Jesus's death and resurrection are the death of absurdity and alienation. Jesus's suffering God's judgment on the cross is the death of guilt and condemnation for every deed, for every secret thing, for every evil. All this is promised to all who believe and only those who believe.

Everything is never enough, but Jesus is. Jesus is enough to satisfy God's judgment on your behalf. And Jesus is enough to satisfy your soul forever.

Jesus alone is God's answer to your life's absurdity.

▪ ▪ ▪

Each level of Ecclesiastes' three-story building reveals a crucial part of the path to happiness. On the ground floor, as we discovered in the first part of this book, Qohelet bangs his head on the immanent frame. He finds and laments the limits of everything that promises happiness here below.

Only by realizing that every earthly good is finite and fleeting can you begin to enjoy any of them rightly. Only by refusing to grasp for gain can you begin to receive each good as a gift. Don't wrap your heart as tight as you can around your most cherished good, or you'll break both. Don't try to satisfy your soul with work or knowledge or pleasure or money or power, or each one will leave you emptier. Happiness comes not from storing gain (you can't) or wishing time would freeze (it won't) but from renouncing control. Happiness dawns in the faint glow of the absurd.

But happiness doesn't stop there. Every good in your life is tinged with the absurd, but these absurd goods are still gifts. As we saw in the book's second part, the view from Ecclesiastes' second story shows that life itself is a gift, and so is every good thing in it.

Gift implies giver. Already from this second floor, Qohelet sees through the immanent frame. He sees that every good thing inside this immanent frame comes from beyond it. Gifts don't simply appear; they're given. Each lawful delight—food and drink and work and marriage, the slow joys of nurture, everything that makes the wire between your heart and the world hum—is sent into your life by the same gleeful giver who gave you life. Every source of happiness in your life is a comet, trailing celestial glory that discloses an origin beyond all you can see. A gift is undeserved and undemandable. You can't summon a gift by scheduling it, purchasing it, or earning it. All you can do with a gift is receive and enjoy it. And the better you know the giver, the more of him you'll see in each gift and the better you'll receive each gift. God is happy, and he created the world so that creatures could share his joy. God created the world not from a deficit of happiness but from an abundance. Happiness comes from receiving the gift and recognizing the giver.

The view from Ecclesiastes' third story looks clear past the immanent frame. Up there Qohelet directs your gaze up and away from the limits of this world and your life. Because God alone is the transcendent framer, you should revere him and live for him. Because God alone gave you life, he is the final authority on what it means to live well.

Happiness comes from knowing God, submitting to God, and living for God. One day, for all who trust in Jesus, happiness will come from living not just for God but with God in a world perfectly remade by God.

Three stories; each tells a crucial part of happiness's story. The contentment of limits; the joys of resonance; the happiness that can't be taken by the world because it wasn't given by the world. Everything is never enough. Learning that truth keeps you from trying to make anything in this life enough to fill your heart. And it aims your heart at the God who alone is enough, and more than enough, to satisfy you forever.

ACKNOWLEDGMENTS

When the idea for this book first started to rattle around my head, and I wasn't sure whether it was worth writing or when or how to write it, my old friend Matt McCullough offered unnervingly Ecclesiastean advice: "Write it while you're still young enough to believe in yourself." Around that time, on one of the painfully rare occasions when the three of us were together, Matt and Drew Bratcher teamed up to insist that I read Annie Dillard's *Pilgrim at Tinker Creek,* a book I had no business not reading all these years. Without the fire that book lit in me I could not have written this one. Drew and Matt, this book is dedicated to you because without friends like you I never could have written a book like this.

Ecclesiastes first got under my skin when I preached through the book, in the depths of Covid, in 2021. I had planned to start the series a year prior. When one church member heard that I was beginning a series on Ecclesiastes the first Sunday of the year, she said to another pastor of our church, "A series on Ecclesiastes is the last thing I need." Scattered early hesitations notwithstanding, the members of Capitol Hill Baptist Church received those sermons with heartening warmth and affection. Their enthusiasm for Ecclesiastes fired mine, their generous sabbatical provision enabled me to write, and their eagerness to see the book completed (especially you, Hope Wilson!) helped dissolve my doubts about it. Members of CHBC, thank you.

Eric Beach enriched this book's soil by helping me locate sources that were beyond my reach. My old partner in academic crime, Tyler Wittman, eagerly supported the project, sharpened me in fruitful conversations at key points, and, by recommending that I read Norman Wirzba, started me down a rabbit trail I'm nowhere near the end of. An invitation to remotely present at Southern Seminary's 1892 Club allowed me to test-drive chapter 7 and the broader project before an audience of keen PhD students. Taylor Hartley, John Sarver, Ben Robin, and Ryan Curia each read the full manuscript (some more than once), gave feedback that improved it, and gave encouragement that improved me. Ryan deserves special thanks for helping me brainstorm new material late in the fourth quarter. My older daughters, Rose and Lucy, read many chapters as they came. Not to mention they baked and delivered cookies to power my writing. Thank you all.

The works of Robert Macfarlane and Johnny Flynn, especially their collaboration, inspired this book in surprisingly direct ways. Their song "Nether" somehow catalyzed both this book's shape and, well, vibe. Fittingly, the song left no visible trace on the book's surface, but its influence is everywhere beneath.

I owe Paul Pastor an extra measure of thanks, pressed down and running over, for responding to an unsolicited email with striking generosity and kindness, and even greater thanks for connecting me with a wonderful agent. Keely Boeving deserves yet more thanks for being that wonderful agent—her very name is a blessing in the Jamieson home.

I'm deeply grateful to the whole team at WaterBrook for taking on this book and investing so much skillful effort in it. Especially: Thank you, Drew Dixon, for helping this book become a far better version of itself.

Finally, thank you, Kristin, for sixteen years and counting of toil and joy in our absurd days together under the sun. " 'Cause there ain't no California without you."

NOTES

PREFACE: SHOULDN'T YOU BE HAPPIER?

ix **only 12 percent of people:** Max Roser and Esteban Ortiz-Ospina, "Literacy," Our World in Data, updated March 2024, https://ourworldindata.org/literacy.

ix **"Those who enjoy bemoaning their fate":** Darrin M. McMahon, *Happiness: A History* (New York: Grove, 2006), 466.

x **The first perspective sees happiness:** I borrow the image of happiness as health from Peter Kreeft, *Christianity for Modern Pagans: Pascal's "Pensées" Edited, Outlined and Explained* (San Francisco: Ignatius Press, 1993), 27. For a recent philosophical treatment that prioritizes the subjective sense of happiness and attempts to integrate it with various features of a good life, see Mike W. Martin, *Happiness and the Good Life* (Oxford: Oxford University Press, 2012). On some of the paradoxes of happiness, see Martin's chapter 7.

xii **Ecclesiastes was written well over:** The observation that Ecclesiastes is the Bible's only work of philosophy is fairly common. See, for instance, Nili Samet, "Qoheleth's Idiolect and Its Cultural Context," *Harvard Theological Review* 114, no. 4 (2021): 451–68, at 454.

xii **Its primary author and protagonist:** I say "primary author" because the final section, which sums up Qohelet's life's work and adds an exclamation mark to his main message, seems to be written by Qohelet's editor, who gave the book its final shape. (The same might be true of its opening sentence and a transitional statement reflecting on Qohelet's quest for wisdom in Ecclesiastes 7:27.) Throughout, I use "Ecclesiastes" to refer to the book and "Qohelet" for the man speaking to us in it. For a brief discussion of the debated relationship between Qohelet and the so-called "epilogist" (whom I call Qohelet's editor), see the note in chapter 21 that starts with the key phrase, "Besides being wise, Qohelet also taught."

xii **The Hebrew word *qohelet:*** For brief discussions of the meaning of the Hebrew word *qohelet,* see, e.g., Thomas Krüger, *Qoheleth,* Hermeneia—A Critical and Historical Commentary on the Bible (Minneapolis, Minn.: Fortress, 2004), 40–41; Craig G. Bartholomew, *Ecclesiastes,* Baker Commentary on the Old Testament Wisdom and Psalms (Grand Rapids, Mich.: Baker Academic, 2009), 103–4.

xii **"The good teacher imparts":** Richard Sennett, *The Craftsman* (New Haven: Yale University Press, 2008), 6.

xiii **Does life have a meaning:** Michael V. Fox, "The Inner Structure of Qohelet's Thought," in *Qohelet in the Context of Wisdom,* ed. Antoon Schoors (Leuven, Belgium: Peeters, 1998), 225 (emphasis original), "My basic thesis is that the central concern of the book of Qohelet is *meaning*—not transience, not work, not values, not mortality. These themes are there, but they are all ways of approaching the more fundamental issue, the meaning of life." For an illuminating, nuanced discussion of the meaning of life in Ecclesiastes in comparison with other ancient texts, which draws on modern psychological concepts of meaning that combine coherence, purpose, and significance, see Arthur Jan Keefer, *Ecclesiastes and the Meaning of Life in the Ancient World* (Cambridge: Cambridge University Press, 2022).

xiii **First, Ecclesiastes is a quest:** For Ecclesiastes as the record of Qohelet's quest, see, among many others, Leo G. Perdue, *The Sword and the Stylus: An Introduction to Wisdom in the Age of Empires* (Grand Rapids, Mich.: Eerdmans, 2008), 208.

xiii **Qohelet sought to discover:** Ecclesiastes 1:13, 17. The following quote is from Ecclesiastes 2:3. Unless otherwise noted, Scripture references are from the ESV, which I occasionally alter in minor ways. For reasons I will provide in chapter 11, I regularly alter the ESV's "vanity" to "absurd." Throughout the book, in the rare instances where Hebrew verse numbering differs from English, I list the English.

xiv **Second, Ecclesiastes is a question:** Peter Kreeft, *Three Philosophies of Life* (San Francisco: Ignatius Press, 1989), 19, "There is nothing more meaningless than an answer without its question. That is why we need Ecclesiastes."

xiv **"What does man gain by all the toil":** Ecclesiastes 1:3. The following question is from Ecclesiastes 6:12.

xiv **"Who knows whether the spirit of man":** Ecclesiastes 3:21, 22 (which I have translated freely to give the sense; cf. 10:14); 7:13, 24.

xv **Third, Qohelet is a stand-up comic:** I came to this insight independently (by listening to the audiobook of Jerry Seinfeld's *Is This Anything?* while preaching through Ecclesiastes), and I disagree with the precise parallels he draws, but it is worth noting that Knut Heim discovered profound similarities between Qohelet's rhetoric and that of stand-up comedians after attending a Jim Gaffigan show. See Knut Martin Heim, *Ecclesiastes,* Tyndale Old Testament Commentaries (Downers Grove, Ill.: InterVarsity Press Academic, 2019), ix–x. Speaking of stand-up comics, the hypothetical Qohelet quote below, "Death comes to us all," is borrowed from James Acaster's feature *Repertoire,* specifically the episode, "Recognise."

xv **"When I say I love being a parent":** Jerry Seinfeld, *Is This Anything?* (New York: Simon & Schuster, 2020), 346.

xvi **Fifth, Qohelet is a photographer:** Here I am indebted to Robert L. Short, *A Time to Be Born—A Time to Die* (New York: Harper & Row, 1973), 3–5; and Kreeft, *Three Philosophies,* 19.

xvi **Namely, Ecclesiastes is like the view:** The idea that Ecclesiastes is like the view from a three-story building dawned on me while preparing the final sermon in a series through the book. The largest single contribution to this idea is Craig Bartholomew's insight, discussed four notes below, that Qohelet toggles between two ways of looking at the world: one guided by observation, the other by his confession of faith in God the creator. While preparing that sermon, I read Andrew G. Shead, "Reading Ecclesiastes 'Epilogically,'" *Tyndale Bulletin* 48, no. 1 (1997): 67–91. On pages 88–89, Shead observes that Ecclesiastes' treatment of both "work/deed" (the Hebrew word *ma'aseh*) and "judgment" (the Hebrew word *mishpat*) operates on three levels: (1) observation of phenomena (which are hevel); (2) the way we should live, namely enjoyment and righteousness; (3) God's activity, which is beyond our understanding but ultimately just. These three levels correspond to my three-story structure. Late in the writing of this book, I came across Ryan Ball, "*Hebel,* Joy, and the Fear of God: Qoheleth's Design and Message" (PhD thesis, Wycliffe College and the University of Toronto, 2022). Ball argues that a satisfying, holistic reading of Ecclesiastes must integrate each of those three titular elements without subordinating any to another, which is essentially my point. In other words, it is not the case that either "everything is hevel" or "rejoice in everything" is Ecclesiastes' main message. Instead, Ecclesiastes' vision of life emerges at the intersection of seeing all as hevel, all as a gift (and therefore to be received with joy), and all as subject to the judgment of God (who must therefore be feared).

xvii **At one point he tells us:** Ecclesiastes 2:17, 20.

xvii **But at several points in the book:** The passages cited later in this paragraph are Ecclesiastes 2:24; 5:18; 8:15; 9:7; 11:8.

xviii **Accounting for the contradiction:** This point is a scholarly commonplace. See, for instance, Michael V. Fox, *A Time to Tear Down and a Time to Build Up: A Rereading of Ecclesiastes* (1999; repr., Eugene, Ore.: Wipf & Stock, 2010), 3, 138–40; Eunny P. Lee, *The Vitality of Enjoyment in Qohelet's Theological Rhetoric* (Berlin: de Gruyter, 2005), 8; Bartholomew, *Ecclesiastes,* 81. For surveys of ways scholars have addressed the tension between Ecclesiastes' bleak verdict that all is hevel and its commendations of enjoyment, along with the role of the fear of God in its ethic, see Lee, *Vitality,* 1–8; Ball, "*Hebel,* Joy, and the Fear of God," 3–29.

xviii **To put it in the language of epistemology:** According to Michael V. Fox, "Qohelet's Epistemology," *Hebrew Union College Annual* 58 (1987): 137–56, at 141, "Qohelet's epistemology is essentially empirical." Craig Bartholomew advances on Fox in two respects, one major, one minor. The minor one is terminological: Bartholomew prefers the term *autonomous* to *empirical* to avoid both anachronism and possibly implying a too-rigid understanding of Qohelet's method. (See his *Ecclesiastes,* 271, revising his earlier use of *empirical.*) But Bartholomew's major contribution is to recognize that Qohelet switches, without warning, between an autonomous empirical mode and a confessional one, which Qohelet sets side by side in "deliberate contradictory juxtaposition" (*Ecclesiastes,* 153). That is, Qohelet switches viewpoints from what unaided sense and reason can tell him to what his faith in the creator God of Israel tells him. See especially Craig G. Bartholomew, *Reading Ecclesiastes: Old Testament Exegesis and Hermeneutical Theory* (Rome: Editrice Pontifico Instituto Biblico, 1998), 230–37, 253–64; also Bartholomew, *Ecclesiastes,* 87, 95, 115, 152–53. Though he does not offer a unifying synthesis as Bartholomew does, James L. Crenshaw, "Qohelet's Understanding of Intellectual Inquiry," in *Qohelet in the Context of Wisdom,* ed. Antoon Schoors (Leuven, Belgium: Peeters, 1998), 212–13, also recognizes that Qohelet speaks from two strikingly different sources of knowledge.

xviii **On the second floor, Qohelet also tells us:** Ecclesiastes 2:24; 3:12, 22.

xix **They function like parallel tracks:** This distillation of Ecclesiastes' two main intellectual movements is informed by Jesse M. Peterson, " 'What Is Good': Qoheleth and the Philosophy of Value" (PhD diss., Durham University, 2020), 204–5, who summarizes, "The two run along separate tracks, as it were. The questions about *yitron* [gain] and meaning are never answered affirmatively and only denied (implicitly and explicitly), while the questions about what is good are in fact answered by the joy statements."

xix **These two key themes:** I owe this insight to Stuart Weeks, "The Inner-Textuality of Qoheleth's Monologue," in *Reading Ecclesiastes Intertextually,* ed. Katharine Dell and Will Kynes (London: Bloomsbury T&T Clark, 2014), 143–44.

xix **Another way to account for the difference:** On the influence of the early chapters of Genesis on Ecclesiastes, see, e.g., Charles C. Forman, "Koheleth's Use of Genesis," *Journal of Semitic Studies* 5, no. 3 (1960): 256–63. See also H. W. Hertzberg, *Der Prediger,* KAT 17 (Gütersloh: Gütersloher Verlagshaus, 1963), 230, "There is no doubt: The book of Qohelet is written with Gen 1–4 before the eyes of its author; Qohelet's view of life is formed by the creation narrative" (translation mine). For a recent, learned exploration of links between Ecclesiastes and Genesis 1–11 that seems to me slightly overcautious, especially in its denial of a "fall" in Ecclesiastes' account of the human condition, see Katharine Dell, "Exploring Intertextual Links between Ecclesiastes and Genesis 1–11," in *Reading Ecclesiastes Intertextually,* 3–14.

xix **For most of the book:** On the structural significance of the seven joy-refrains, see Tyler Atkinson, *Singing at the Winepress: Ecclesiastes and the Ethics of Work* (London: Bloomsbury T&T Clark, 2015), 46–47. Within these seven second-story "panels," one can detect some progression and intensification. Qohelet seems to grow more joyful and insistent as they tick by. And, while the third-story themes of judgment and the fear of God are sprinkled in sparsely, they become more prominent toward the end. These two subtle progressions point to the significance of both themes for the book's overall message.

xx **For long years now:** For a discussion of the senses in which Ecclesiastes can fruitfully be understood as modern, see Jennie Grillo, "Qohelet and the Marks of Modernity: Reading Ecclesiastes with Matthew Arnold and Charles Taylor," *Religions* 7, no. 6 (2016): 77, https://doi.org/10.3390/rel7060077.

xxi **"In my view, sociology":** Hartmut Rosa, "Capitalism as a Spiral of Dynamisation: Sociology as Social Critique," in Klaus Dörre, Stephan Lessenich, and Hartmut Rosa, *Sociology, Capitalism, Critique,* trans. Jan-Peter Herrmann and Loren Balhorn (London: Verso, 2014), 68. Rosa describes his project as elaborating a "sociology of the good life" in *Resonance: A Sociology of Our Relationship to the World,* trans. James C. Wagner (Medford, Mass.: Polity, 2019), 2. On "social acceleration," see Rosa's *Social Acceleration: A New Theory of Modernity,* trans. Jonathan Trejo-Mathys (New York: Columbia University Press, 2013). The conversation between Ecclesiastes and contemporary sociology that I facilitate in this book chimes with church fathers' classification of Ecclesiastes under the ancient rubric of "natural science." See Jennie Barbour, *The Story of Israel in the Book of Qohelet: Ecclesiastes as Cultural Memory* (Oxford: Oxford University Press, 2012), 181.

xxi **Who is Hartmut Rosa:** If you would like to read Hartmut Rosa for yourself, I would start with *The Uncontrollability of the World,* trans.

James C. Wagner (Medford, MA: Polity, 2020), Rosa's most concise, accessible exposition of many of his key ideas.

xxii **"The statement of a terrible truth":** Kathleen Raine, cited (without documentation) in Wendell Berry, "The Way of Ignorance," in *The World-Ending Fire: The Essential Wendell Berry* (Berkeley, Calif.: Counterpoint, 2017), 329.

xxii **"If the book we're reading":** Franz Kafka, *Letters to Friends, Family, and Editors* (New York: Schocken, 1977), 16.

"A MEMORY OF THE WORLD UNBROKEN"

3 **"The world is so big":** Michael Chabon, "Wes Anderson's Worlds," in *Bookends: Collected Intros and Outros* (New York: HarperCollins, 2018), 3–4, 7.

CHAPTER 1—HEVEL (I): UNCONTROLLABLE

5 **"I applied my heart to seek":** The two statements of Qohelet's observational program are from Ecclesiastes 1:13–14 and 7:25; the selections of what he saw are in 1:14; 4:1; 9:11; 10:6.

6 **"Vanity of vanities, saith the Preacher":** Ecclesiastes 1:2, KJV.

6 **The most concrete sense of hevel:** This initial survey of uses of *hevel* in the Old Testament and Ecclesiastes draws particularly on the discussion of Stuart Weeks, *Ecclesiastes and Scepticism* (New York: T&T Clark, 2012), 104–20 and the snapshot in Keefer, *Ecclesiastes and the Meaning of Life,* 90n2. For the important insight that *hevel* in Ecclesiastes is a live metaphor, see especially Douglas B. Miller, "Qohelet's Symbolic Use of הבל," *Journal of Biblical Literature* 117, no. 3 (1998): 437–54. For *hevel* as "breath" or "air," see Isaiah 57:13 and Psalm 62:9. For a fuller discussion of literature on *hevel* in Ecclesiastes, see the sixth note to chapter 11, on the text beginning "Hevel names something dissonant."

6 **For ancient Israel, a political alliance:** For this sentence and the next three, see Isaiah 30:7; Proverbs 31:30; Job 27:12; Psalm 39:5 (verse 6 in Hebrew). As Keefer summarizes in *Ecclesiastes and the Meaning of Life,* 90n2, "The lexeme includes senses of breath and brevity, and something of no consequence, substance or worth."

6 **And throughout the book Qohelet custom molds hevel:** Scholars who recognize that Qohelet pushes *hevel* into new territory include Michael V. Fox, "The Meaning of *Hebel* for Qohelet," *Journal of Biblical Literature* 105, no. 3 (1986): 409–27; Phillip Michael Lasater, "Subordination and the Human Condition in Ecclesiastes," *The Journal of Religion* 100, no. 1 (2020): 75–102, at 93; and Samet, "Qoheleth's Idiolect," 461.

6 **You could translate Qohelet's opening thesis:** The following translations of Ecclesiastes 1:2 are from the NIV; CEB; CSB; Bartholomew, *Ecclesiastes,* 101; Weeks, *Ecclesiastes and Scepticism,* 106; Fox, *A Time to Tear Down,* 159.

8 **the central drive of modernity:** Rosa, *Uncontrollability,* viii. The following citation is from page 16.

8 **these technologically aided efforts:** For this citation and the following, see Rosa, *Uncontrollability,* 61.

9 **"We seek out guilty or responsible parties":** Rosa, *Uncontrollability,* 94 (emphasis original).

9 **"for late modern human beings":** Rosa, *Uncontrollability,* 6.

9 **"He feels within him his longing":** Albert Camus, *The Myth of Sisyphus,* trans. Justin O'Brien (New York: Vintage, 1955), 28. See discussion in Rosa, *Uncontrollability,* 26–27, on which the wording of my introduction of Camus's point draws.

10 **"it is only in encountering the *uncontrollable*":** Rosa, *Uncontrollability,* 2 (emphasis original).

10 **In the most meaningful experiences:** See the account of "resonance" throughout Rosa, *Uncontrollability,* especially the relationship between resonance and controllability on pages 40–59, as well as the full treatment in Hartmut Rosa, *Resonance.*

10 **the driving urge of modernity is to control:** Rosa, *Uncontrollability,* 4.

10 **"And I applied my heart to seek":** Ecclesiastes 1:13–18.

11 **Striving after wind is trying to control the uncontrollable:** Using the same German word for "uncontrollability" (*unverfügbarkeit*) as Rosa does, Tilmann Zimmer, *Zwischen Tod und Lebensglück: eine Untersuchung zur Anthropologie Kohelets* (Berlin: de Gruyter, 1999), 32 comments, "With his frequent hevel-judgments, Qohelet makes clear the uncontrollability of human life and all its realms, and so refers to the sovereignty of God" (translation mine).

11 **"At the heart of all beauty":** Camus, *Myth,* 14.

12 **In an uncontrollable world:** See Weeks, *Ecclesiastes and Scepticism,* 98.

12 **"Again I saw that under the sun":** Ecclesiastes 9:11–12.

12 **Qohelet's point is not that the fastest:** For apt comments on these verses, see, e.g., Fox, *A Time to Tear Down,* 296.

13 **"That it's rough out there":** Annie Dillard, *Pilgrim at Tinker Creek* (New York: Harper Perennial, 1998), 9.

13 **In Qohelet's survey of everything:** For a well-rounded statement of this point, see Choon-Leong Seow, *Ecclesiastes: A New Translation with Introduction and Commentary* (New York: Doubleday, 1997), 55.

13 **"Reality escapes hope the way wet soap":** Amit Majmudar, *Twin A: A Memoir* (Seattle: Slant, 2023), 149. The examples that follow are from Ecclesiastes 2:14–16, 18–21; 3:16; 5:13–16; 6:1–2.

14 **The obligation to make something:** Paraphrasing Rosa, *Resonance,* 133.

15 **"I have a terrible premonition":** Kate Bowler, *Everything Happens for a Reason: And Other Lies I've Loved* (New York: Random House, 2018), 93–94.

15 **"categorical imperative of late modernity":** The phrase "categorical

imperative of late modernity" is from Rosa, *Uncontrollability,* 11, as is the sentence following the colon (with formatting adapted). My paragraph draws on his broader discussion on the same page.

15 **"Triple-A Approach" to the good life:** For this citation and the next two, see Hartmut Rosa, "Available, Accessible, Attainable: The Mindset of Growth and the Resonance Conception of the Good Life," in *The Good Life Beyond Growth: New Perspectives,* ed. Hartmut Rosa and Christoph Henning (London: Routledge, 2017), 42–43.

16 **"Control is a drug":** Bowler, *Everything,* 84.

CHAPTER 2—GAIN

17 **"What does man gain by all the toil":** Ecclesiastes 1:3.

17 **"It is what one carries away":** Weeks, *Ecclesiastes and Scepticism,* 35.

18 **"A generation goes, and a generation comes":** Ecclesiastes 1:4–11. I was convinced of the chiastic ($ABCB^1A^1$) structure of Ecclesiastes 1:4–11 by Bartholomew, *Ecclesiastes,* 110.

19 **Having been assembled from dust:** This sentence and the next adapt phrases from, and are informed by the exegesis of, Nili Samet, "Qohelet 1,4 and the Structure of the Book's Prologue," *Zeitschrift für die Alttestamentliche Wissenschaft* 126, no. 1 (2014): 92–100, at 97–98.

20 **Like the natural forces that sustain it:** This sentence and the next paraphrase Fox, *A Time to Tear Down,* 113, and Ardel B. Caneday, "'Everything Is Vapor': Grasping for Meaning Under the Sun," *Southern Baptist Journal of Theology* 15, no. 3 (2011): 26–40, at 30. See also Jesse M. Peterson, "Times as Task, Not Timing: Reconsidering Qoheleth's Catalogue of the Times," *Vetus Testamentum* 72, no. 3 (2022): 444–73, at 456.

21 **Qohelet tells us that he systematically:** Ecclesiastes 2:1–11. This paragraph quotes verses 10 and 11.

21 **A man heaped up an inheritance:** Ecclesiastes 5:13–16. This paragraph quotes verses 15 and 16.

22 **"Then I saw that there is more gain":** Ecclesiastes 2:13. The following quotation is from 2:14–15.

22 **"wisdom is good with an inheritance":** Ecclesiastes 7:11–15, citing verses 11 and 13. My use of "gain" reflects the Hebrew of verse 12; the ESV's "advantage" is less transparent to the Hebrew *yitrôn.*

22 **So what gain is wisdom:** This conclusion and the preceding analysis of Qohelet's no-gain economy are informed by Scott C. Jones, "The Values and Limits of Qohelet's Sub-Celestial Economy," *Vetus Testamentum* 64 (2014): 21–33.

23 **"We are driven ceaselessly onward":** Christian Wiman, *My Bright Abyss: Meditation of a Modern Believer* (New York: Farrar, Straus and Giroux, 2013), 97.

23 **1915 poem "Sunday Morning":** Wallace Stevens, "Sunday Morning," *Poetry,* November 1915, 82–83, www.poetryfoundation.org/poetrymagazine/browse?volume=7&issue=2&page=28.

27 **for this condition is "social acceleration":** See especially Hartmut Rosa, *Social Acceleration.*

27 **The shape of late modern life:** Rosa, *Social Acceleration,* 156. See also Hartmut Rosa, *Alienation and Acceleration: Towards a Critical Theory of Late-Modern Temporality* (Malmö, Sweden: NSU Press, 2010), 33.

27 **Under conditions of social acceleration:** So Peter Conrad, *Modern Times, Modern Places* (New York: Knopf, 1999), 6.

27 **"If you do not constantly strive":** Rosa, *Social Acceleration,* 117.

28 **This walking-up-a-down-escalator existence:** See Rosa, *Resonance,* 122. See also Rosa, *Alienation and Acceleration,* 32, 60, 81; and Rosa, "Available, Accessible, Attainable," 42. The following citation is from Rosa, "Escalation: The Crisis of Dynamic Stabilisation and the Prospect of Resonance," in *Sociology, Capitalism, Critique,* 282.

CHAPTER 3—WORK

29 **"economists of the early 20th century":** Derek Thompson, "Workism Is Making Americans Miserable," *The Atlantic,* February 24, 2019, www.theatlantic.com/ideas/archive/2019/02/religion-workism-making-americans-miserable/583441. Subsequent citations of Thompson are from this article, as is the 2005 statistic on workweeks.

30 **Americans "work longer hours":** Samuel P. Huntington, *Who Are We? The Challenges to America's National Identity* (New York: Simon & Schuster, 2004), 30.

30 **compared to women who graduated:** See discussion in Derek Thompson, "Does It Matter Where You Go to College?," *The Atlantic,* December 11, 2018, www.theatlantic.com/ideas/archive/2018/12/does-it-matter-where-you-go-college/577816.

30 **work has become "the chief repository":** Mary S. Hartman, *The Household and the Making of History: A Subversive View of the Western Past* (Cambridge: Cambridge University Press, 2004), 198.

30 **"In my opinion, second-wave feminism":** Camille Paglia, *Free Women, Free Men: Sex, Gender, Feminism* (New York: Vintage, 2017), 240.

31 **"the career mystique—a set of ideas":** Scott Yenor, *The Recovery of Family Life: Exposing the Limits of Modern Ideologies* (Waco, Tex.: Baylor University Press, 2020), 120. Yenor's point is that Betty Friedan and other second-wave feminists promoted the formation and culture-wide embedding of this career mystique.

31 **"collective anxiety, mass disappointment":** Thompson, "Workism."

31 **"What does man gain by all the toil":** Ecclesiastes 1:3.

31 **By "toil" (Hebrew *'amal*):** Ecclesiastes also frequently uses a broad, neutral word for work (the verb *'asah,* with its cognate noun), which maps onto our words "make," "work," and "do."

31 **Elsewhere in the Old Testament:** For *'amal* as "distress" or "anguish," see Isaiah 53:11; as "misfortune" or "disaster," see Numbers 23:21 and Psalm 7:14.

32 **"I made great works":** Ecclesiastes 2:4–7.

32 **He describes the work:** This sentence borrows wording from Stuart Weeks, *Ecclesiastes 1–5: A Critical and Exegetical Commentary* (London: T&T Clark, 2020), 387.

32 **"Qohelet's business is not ephemeral":** Weeks, *Ecclesiastes 1–5,* 388, which also informs the next three sentences.

32 **"Then I considered all that my hands":** Ecclesiastes 2:11.

32 **Qohelet here appraises not just his labor:** The phrase "the infrastructure of his fortune" is from Weeks, *Ecclesiastes 1–5,* 418.

33 **He calls work absurd:** This sentence paraphrases Fox, "The Meaning of *Hebel,*" 416; the next sentence goes beyond Fox, though he makes a similar point in *A Time to Tear Down,* 122.

33 **"I hated all my toil":** Ecclesiastes 2:18–23.

34 **Both toil and wisdom are irrelevant:** Paraphrasing Fox, *A Time to Tear Down,* 188.

34 **"Then I saw that all toil":** Ecclesiastes 4:4–8.

35 **Most translations and commentators:** For Ecclesiastes 4:4 as speaking of not envy but "an all-consuming passion . . . that isolates people from those around them," see Weeks, *Ecclesiastes 1–5,* 580, also 584.

37 **"There is a realm of time":** Abraham Joshua Heschel, *The Sabbath* (New York: Farrar, Straus and Giroux, 2005), 3.

37 **"What has a man from all the toil":** Ecclesiastes 2:22–23.

37 **"Whoever begins a career at Microsoft":** Cited in Zygmunt Bauman, *Liquid Modernity* (Cambridge, Mass.: Polity, 2000), 116. See discussion of this point in Rosa, *Social Acceleration,* 112, 230–31, 360n16.

38 **"Today, a young American":** Richard Sennett, *The Corrosion of Character: The Personal Consequences of Work in the New Capitalism* (New York: Norton, 1998), 25; this page also informs the preceding sentence. The following two citations are from pages 87 and 94, and the sentence beginning "When past experience" is informed by page 97.

38 **"To be a workist is to worship":** Thompson, "Workism."

CHAPTER 4—KNOWLEDGE

39 **In London, on July 9, 1955:** The text of the manifesto, along with an account on which I draw, can be found at "Russell-Einstein Manifesto," Atomic Heritage Foundation, accessed July 11, 2022, www.atomicheritage

.org/key-documents/russell-einstein-manifesto. I learned of the manifesto through Sennett, *The Craftsman,* 295.

40 **But today in the West:** This paragraph draws on Michael J. Sandel, *The Tyranny of Merit: What's Become of the Common Good?* (New York: Farrar, Straus and Giroux, 2020), 81–111.

40 **A college degree is the primary path:** Sandel, *Tyranny,* 73. For the next sentence, see Sandel, *Tyranny,* chapter 4.

40 **"And I applied my heart to seek":** Ecclesiastes 1:13–18.

41 **basically means his independent:** I borrow the phrase "independent rational intellect" from Fox, *A Time to Tear Down,* 76.

42 **"So I turned to consider":** Ecclesiastes 2:12–17.

42 **But a path is only as good:** This imagery is influenced by Weeks, *Ecclesiastes 1–5,* 434.

43 **"All this I have tested":** Ecclesiastes 7:23–29.

43 **Qohelet tested everything:** On the paradox of Qohelet seeking wisdom by wisdom yet failing to find wisdom, see Michael V. Fox and Bezalel Porten, "Unsought Discoveries: Qohelet 7:23-8:1a," *Hebrew Studies* 19 (1978): 26–38, at 27–28.

43 **No master of what he surveys:** This sentence adapts wording from Fox, *A Time to Tear Down,* 265; Fox also includes the passage I cite from Camus, *Myth,* 6.

44 **"While adding one thing to another":** Ecclesiastes 7:27–28.

44 **Qohelet's confession that his autonomous:** My reading of Ecclesiastes 7:23–29 is indebted to A. D. Spears, "The Theological Hermeneutics of Homiletical Application and Ecclesiastes 7:23–29" (PhD diss., University of Liverpool, 2006). See also Bartholomew, *Ecclesiastes,* 263–77.

45 **"When I applied my heart":** Ecclesiastes 8:16–17.

45 **It isn't that we can know nothing:** Jones, "Values and Limits," 29.

45 **Wisdom prepares persuasive rebukes:** Ecclesiastes 7:5, 11–12, 19. The following citations in this paragraph and the following paragraphs are from Ecclesiastes 9:11, 13–16, 18; 10:1.

46 **Wisdom is mightier than weapons:** Paraphrasing Fox, *A Time to Tear Down,* 89.

48 **"No predictive science of human behavior":** Jason Blakely, *We Built Reality: How Social Science Infiltrated Culture, Politics, and Power* (New York: Oxford University Press, 2020), xxiv; my exposition of the point draws on his previous page as well.

48 **"What methods hold out":** Blakely, *We Built Reality,* 73.

CHAPTER 5—PLEASURE

49 **"Man's great affliction":** Simone Weil, *Gravity and Grace,* trans. Emma Crawford and Mario von der Ruhr (London: Routlege, 2002), 100; the

following citation too. I was alerted to the resonance between Ecclesiastes and this point of Weil's by Bartholomew, *Ecclesiastes,* 99.

50 **"I said in my heart":** Ecclesiastes 2:1–2. Verse 3 follows in the next paragraph.

50 **The directive guiding Qohelet's inquiry:** My account of the structure of Ecclesiastes 2:1–11 follows Fox, *A Time to Tear Down,* 175.

50 **In his inquiry into pleasure's value:** On Qohelet's "fortifying" use of wine in his existential trial of life's pleasures, see Weeks, *Ecclesiastes 1–5,* 377.

50 **"I made great works":** Ecclesiastes 2:4–9. For the second half of verse 8, I adapt the translation of Weeks, *Ecclesiastes 1–5,* 328. For Weeks's rationale for his rendering see pages 395–96, 406–13.

51 **"And whatever my eyes desired":** Ecclesiastes 2:10.

51 **"Then I considered all that my hands":** Ecclesiastes 2:11.

52 **Americans across a vast range:** See the reporting in Joe Pinsker, "The Pay Raise People Say They Need to Be Happy," *The Wall Street Journal,* November 19, 2023, www.wsj.com/personal-finance/income-raise-happiness-06a70900.

52 **"There is an evil that I have seen":** Ecclesiastes 6:1–2.

53 **"But God does not allow him":** My translation is that of Bartholomew, *Ecclesiastes,* 234. Other scholars who note that here the idiom "eat" means "enjoy" include Robert Alter, *The Wisdom Books: Job, Proverbs, and Ecclesiastes* (New York: Norton, 2010), 366; and Jesse M. Peterson, "Is Coming into Existence Always a Harm? Qoheleth in Dialogue with David Benatar," *Harvard Theological Review* 112, no. 1 (2019): 33–54, at 40–41.

53 **Qohelet then works a variation:** Roland E. Murphy, *Ecclesiastes* (Dallas: Word, 1992), 53, observes that Ecclesiastes 6:3–6, which is cited in the block quote that follows, is "an extension or an intensification of vv. 1–2 in that the failure to enjoy one's possessions and to fulfill one's desires remains the problem." My translation of verses 4–5 is informed by Peterson, "Coming into Existence," 39–41, as is the exegesis that follows.

54 **"All the toil of man":** Ecclesiastes 6:7–9.

54 **"If we are enjoying a good meal":** Michael V. Fox, *Ecclesiastes* (Philadelphia: Jewish Publication Society, 2004), 41.

CHAPTER 6—MONEY

56 **Stefan Thomas, a computer programmer:** Nathaniel Popper, "Lost Passwords Lock Millionaires Out of Their Bitcoin Fortunes," *The New York Times,* January 12, 2021, www.nytimes.com/2021/01/12/technology/bitcoin-passwords-wallets-fortunes.html. Popper's lede is hard to improve, so I paraphrase it. My account follows his closely.

57 **"I also gathered for myself":** Ecclesiastes 2:8.

57 **Qohelet is "*the* accumulator":** Kumiko Takeuchi, *Death and Divine Judgment in Ecclesiastes* (Winona Lake, Ind.: Eisenbrauns, 2019), 79 (emphasis original).

57 **"I hated all my toil":** Ecclesiastes 2:18–19.

57 **"Again, I saw an absurdity":** Ecclesiastes 4:7–8.

57 **"He who loves money will not":** Ecclesiastes 5:10.

57 **"When goods increase":** Ecclesiastes 5:11.

58 **The more that is gained:** My wording here riffs on that of Stuart Weeks, *Ecclesiastes 5–12: A Critical and Exegetical Commentary* (London: T&T Clark, 2021), 7.

58 **The more wealth you have:** This sentence and the next are indebted to Bartholomew, *Ecclesiastes,* 219.

58 **"Sweet is the sleep":** Ecclesiastes 5:12. My translation of verse 12 adapts the ESV in light of Seow, *Ecclesiastes,* 201, 206. On the translation difficulties in Ecclesiastes 5:12 (5:11 in Hebrew), see Seow, *Ecclesiastes,* 205–6; Weeks, *Ecclesiastes 5–12,* 29–31.

58 **"There is a grievous evil":** Ecclesiastes 5:13–16.

59 **"There is an evil that I have seen":** Ecclesiastes 6:1–2.

59 **If your desired destination:** I adapt this image from the comment of Fox, *A Time to Tear Down,* 235, on Ecclesiastes 5:10 (5:9 in Hebrew), "Money should be a means, not an end in itself, for if one heads for riches the horizon ever recedes."

60 **But in a modern market society:** I draw the phrase "market society" from Michael J. Sandel, *What Money Can't Buy: The Moral Limits of Markets* (New York: Farrar, Straus and Giroux, 2012), 10–11.

60 **"Thus—and this is very important—money becomes":** Georg Simmel, "Money in Modern Culture," *Theory, Culture and Society* 8, no. 3 (1991): 17–31, at 27.

60 **"the notion arises that all happiness":** The citations in this sentence and the next are from Simmel, "Money in Modern Culture," 25.

61 **Money promises security and calm:** Here I paraphrase Simmel, "Money in Modern Culture," 28, "This feeling of security and calm which the possession of money provides, this conviction of possessing the intersection of all values in the form of money, thus contains in a purely psychological sense, formally one could say, the equalization point which gives the deeper justification to that complaint about money as the God of our times."

61 **money "serves secularized capitalist":** Rosa, *Social Acceleration,* 178 (emphasis original).

61 **Aristotle distinguished between:** For an application of Aristotle's use value/exchange value distinction to Ecclesiastes' teaching on wealth, see Milton P. Horne, "Intertextuality and Economics: Reading Ecclesiastes with Proverbs," in *Reading Ecclesiastes Intertextually,* 106–17.

61 **Qohelet anticipates this distinction:** See Horne, "Intertextuality and Economics," 114, on Ecclesiastes 6:1–6.

61 **"This colonization of ends by means":** The citation in this sentence and the next citation are from Simmel, "Money in Modern Culture," 25. Simone Weil makes the same point in her oracular idiom in *Gravity and Grace,* 52.

62 **"In globalized capitalism, exchange value":** William T. Cavanaugh, *Being Consumed: Economics and Christian Desire* (Grand Rapids, Mich.: Eerdmans, 2008), 69.

62 **"The richer we are . . . the more":** Rosa, "Available, Accessible, Attainable," 42.

62 **"Money, by itself, has an individualizing":** Byung-Chul Han, *The Disappearance of Rituals: A Topology of the Present* (Medford, Mass.: Polity, 2020), 43.

62 **"My life is full of convenience":** Andy Crouch, *The Life We're Looking For: Reclaiming Relationship in a Technological World* (New York: Convergent, 2022), 26. The following quote is from page 73. Simmel anticipates Crouch's latter point in "Money in Modern Culture," 18.

64 **"Two are better than one":** Ecclesiastes 4:9–12.

64 **"wealth radiant and wealth reflective":** John Ruskin, "Unto This Last," in *Unto This Last and Other Writings* (New York: Penguin, 1997), 162. The next three citations are from pages 187, 220, and 222 (small capitals original). I first learned of Ruskin's treatment of these subjects through Alastair Roberts, "Ruskin and the Illusion of Value," The Kitchen Table (blog), November 3, 2017, https://ddcasp.weebly.com/the-kitchen-table/ruskin-and-the-illusion-of-value.

CHAPTER 7—TIME

67 **Time is our native habitat:** The way I put this point is inspired by James K. A. Smith, *How to Inhabit Time: Understanding the Past, Facing the Future, Living Faithfully Now* (Grand Rapids, Mich.: Brazos, 2022), 27, 51; and Oliver Burkeman, *Four Thousand Weeks: Time Management for Mortals* (New York: Farrar, Straus and Giroux, 2021), 216. Both draw on Martin Heidegger.

67 **"Let each of us examine":** Blaise Pascal, *Pensées,* trans. A. J. Krailsheimer (New York: Penguin, 1995), 13 §47 (page number then pensée number). For fruitful studies of Pascal's thought, see Alban Krailsheimer, *Pascal* (Oxford: Oxford University Press, 1980); Thomas V. Morris, *Making Sense of It All: Pascal and the Meaning of Life* (Grand Rapids, Mich.: Eerdmans, 1992); Kreeft, *Christianity for Modern Pagans;* Paul J. Griffiths, *Why Read Pascal?* (Washington, D.C.: Catholic University of America Press, 2021); Benjamin Storey and Jenna Silber Story, *Why We Are Restless:*

On the Modern Quest for Contentment (Princeton, N.J.: Princeton University Press, 2021), 50–98.

68 **"For everything there is a season":** Ecclesiastes 3:1–8.

68 **Qohelet's poem of times:** My discussion of conflicting interpretations of Ecclesiastes 3:1–8 is indebted to Peterson, "Times as Task," 445–50, though I demur from his theological criticisms of what he calls the "common determinist" reading. For representatives of the "proper times" reading see, e.g., Fox, *A Time to Tear Down,* 191–214; Mette Bundvad, *Time in the Book of Ecclesiastes* (Oxford: Oxford University Press, 2015), 90–109. For the "common determinist" reading, see, e.g., Murphy, *Ecclesiastes,* 39; Seow, *Ecclesiastes,* 169.

68 **"I perceived that whatever God does":** Ecclesiastes 3:14.

69 **What pattern:** See especially Peterson, "Times as Task," 460, 469. Similarly John Jarick, "The Hebrew Book of Changes: Reflections on *Hakkōl Hebel* and *Lakkōl Zemān* in Ecclesiastes," *Journal for the Study of the Old Testament* 90 (2000): 79–99, at 98, "In his catalogue of times he excels himself in setting out a remarkably complex pattern of change that at one and the same time speaks of order and of chaos: there are wheels within wheels that suggest regularity and design, yet each on-rushing time cancels out its opposite in meaningless ambiguity."

69 **Why can't you keep to the present:** This series of four short paragraphs borrows from Pascal, *Pensées,* 13 §47, "We never keep to the present. We recall the past; we anticipate the future as if we found it too slow in coming and were trying to hurry it up, or we recall the past as if to stay its too rapid flight. We are so unwise that we wander about in times that do not belong to us, and do not think of the only one that does; so vain that we dream of times that are not and blindly flee the only one that is. The fact is that the present usually hurts. We thrust it out of sight because it distresses us, and if we find it enjoyable, we are sorry to see it slip away. We try to give it the support of the future, and think how we are going to arrange things over which we have no control for a time we can never be sure of reaching."

71 **After hanging his time tapestry:** Peterson, "Times as Task," 468. The citations of Ecclesiastes in this paragraph and the next consist of 3:9–11.

72 **"Time is the continuous loop":** Dillard, *Pilgrim,* 77.

72 **"I perceived that whatever God does":** Ecclesiastes 3:14–15.

72 **God writes time in permanent marker:** The rest of this paragraph borrows imagery from Peterson, "Times as Task," 467; and Jarick, "The Hebrew Book of Changes," 91.

74 **Under the clock's reign:** See John Urry, "Speeding Up and Slowing Down," in *High-Speed Society: Social Acceleration, Power, and Modernity,* ed. Hartmut Rosa and William E. Scheuerman (University Park, Pa.: Pennsylvania State University Press, 2009), 186.

74 **in our modern market society, time:** Here I paraphrase Rosa, *Social Acceleration,* 377n9. Similarly Burkeman, *Four Thousand Weeks,* 24.

74 **"We all try and save time":** Jerry Seinfeld, *Is This Anything?,* 67.

75 **"the contraction of the present":** See Hermann Lübbe, "The Contraction of the Present," in *High-Speed Society: Social Acceleration, Power, and Modernity,* ed. Hartmut Rosa and William E. Scheuerman (University Park, Pa.: Pennsylvania State University Press, 2009), 159–78. See also Rosa, *Social Acceleration,* 76. The following quote is from Lübbe, "The Contraction of the Present," 159.

75 **What does this clocked, contracted time:** This paragraph is indebted to Burkeman, *Four Thousand Weeks,* 9, 13, 26.

76 **present-day Americans, for instance, feel more harried:** According to Judy Wajcman, *Pressed for Time: The Acceleration of Life in Digital Capitalism* (Chicago: The University of Chicago Press, 2015), 4. The phrase later in this paragraph, "the time-pressure paradox," comes from page 5. See also Rosa, *Social Acceleration,* xxxv.

76 **"One very curious but consistent fact":** Rosa, "Available, Accessible, Attainable," 39.

77 **"Be not overly wicked":** Ecclesiastes 7:17, followed by 9:12.

77 **"'Look there,' she said, and gestured to the keys":** A. E. Stallings, "Lost and Found," in *Like: Poems* (New York: Farrar, Straus and Giroux, 2018), 63.

78 **The ancient Chinese poet Wang Wei:** Wang Wei, "Source of the Peach Blossom Stream"; translation by Kim Stanley Robinson, *The High Sierra: A Love Story* (New York: Little, Brown and Company, 2022), 446–47.

CHAPTER 8—ENOUGH

79 **an expert in "behavioral engineering":** For Nir Eyal's expertise in "behavioral engineering," see Nir Eyal with Ryan Hoover, *Hooked: How to Build Habit-Forming Products* (New York: Penguin, 2014); the citation in this paragraph is from page 97. For an exposition of Eyal's work on which my description draws, see Laura Entis, "How the 'Hook Model' Can Turn Customers into Addicts," *Fortune,* January 11, 2017, https://fortune.com/2017/01/11/nir-eyal-hook-model. In his most recent book, Eyal has apparently converted from dealer to doctor. See Nir Eyal with Julie Li, *Indistractable: How to Control Your Attention and Choose Your Life* (Dallas: BenBella, 2019). My engagement with Eyal is informed by Matt Feeney, *Little Platoons: A Defense of Family in a Competitive Age* (New York: Basic Books, 2021), 138–41; the quote about "Dopamine Labs" is from page 141.

80 **"All things are full of weariness":** Ecclesiastes 1:8.

80 **"Again, I saw an absurdity":** Ecclesiastes 4:7–8.

81 **He is insatiable:** This sentence and the next echo Fox, *A Time to Tear Down,* 122.

81 **"He who loves money":** Ecclesiastes 5:10.

81 **Remember Qohelet's man:** Ecclesiastes 6:1–5.

81 **Not rest from hard labor:** I adapt the phrase "psychological rest" from Peterson, "Coming into Existence," 45–46, who speaks of "psychological unrest"; pages 39–47 inform this section's whole discussion.

81 **"You have made us for yourself":** Augustine, *Confessions,* 1.1.1, translation mine.

81 **"No psychic equilibrium is possible":** Storey and Storey, *Why We Are Restless,* 66.

82 **"All the toil of man":** Ecclesiastes 6:7, 9.

82 **humans don't have appetites:** For the Old Testament's construal of humanity as intrinsically needy and appetitive through its use of the word *nephesh,* see Hans Walter Wolff, *Anthropology of the Old Testament,* trans. Margaret Kohl (London: SCM Press, 1974), 10–25.

82 **"A test which has gone on so long":** Pascal, *Pensées,* 45 §148.

83 **"He has made everything beautiful":** Ecclesiastes 3:11.

83 **"If there were no echo":** Eric Ortlund, "Deconstruction in Qohelet: A Response to Mark Sneed," *Journal for the Study of the Old Testament* 40, no. 2 (2015): 239–56, at 255; the following sentence is informed by page 254.

84 **"Capable of feelings that embrace":** Jeffrey Gordon, "Nagel or Camus on the Absurd?," *Philosophy and Phenomenological Research* 45, no. 1 (1984): 15–28, at 26. For more on this theme, one could profitably meditate on Abraham Joshua Heschel, *Man Is Not Alone: A Philosophy of Religion* (New York: Farrar, Straus and Giroux, 1951), 253, "All thoughts and feelings about the tangible and knowable world do not exhaust the endless stirring within us. There is a surplus of restlessness over our palpable craving. We are lonely with men, with things, with our own cravings. The goals are greater than the grasp."

84 **"What else does this craving":** Pascal, *Pensées,* 45 §148.

84 **"The sense that in this universe":** C. S. Lewis, *The Weight of Glory: And Other Addresses* (New York: HarperCollins, 2001), 40. The following quotation is from page 42.

84 **this huge world is so stuffed with marvels:** Chabon, "Wes Anderson's Worlds."

CHAPTER 9—POWER

86 **In October 2004, political philosopher:** For this paragraph and the next see Michael Ignatieff, *Fire and Ashes: Success and Failure in Politics* (Cambridge, Mass.: Harvard University Press, 2013), 1–2. My account

closely follows Ignatieff's. Dates and figures in this section come from "Michael Ignatieff," Wikipedia, last modified January 29, 2023, https://en.wikipedia.org/wiki/Michael_Ignatieff#Political_career.

87 **"There were times when I felt":** Ignatieff, *Fire and Ashes,* 3.

87 **He was "king over Israel":** Ecclesiastes 1:12.

87 **"Moreover, I saw under the sun":** Ecclesiastes 3:16–17.

88 **"Again I saw all the oppressions":** Ecclesiastes 4:1–3.

89 **"Better was a poor and wise youth":** Ecclesiastes 4:13–16.

89 **"No one is strong forever":** Richard Sennett, *Authority* (New York: Norton, 1980), 167.

90 **"the solitary reality":** Ignatieff, *Fire and Ashes,* 166–67.

90 **"I say: Keep the king's command":** Ecclesiastes 8:2–4, 8–9.

91 **"I have also seen this example":** Ecclesiastes 9:13–16.

92 **"You imagine that fortune's attitude":** Boethius, *The Consolation of Philosophy,* trans. H. F. Stewart, E. K. Rand, and S. J. Tester, Loeb Classical Library (Portsmouth, N.H.: Heinemann, 1973), II.1–2.

93 **"For me, as Rosalynn and I approach":** President Jimmy Carter, "A Letter from Home," *The Bitter Southerner,* March 30, 2021, https://bittersoutherner.com/a-letter-from-home/jimmy-carter.

CHAPTER 10—DEATH

96 **Death practices an unjust equity:** I borrow the phrase "unjust equity" from Peterson, " 'What Is Good,' " 91. See also Takeuchi, *Death and Divine Judgment,* 102, "Death visits every person and negates whatever is done on this earth to an absurd equality." Throughout this section, my exposition of Ecclesiastes' treatment of death's harms is informed by pages 87–98 of Peterson's work.

96 **"The wise person has his eyes":** Ecclesiastes 2:14–16.

96 **Qohelet takes this as an insult:** Fox, "Inner Structure of Qohelet's Thought," 230 (emphasis original), "This is not a failing of wisdom but an injustice done *to* wisdom, the ultimate insult: Wisdom's polar advantage over folly is erased by death's brutal egalitarianism."

97 **"It is the same for all":** Ecclesiastes 9:2–3.

97 **Qohelet reckons death's blindness:** Takeuchi, *Death and Divine Judgment,* 121.

97 **"What happens to the children of man":** Ecclesiastes 3:19–20.

98 **"I hated all my toil":** Ecclesiastes 2:18–22.

98 **"For of the wise as of the fool":** Ecclesiastes 2:16.

98 **people deeply settled in a place:** According to Wendell Berry, *The Need to Be Whole: Patriotism and the History of Prejudice* (Berkeley, Calif.: Shoemaker & Company, 2022), 203.

99 **"There is no remembrance":** Ecclesiastes 1:11.

99 **"Again I saw that under the sun":** Ecclesiastes 9:11–12.

99 **Its unannounced advent mocks:** This sentence and the next two riff on Peterson, "'What Is Good,'" 98, "For one thing, just as one would not presume to show up at a king's door for an impromptu meeting, death's unannounced arrival mocks the apparent dignity of persons, treating them instead like baited varmint suddenly pounced on by their trappers."

99 **"But he who is joined":** Ecclesiastes 9:4–6, 10. When Qohelet says that there is no work in Sheol, I take his point to be simply that death ends earthly labor. As I understand him, Qohelet uses "Sheol" as a metaphor meaning "the place where dead people go." Michael A. Eaton, *Ecclesiastes: An Introduction and Commentary* (Downers Grove, Ill.: InterVarsity Press, 1983), 147, observes, Sheol is "no more than the state of death pictured in visible terms." As we will explore in chapter 21, Qohelet's perspective here does not rule out the hope of a blessed afterlife for those who fear God. For a careful, nuanced discussion of Sheol in the Old Testament, see T. Desmond Alexander, "The Old Testament View of Life After Death," *Themelios* 11, no. 2 (1986): 41–46.

100 **old age a ceremony of losses:** "A ceremony of losses" is from Donald Hall, *Essays After Eighty* (New York: Mariner, 2015), 4. "A carnival of losses" and the quote that follows are from Donald Hall, *A Carnival of Losses: Notes Nearing Ninety* (New York: Mariner, 2019), 3.

100 **"Remember also your Creator":** Ecclesiastes 12:1–7.

101 **Scholars haggle endlessly over the details:** Many interpreters have understood Ecclesiastes 12:1–7 as an allegory of old age; Fox, *A Time to Tear Down,* 333–49 suggests that three levels of meaning coexist in it (literal, symbolic, and allegorical); Choon-Leong Seow, "Qohelet's Eschatological Poem," *Journal of Biblical Literature* 118, no. 2 (1999): 209–34 reads the poem as depicting an apocalyptic end to human existence as a whole. My understanding is most informed by Peterson, "'What Is Good,'" 90, who suggests that the process of aging and death is in view until verse 6, "where a distinctly jolting, even violent moment occurs—a 'snapping,' a 'breaking,' a 'shattering.'"

101 **"In your eighties it gets hard to walk":** This quote and the following are from Hall, *A Carnival of Losses,* 3.

101 **Death is a brute:** Weeks, "Inner-Textuality," 144, "There is, perhaps, no stronger evocation in ancient literature of death's brutality and finality than in the climax of Qohelet's words at 12:6–7."

101 **"The last act is bloody":** Pascal, *Pensées,* 53 §165.

102 **Because for the one who dies:** Fox, *A Time to Tear Down,* 342, "In one sense this is the extinction of an individual life; in another, the extinction of a universe. Every individual is a microcosm and every death the end of a world. For the person who dies, the stars blink out, the sun goes dark (only the living 'see the sun'), rigor mortis sets in, and all sound ceases."

102 **"What do all these people see":** Fox, *A Time to Tear Down,* 338. See also Bundvad, *Time,* 73.

103 **While death betrays no intent:** My account in this section draws on L. S. Dugdale, *The Lost Art of Dying: Reviving Forgotten Wisdom* (New York: HarperOne, 2020), especially pages 83–84.

103 **"Being unable to cure death":** Pascal, *Pensées,* 37 §133.

104 **"One will never be sufficiently surprised":** Camus, *Myth,* 15.

104 **"Our generations rise and break":** Annie Dillard, *For the Time Being* (New York: Knopf, 1999), 118.

104 **"One of the main reasons":** Ernest Becker, *The Denial of Death* (New York: Simon & Schuster, 1997), 120.

104 **That is why diversion is a vastly:** Pascal, *Pensées,* 42 §138, "*Diversion.* It is easier to bear death when one is not thinking about it than the idea of death when there is no danger."

104 **Modern life is like a designer home:** I adapt the two illustrations in this paragraph from Kreeft, *Christianity for Modern Pagans,* 169; the following paragraph's image of pleasures as sedatives is adapted from page 186.

105 **"Processes of bodily decay":** Rosa, *Uncontrollability,* 80, 83.

105 **"On the radio I hear":** Wiman, *My Bright Abyss,* 7–8. The following quotation is from page 142 (emphasis original).

CHAPTER 11—HEVEL (II): ABSURD

107 **"So I hated life":** Ecclesiastes 2:17.

107 **"So I turned about and gave":** Ecclesiastes 2:20.

108 **growing number of "deaths of despair":** See, for instance, Richard V. Reeves, *Of Boys and Men: Why the Modern Male Is Struggling, Why It Matters, and What to Do About It* (Washington, D.C.: Brookings Institution Press, 2022), 60–63, who cites the seminal work of Anne Case and Angus Deaton, *Deaths of Despair and the Future of Capitalism* (Princeton, N.J.: Princeton University Press, 2020).

108 **Instead, what Qohelet means by *hevel:*** Camus's fullest exposition of the absurd is *The Myth of Sisyphus.* For philosophical works that critically engage the absurd and Camus's notion of it, see, for instance, Thomas Nagel, "The Absurd," *The Journal of Philosophy* 68, no. 20 (1971): 716–27; Gordon, "Nagel or Camus on the Absurd?"; Duncan Pritchard, "Absurdity, Angst, and the Meaning of Life," *The Monist* 93, no. 1 (2010): 3–16; Ryan Gillespie, "Cosmic Meaning, Awe, and Absurdity in the Secular Age: A Critique of Religious Non-Theism," *Harvard Theological Review* 111, no. 4 (2018): 461–87; Grace Whistler, "The Absurd," in *Brill's Companion to Camus: Camus Among the Philosophers,* ed. Matthew Sharpe, Maciej Kałuża, and Peter Francev (Leiden: Brill, 2019), 271–84; James Nikopolous, "Our Singular Absurdities," *Journal of Philosophical Research* 46 (2021): 105–23.

108 **What unites Qohelet's hevel:** This sentence and the following draw especially on Peterson, " 'What Is Good,' " 49, 51 (emphasis original), "Apart from 'absurd,' none of the other proposed translations for *hebel* can account for this *situational* aspect of Qoheleth's *hebel*-usage. The most important claim here is not that the word 'absurd' must be utilized for translations of *hebel* or that *hebel* must be read through the philosophy of Albert Camus. Rather, what is crucial is the recognition that in all of the cases charted above Qoheleth finds problematic the unfit relation between the two parts. The left-side action (or fact) sets up a certain expectation that is stymied by the right-side result. 'Absurd,' derived from the Latin *absurdus,* meaning 'dissonant,' 'incongruous,' 'out of tune,' is a natural term for expressing this sense of impropriety. . . . So then, 'absurdity' is a way of describing the *environment* or *context* in which any attempted actions are met with frustration and inevitably result in futility."

108 **Hevel names something dissonant, incongruous:** For literature that takes the primary and predominant meaning of *hevel* in Ecclesiastes to be "absurd" in the sense discussed here, see, among others, Fox, "The Meaning of *Hebel*"; Fox, *A Time to Tear Down,* 30–49; Antoon Schoors, *The Preacher Sought to Find Pleasing Words: A Study of the Language of Qohelet; Part II: Vocabulary* (Leuven, Belgium: Peeters, 2004), 119–29; Philip Michael Lasater, "Not So Vain After All: Hannah Arendt's Reception of Ecclesiastes," *Journal of the Bible and Its Reception* 6, no. 2 (2019): 163–96, at 171–72; Lasater, "Subordination," 87, 93; Peterson, " 'What Is Good,' " 36–53. Peterson's treatment is especially illuminating and rigorous. He points out that in Ecclesiastes, *hevel* frequently means "futile," describing a situation in which toil intended some goal but did not obtain it (e.g., Ecclesiastes 1:14; 2:1, 11, 15; see " 'What Is Good,' " 43). But, as the book progresses, Qohelet begins to identify as hevel not only actions but situations, and "absurd" is a way of describing the environment or context in which attempted actions are frustrated and result in futility (49–51). Therefore, the meaning "absurd" for *hevel* is not an anachronistic imposition of twentieth-century existentialist philosophy but arises from the way Qohelet generalizes and abstracts from the futility he perceives. "Absurdity is futility run amok and raised to a metalevel perspective. . . . Absurdity, then, transcends yet still includes futility" (52). Scholars who agree that "absurd" is *hevel*'s primary sense, while also pointing to a variety of secondary connotations, include Gary D. Salyer, *Vain Rhetoric: Private Insight and Public Debate in Ecclesiastes* (Sheffield: Sheffield Academic Press, 2001), 254; and, following him, Bundvad, *Time,* 80–81n121. For an influential criticism of *hevel* as "absurd," followed by a convincing rejoinder, see Mark Sneed, "Hebel as 'Worthless' in Qoheleth: A Critique of Michael V. Fox's 'Absurd' Thesis," *Journal of Biblical Literature* 136, no. 4 (2017): 879–94; Michael V. Fox, "On הבל in Qoheleth: A Reply to Mark

Sneed," *Journal of Biblical Literature* 138, no. 3 (2019): 559–63. For a survey of scholarship on the meaning of *hevel* in Ecclesiastes, see Russell L. Meek, "Twentieth- and Twenty-first-century Readings of *Hebel* (הֶבֶל) in Ecclesiastes," *Currents in Biblical Research* 14, no. 3 (2016): 279–97.

109 **"I said that the world is absurd":** Camus, *Myth,* 21, 28.

109 **Hevel is the tragic divorce:** This sentence paraphrases Fox, "The Meaning of *Hebel,*" 410; the following sentence draws on C. B. Peter, "In Defense of Existence: A Comparison Between Ecclesiastes and Albert Camus," *Bangalore Theological Forum* 12 (1980): 26–43, at 37; cited by N. Karl Haden, "Qoheleth and the Problem of Alienation," *Christian Scholars Review* 17 (1987): 52–66, at 55.

109 **"I said in my heart":** Ecclesiastes 2:1, which serves as a heading for verses 1–11.

110 **"Again, I saw an absurdity":** Ecclesiastes 4:7–8. As Fox ("The Meaning of *Hebel,*" 418) comments on these verses, "It is not the transitoriness of the gain that makes this labor *hebel* but its failure to provide even fleeting satisfaction."

110 **"Better is the sight of the eyes":** Ecclesiastes 6:9.

110 **"He who loves money will not be satisfied":** Ecclesiastes 5:10. Choon-Leong Seow comments, "One ought not to ask here if money itself or the situation is *hebel,* for both are; because money is *hebel* (evanescent and unreliable), the case of people not being satisfied to have it is *hebel* (incomprehensible, absurd)." In Choon-Leong Seow, "Beyond Mortal Grasp: The Usage of *Hebel* in Ecclesiastes," *Australian Biblical Review* 48 (2000): 1–16, at 12.

110 **"There is an evil that I have seen":** Ecclesiastes 6:1–2. Other repetitions of this theme occur in Ecclesiastes 2:26 and 5:13–17.

111 **"As he came from his mother's womb":** Ecclesiastes 5:15.

111 **"What is it we want when":** Christian Wiman, *He Held Radical Light: The Art of Faith, the Faith of Art* (New York: Farrar, Straus and Giroux, 2018), 7.

111 **"The wise person has his eyes":** Ecclesiastes 2:14–15. The following paragraph cites Ecclesiastes 7:15 and 8:14.

112 **"I said in my heart":** Ecclesiastes 3:18–20.

113 **"The modern objective consciousness":** Walker Percy, *Lost in the Cosmos: The Last Self-Help Book* (New York: Picador, 1983), 254.

113 **depression and burnout are the fastest-growing:** See the discussion in Rosa, "De-Synchronization, Dynamic Stabilization, Dispositional Squeeze: The Problem of Temporal Mismatch," in *The Sociology of Speed: Digital, Organizational, and Social Temporalities,* ed. Judy Wajcman and Nigel Dodd (Oxford: Oxford University Press, 2017), 39.

113 **"The depressed individual is unable":** Alain Ehrenberg, *The Weariness of the Self: Diagnosing the History of Depression in the Contemporary Age* (Mon-

treal: McGill-Queen's University Press, 2010), 4. The preceding sentence paraphrases one from this page as well. For the following sentence, see page 11, "If neurosis is the tragedy of guilt, depression is the tragedy of inadequacy." The remainder of the paragraph is informed by page 219 (emphasis original), "Depression, then, is melancholia plus equality, the perfect disorder of the democratic human being. It is *the inexorable counterpart of the human being who is his/her own sovereign.* We are not speaking of the human being who has acted badly but, rather, of the human being who cannot act. Depression is not conceived in terms of law, what is allowed and what is forbidden, but in terms of *capacity.*" The paragraph's final sentence borrows its image from page 9.

113 **Depression is an inevitable by-product:** This paragraph draws on ideas and language in Ehrenberg, *Weariness,* xvi, xxx, 9, 185, 218, 221.

114 **Depression is the shattering sense:** For two compassionate, hopeful, practical responses to depression, see David Murray, *Christians Get Depressed Too: Hope and Help for Depressed People* (Grand Rapids, Mich.: Reformation Heritage Books, 2010); and Alan Noble, *On Getting Out of Bed: The Burden and Gift of Living* (Downers Grove, Ill.: InterVarsity Press, 2023).

114 **Depending on your vantage point:** This paragraph draws on Byung-Chul Han, *The Burnout Society* (Stanford, Calif.: Stanford University Press, 2015), 8, 10, 23. Burkeman, *Four Thousand Weeks,* 9, makes similar points as well. The paragraph's final two sentences echo Han, *The Disappearance of Rituals,* 14, "The narcissistic subject of performance breaks apart because of a fatal accumulation of ego-libido. It exploits itself voluntarily and passionately until it breaks down. It optimizes itself to death. Its failing is called depression or burnout." See also Jonathan Malesic, *The End of Burnout: Why Work Drains Us and How to Build Better Lives* (Oakland, Calif.: University of California Press, 2022).

114 **"the perfect disorder of the democratic":** Ehrenberg, *Weariness,* 219. The following sentence cites Rosa, *Social Acceleration,* 248 (emphasis original).

115 **"So I hated life":** Ecclesiastes 2:17. The citation in the next paragraph is Ecclesiastes 2:20.

116 **"What is this world that we are so":** Wiman, *My Bright Abyss,* 145–46.

116 **"You are depressed because you have":** Percy, *Lost in the Cosmos,* 76. Richard Sennett, *Together: The Rituals, Pleasures and Politics of Cooperation* (New York: Penguin, 2013), 254, registers a similar point: "The psychoanalyst Darian Leader is sceptical of the WHO statistics, believing that the epidemic of depression reformats the sadness and injustice which attend real life into a disease."

116 **A useful modern name:** For a genealogy of the concept of alienation and an exposition of it from an anti-essentialist critical theory stance (a stance

obviously far from mine), see Rahel Jaeggi, *Alienation,* trans. Frederick Neuhouser and Alan E. Smith (New York: Columbia University Press, 2014). For a discussion of Ecclesiastes through the lens of alienation see Haden, "Qoheleth and the Problem of Alienation."

116 **Alienation is the opposite:** See, for instance, Rosa, *Alienation and Acceleration,* 87–88, "If the opposite of feeling alienated is 'feeling at home' (at a certain place, with certain people or with certain actions, for example), then we might actually say that very often, we do not feel at home in doing the things we do."

116 **"Alienation has come to serve":** Rosa, "Available, Accessible, Attainable," 44.

117 **alienation describes a state:** Rosa, *Resonance,* 178.

117 **Imagine that Martians exist:** I adapt this illustration from Jaeggi, *Alienation,* 25.

117 **alienation is an umbrella:** As Jaeggi, *Alienation,* 5 recognizes.

118 **"If human life is indeed absurd":** Gordon, "Nagel or Camus on the Absurd?," 28.

118 **The answer is simple:** For the biblical background Qohelet assumes, see, of course, Genesis 1–3. On the curse of Genesis 3 as the background of Ecclesiastes' reflections on toil, see, e.g., Christopher J. H. Wright, *Old Testament Ethics for the People of God* (Downers Grove, Ill.: IVP Academic, 2004), 151; Keefer, *Ecclesiastes and the Meaning of Life,* 204, 206. The phrase "aboriginal catastrophe" is from Percy, *Lost in the Cosmos,* 11.

119 **"See, this alone I found":** Ecclesiastes 7:29. Scholars who detect an allusion to the fall here include Eaton, *Ecclesiastes,* 133; William P. Brown, *Ecclesiastes* (Louisville, Ky.: Westminster John Knox, 2000), 84–85; and Krüger, *Qoheleth,* 149.

119 **"Surely there is not a righteous man":** Ecclesiastes 7:20.

119 **A consequence of the fall is original sin:** For a masterful account of the historical career of original sin in the West, and a subtle defense of the doctrine addressed to its cultured despisers, see Alan Jacobs, *Original Sin: A Cultural History* (New York: HarperOne, 2008).

119 **"Actual sin is simple: it means":** Kreeft, *Christianity for Modern Pagans,* 148.

120 **"all of us arrive in this world":** Jacobs, *Original Sin,* 155.

120 **"All go to one place":** Ecclesiastes 3:20. The following quotation is from Genesis 3:19.

120 **"What is crooked cannot be":** Ecclesiastes 1:15; 7:13.

120 **Like Qohelet, sober-minded secular:** See, for instance, Rosa, *Alienation and Acceleration,* 98–99, "As critiques of the idea of a 'true authenticity' from Helmuth Plessner through Adorno to contemporary post-structuralists have argued convincingly, there can be little doubt that any

attempt for a political and cultural elimination of alienation leads to totalitarian forms of philosophy, culture and politics, and to authoritarian forms of personality."

121 **"All these examples of wretchedness":** Pascal, *Pensées,* 29 §116. As Morris, *Making Sense of It All,* 134, comments, "The nature of our wretchedness reverberates with echoes of our greatness."

121 **"Nature has all the air of a good thing spoiled":** C. S. Lewis, *Miracles: A Preliminary Study* (New York: HarperOne, 1996), 196.

121 **"Who indeed would think himself unhappy":** Pascal, *Pensées,* 30 §117.

122 **"One who had never been a prince":** Kreeft, *Christianity for Modern Pagans,* 60, on which the preceding and following sentences also draw.

122 **"Is it not clear as day that man's":** Pascal, *Pensées,* 35 §131. On this duality, consider Kreeft, *Christianity for Modern Pagans,* 134, "Here are two facts, two pieces of crucial data. Both are equally solid. First, that no thing in this universe is solid, stable, absolute and unchanging, least of all ourselves. Second, that we scream for that solidity. We yearn, we demand, we act like babies deprived of milk, fish of water, birds of air. We act like land creatures sucked from their home by a tidal wave in a past so remote and forgotten that we seem to have been drifting always. But all driftwood originally came from a tree, with roots."

122 **Would you rather believe:** I borrow the phrase "naturally and perfectly innocent" from Alan Jacobs's description of Rousseau's view of humanity in *Original Sin,* 155.

122 **"Certainly nothing jolts us":** Pascal, *Pensées,* 36 §131.

123 **If the world and the human self:** As Cornelius Plantinga, Jr., *Not the Way It's Supposed to Be: A Breviary of Sin* (Grand Rapids, Mich.: Eerdmans, 1995), xii (emphasis original), observes, "Unlike some other identifications of human trouble, a diagnosis of sin and guilt allows hope. Something can be done for this malady. Something *has* been done for it."

"THE PRESENT, AT LAST"

127 **"I never merited this grace":** Dillard, *Pilgrim,* 103.

CHAPTER 12—GIFT

129 **In his work on craftsmanship:** Sennett, *The Craftsman,* 38.

129 **The better your technique:** The five joy-commendations I cite are Ecclesiastes 2:24–26; 3:12; 5:18–20; 8:15; and 9:7–10. The remaining two are 3:22 and 11:7–10.

132 **When he says repeatedly:** Ecclesiastes 2:24; 3:12–13, 22; 8:15.

132 **it is God who grants life:** Though some scholars manage not to see it, the doctrine of creation is crucial to Ecclesiastes. In light of passages like Ecclesiastes 11:5 ("You do not know the work of God who makes every-

thing"), the charge of 12:1 to "Remember . . . your Creator" comes not from blue sky but from the core of Qohelet's theology. For an apt survey of the theme of creation in Ecclesiastes and other so-called wisdom books, see Zoltán Schwáb, "Creation in the Wisdom Literature," in *The Cambridge Companion to Biblical Wisdom Literature,* ed. Katharine J. Dell, Suzanna R. Millar, and Arthur Jan Keefer (Cambridge: Cambridge University Press, 2022), 391–413.

133 **Every gift bears a trace of its giver:** See Peter Leithart, *Gratitude: An Intellectual History* (Waco, Tex.: Baylor University Press, 2014), 16.

133 **To enjoy is not to act as if:** My wording here is inspired by Smith, *How to Inhabit Time,* 115, who comments on these passages in Ecclesiastes (emphasis original), "The Teacher is not Albert Camus, who counsels us to act as *if,* to make meaning where there is none."

133 **Not striving but receiving:** Putting the link between life-as-gift and living-as-receiving into a philosophical idiom is Kenneth L. Schmitz, *The Gift: Creation* (Marquette, Wis.: Marquette University Press, 1982), 57, "The transcendental generosity calls for a transcendental receptivity, availability and openness." The rest of this section is indebted to the rich account of the fundamental posture of receiving life as a gift, contrasted with grasping it as a possession, in Norman Wirzba, *Agrarian Spirit: Cultivating Faith, Community, and the Land* (South Bend, Ind.: University of Notre Dame Press, 2022), 78. The second sentence of this paragraph echoes Norman Wirzba, *This Sacred Life: Humanity's Place in a Wounded World* (Cambridge: Cambridge University Press, 2021), 194.

133 **You can neither give yourself life:** This sentence and the next three paraphrase and riff on Wirzba, *This Sacred Life,* 176.

133 **If life is a gift:** Wendell Berry, *Life Is a Miracle: An Essay Against Modern Superstition* (Berkeley, Calif.: Counterpoint, 2000), 9, "Though we have life, it is beyond us. We do not know how we have it, or why. We do not know what is going to happen to it, or to us. It is not predictable; though we can destroy it, we cannot make it." As Berry says in *The Need to Be Whole,* 481, "So far as I know or can imagine, people who have revered life and those who still revere it would all give the same reason: that it has appeared to them to be a great miracle, unaccountable on the terms of available knowledge. To those who disdain the word 'miracle,' life is still a great mystery."

134 **"What do you have that":** 1 Corinthians 4:7.

134 **"To receive is to trust":** Wirzba, *Agrarian Spirit,* 78.

135 **"a gift the recipient obtains":** Heschel, *Man Is Not Alone,* 291.

135 **Trading control for trust:** Contrast the characteristic modern posture described by Rosa, *Uncontrollability,* 6.

135 **But whatever their weight:** So Leithart, *Gratitude,* 186, summarizing

Heidegger, "The first human stance is one of reception rather than domination, and reception is a hairbreadth away from gratitude."

CHAPTER 13—ENJOY

137 **"In the day of prosperity be joyful":** Ecclesiastes 7:14, which reads in full, "In the day of prosperity be joyful, and in the day of adversity consider: God has made the one as well as the other, so that man may not find out anything that will be after him." But enough already with adversity.

137 **a series of synonymous expressions:** As Choon-Leong Seow, "Theology When Everything Is Out of Control," *Interpretation* 55, no. 3 (2001): 237–49, at 246, observes, "Synonymous expressions for enjoyment in the book are suggestive; the expressions 'see good' (2:24), 'do well' (3:12), 'be in good' (7:14), and 'see life' (9:9) all mean 'enjoy.'"

138 **"There is nothing better for a person":** Ecclesiastes 2:24; 3:12–13; 8:15.

138 **Enjoyment depends on the ability:** Here I echo the comments of Lee, *Vitality,* 51, on Ecclesiastes 7:14.

138 **Enjoyment is only a present experience:** Lee, *Vitality,* 41, "Enjoyment is always contingent upon God's giving, and is an opportunity available only for the moment."

138 **"I kept my heart from no pleasure":** Ecclesiastes 2:10.

139 **That is why he instructs the worker:** Many scholars note this crucial difference. For instance, William P. Brown, "'Whatever Your Hand Finds to Do': Qoheleth's Work Ethic," *Interpretation* 55, no. 3 (2001): 271–84, at 281 (emphasis original), "Unlike gain, which is gleaned *from* one's labors, enjoyment is found *amid* the toiling."

139 **"Not being a hibernating animal":** Heschel, *Man Is Not Alone,* 271. See also Thomas Hurka, *The Best Things in Life: A Guide to What Really Matters* (Oxford: Oxford University Press, 2011), 40, who notes that, strictly speaking, enjoyment is a form of "pleasure-that" in one's own present activity, even if the action consists of observing some pleasurable performance, such as sports or music.

139 **What brings you joy:** This paragraph drafts behind the observations of Mark Johnston, "Is Life a Ponzi Scheme?" *Boston Review,* January 2, 2014, www.bostonreview.net/articles/mark-johnston-samuel-scheffler-death-afterlife-humanity-ponzi-scheme. Especially this: "This kind of joy is wholly legitimate, a proper response to these activities, and also self-standing, in that it does not give hostages to futurity as a condition on its legitimacy." Peterson, "'What Is Good,'" 234, comments on how Johnston encapsulates a central element in Qohelet's idea of joy: "The joy commended by the sage will not 'remain' or be 'left over' after one

has died, but that is no longer a worry. It is indeed 'self-standing,' unbeholden to a master end. It will not be remembered or admired by any future third-person arbiters. It will be entirely spent, used up, poured into its activities—and then gone."

139 **"Behold, what I have seen to be good":** Ecclesiastes 5:18–20.

139 **"This statement is the interpreter":** Martin Luther, *Luther's Works: Volume 15; Notes on Ecclesiastes, Lectures on the Song of Solomon, Treatise on the Last Words of David,* ed. Jaroslav Pelikan (St. Louis: Concordia, 1972), 93.

140 **The joy God gives now:** See, e.g., Lee, *Vitality,* 47.

142 **away from this "sight of the eyes":** Ecclesiastes 6:9, "Better is the sight of the eyes than the wandering of the appetite: this also is absurd and a striving after wind."

142 **Either your circumstances can rise:** For a classic, commendable exposition, which has far more nuance and richness than my stripped-down summary would suggest, see Jeremiah Burroughs, *The Rare Jewel of Christian Contentment* (Edinburgh: Banner of Truth, 1964).

143 **"Joy plunges us into time and the world":** Charles Mathewes, "On Using the World," in *Having: Property and Possession in Religious and Social Life,* ed. William Schweiker and Charles Mathewes (Grand Rapids, Mich.: Eerdmans, 2004), 215. Soon we will consider the tension between plunging participation and the world's inadequacy.

143 **"Perhaps our most serious cultural loss":** Wendell Berry, "Faustian Economics," in *The World-Ending Fire: The Essential Wendell Berry* (Berkeley, Calif.: Counterpoint, 2017), 215. Three sentences later, my assertion that life itself is unfathomable and inexhaustible borrows phrasing from Karl Barth, *Church Dogmatics: Volume III, The Doctrine of Creation, Part 2,* trans. H. Knight et al., ed. G. W. Bromiley and T. F. Torrance (Edinburgh: T&T Clark, 1960), 555.

143 **"this will go with him in his toil":** Ecclesiastes 8:15.

144 **"Go, eat your bread with joy":** Ecclesiastes 9:7.

144 **"Because so many are hungry":** Wendell Berry, "Some Thoughts on Citizenship and Conscience in Honor of Don Pratt," in *The World-Ending Fire: The Essential Wendell Berry* (Berkeley, Calif.: Counterpoint, 2017), 301–2.

144 **"Rejoice, O young man":** Ecclesiastes 11:9. For an insightful study of the use of Numbers 15:39 in Ecclesiastes 11:9, see Will Kynes, "Follow Your Heart and Do Not Say It Was a Mistake: Qoheleth's Allusions to Numbers 15 and the Story of the Spies," in *Reading Ecclesiastes Intertextually,* 15–27.

144 **"Everyone must give an account":** *Y. Qidd.* 4:12, cited in Lee, *Vitality,* 77.

144 **Qohelet's seven shining celebrations:** The passages cited in this paragraph, including the final block quote, are Ecclesiastes 3:12; 5:18; 8:15; 9:9, 10; 11:7–10.

145 **In reading these passages we must resist two temptations:** My reasoning here draws on Susannah Ticciati, "Ecclesiastes, Augustine's *Uti/Frui* Distinction, and Christ as the Waste of the World," in *Reading Ecclesiastes Intertextually,* 259–62.

146 **"Others again, who have indeed":** Pascal, *Pensées,* 46 §148.

147 **Further help comes from the church father Augustine:** My exposition is informed by that of Ticciati, "Ecclesiastes," 255–60.

147 **while created goods are to be "used":** On what "using" created goods in this sense does and doesn't mean, see Mathewes, "On Using the World," 209.

147 **Augustine says Ecclesiastes exposes:** Augustine, *The City of God* (New York: Modern Library, 1999), 713 (XX.3), "This wisest man devoted this whole book to a full exposure of this vanity, evidently with no other object than that we might long for that life in which there is no vanity under the sun, but verity under Him who made the sun."

CHAPTER 14—LOT

149 **That singular magazine ran:** For details and quotes that follow, see Samuel Loncar in conversation with John Wilson, "'A Small Good Thing' An Interview with John Wilson," *Marginalia Review of Books,* November 20, 2020, www.marginaliareviewofbooks.com/post/a-small-good-thing-an-interview-with-john-wilson (emphasis original).

150 **"So I saw that there is nothing":** The three passages cited here are Ecclesiastes 3:22; 5:18–19; and 9:9.

151 **Qohelet uses the term "lot":** Keefer, *Ecclesiastes and the Meaning of Life,* 137.

151 **Because God is the allotter:** Seow, *Ecclesiastes,* 58. The following sentence is indebted to Fox, *A Time to Tear Down,* 110.

151 **Modernity is the illusion:** On Qohelet's side is Berry, *The Need to Be Whole,* 466, "The traditional definition of 'human' is composed of limits as much as privileges."

152 **wholeness that come from:** Here I borrow from Wendell Berry's description of what the rest of us should learn from the Amish but do not, in *The Unsettling of America: Culture & Agriculture* (Berkeley, Calif.: Counterpoint, 2015), 99, "But it cannot be denied that they have mastered one of the fundamental paradoxes of our condition: we can make ourselves whole only by accepting our partiality, by living within our limits, by being human—not by trying to be gods. By restraint they make themselves whole."

CHAPTER 15—EAT AND DRINK

155 **He says there is nothing better:** Ecclesiastes 2:24 (also 8:15); 3:12–13; 5:18; 9:7.

155 **"Sweet is the sleep of a laborer":** Ecclesiastes 5:12.

157 **"Food is the daily sacrament":** Robert Farrar Capon, *The Supper of the Lamb: A Culinary Reflection* (New York: Modern Library, 2002), 40. My next two sentences remold language of Capon's from pages 114 and 123. See also Henry David Thoreau, *Familiar Letters of Henry David Thoreau,* ed. F. B. Sanborn (New York: Houghton Mifflin, 1894), 9, "This curious world which we inhabit is more wonderful than it is convenient; more beautiful than it is useful; it is more to be admired and enjoyed than used."

157 **The sun rises because:** Here, of course, I rip off the justly famous passage of G. K. Chesterton, *Orthodoxy* (New York: Image Books, 2001), 58 (emphasis original), "Now, to put the matter in a popular phrase, it might be true that the sun rises regularly because he never gets tired of rising. His routine might be due, not to a lifelessness, but to a rush of life. The thing I mean can be seen, for instance, in children, when they find some game or joke that they specially enjoy. A child kicks his legs rhythmically through excess, not absence, of life. Because children have abounding vitality, because they are in spirit fierce and free, therefore they want things repeated and unchanged. They always say, 'Do it again'; and the grown-up person does it again until he is nearly dead. For grown-up people are not strong enough to exult in monotony. But perhaps God is strong enough to exult in monotony. It is possible that God says every morning, 'Do it again' to the sun; and every evening, 'Do it again' to the moon. It may not be automatic necessity that makes all daisies alike; it may be that God makes every daisy separately, but has never got tired of making them. It may be that He has the eternal appetite of infancy; for we have sinned and grown old, and our Father is younger than we. The repetition in Nature may not be a mere recurrence; it may be a theatrical *encore.*"

157 **"Whenever people come":** Norman Wirzba, *Food and Faith: A Theology of Eating,* 2nd ed. (Cambridge: Cambridge University Press, 2019), 41. The final sentence of this paragraph is inspired by Wirzba's comment on page 74, "Thoughtful eating reminds us that there is no human fellowship without a table, no table without a kitchen, no kitchen without a garden, no garden without viable ecosystems, no ecosystems without the forces productive of life, and no life without its source in God."

157 **Your life is not self-contained:** The thesis that human life is well conceived as a meshwork within the larger meshwork of creation, against modern notions of constitutive autonomy, is convincingly argued in Wirzba, *This Sacred Life.* My phrase "Life is not a power or possession" borrows from pages 66–67. See also Berry, *The Unsettling of America,* 116,

"There is, in practice, no such thing as autonomy. Practically, there is only a distinction between responsible and irresponsible dependence."

158 **"Food is God's love made nutritious and delicious":** Wirzba, *Food and Faith,* 46.

CHAPTER 16—TOIL

161 **Three times he uses neutral Hebrew:** Ecclesiastes 3:22; 9:10.

161 **The other seven speak of "toil":** Here citing Ecclesiastes 2:24 and 5:18; the remaining references are in 3:13; 5:19; 8:15; 9:9.

162 **To enjoy toil, the first thing you have to learn:** Here I adapt a comment of Ellen F. Davis, "Slaves or Sabbath-Keepers? A Biblical Perspective on Human Work," *Anglican Theological Review* 83, no. 1 (2001): 25–40, at 33.

162 **Rest does not exist for the sake of work:** See, for instance, Han, *The Disappearance of Rituals,* 36. Davis, "Slaves or Sabbath-Keepers?," 31 is also insightful: "The slave system, the industrial system, is work without Sabbath. And in the theological framework of Exodus, that means work that takes no account of God the Creator." Similarly Brown, " 'Whatever Your Hand Finds to Do,' " 273.

163 **One of the rewards of a craft:** The point in the first half of this sentence is made by J. Budziszewski, *How and How Not to Be Happy* (Washington, D.C.: Regnery, 2022), 31.

163 **The essence of craftsmanship:** Sennett, *The Craftsman,* 9, "Craftsmanship names an enduring, basic human impulse, the desire to do a job well for its own sake." The quote that follows is from page 24.

CHAPTER 17—WEALTH

164 **When you buy something:** Rosa, *Resonance,* 255, 419. My observation that we are not strictly a consumer society but an acquirer society is informed both by Rosa and by Cavanaugh, *Being Consumed,* especially pages xi, 15 (which the last sentence of my paragraph paraphrases), 34, 48, 90–91, 93.

165 **Jesus warns:** The biblical passages this paragraph alludes to, including the block quote from Paul, are Matthew 19:23–24; Mark 10:21; Luke 12:20; 1 Timothy 6:10, 17–19.

165 **"Everyone also to whom God":** Ecclesiastes 5:19. Qohelet's clear-eyed acceptance of limits, including death as the hardest limit, and his continual polemic against the effort to accumulate gain that can somehow withstand death's zeroing effect, undermine the claim of Matthew S. Rindge, "Mortality and Enjoyment: The Interplay of Death and Possessions in Qohelet," *Catholic Biblical Quarterly* 73, no. 2 (2011): 265–80, at 268, that "the advice to enjoy possessions reflects an effort to find some way of

exerting control on the face of the loss of control represented by death." It is also worth noting here that, in Qohelet's isolated comment on money in Ecclesiastes 10:19, he clearly intends ironic realism, not mercenary obsession: "Bread is made for laughter, and wine gladdens life, and money answers everything."

166 **"Wise consumption is a far":** Ruskin, "Unto This Last," 217.

166 **such astronomical accumulation:** See Aristotle, *Politics* 1256b40ff., cited and discussed in Scott Meikle, *Aristotle's Economic Thought* (Oxford: Oxford University Press, 1995), 46–47.

167 **"Most people hold that owning property":** The rest of this paragraph and the next closely follow the exposition of Augustine's view of possession in David E. Klemm, "Material Grace," in *Having: Property and Possession in Religious and Social Life,* ed. William Schweiker and Charles Mathewes (Grand Rapids, Mich.: Eerdmans, 2004), 226, which I cite here twice.

168 **No matter how hard you worked:** Deuteronomy 8:17–18, "Beware lest you say in your heart, 'My power and the might of my hand have gotten me this wealth.' You shall remember the LORD your God, for it is he who gives you power to get wealth, that he may confirm his covenant that he swore to your fathers, as it is this day."

CHAPTER 18—MARRIAGE

170 **Americans, Westerners, and people throughout the so-called developed world:** For global data, see Esteban Ortiz-Ospina and Max Roser, "Marriages and Divorces," Our World in Data, last revised April 2024, https://ourworldindata.org/marriages-and-divorces. For the changing share of Americans who never marry, see Wendy Wang, "The Share of Never-Married Americans Has Reached a New High," Institute for Family Studies (blog), September 9, 2020, https://ifstudies.org/blog/the-share-of-never-married-americans-has-reached-a-new-high. For change in age at first marriage in the United States, see the United States Census Bureau, "Figure MS—2: Median Age at First Marriage: 1890 to Present," accessed July 25, 2023, www.census.gov/content/dam/Census/library/visualizations/time-series/demo/families-and-households/ms-2.pdf. Between my drafting this chapter and this book coming to publication, Brad Wilcox, *Get Married: Why Americans Must Defy the Elites, Forge Strong Families, and Save Civilization* (New York: Broadside, 2024), made a large and deserved splash. Perhaps a couple more out of the hypothetical hundred people you ask would now tell you that marriage and children are a fast track to happiness.

170 **"Enjoy life with the wife whom you love":** Ecclesiastes 9:9.

170 **Throughout the modern era:** This paragraph is informed by, though also goes beyond, Eva Illouz, "Is Love Still Part of the Good Life?," in *The*

Good Life Beyond Growth: New Perspectives, ed. Hartmut Rosa and Christoph Henning (London: Routledge, 2017), 177–87.

171 **A second problem is that the quest:** My paradigm of the quest versus the toil of nurture was inspired by Antti Kauppinen, "Against Seizing the Day," in *Oxford Studies in Normative Ethics: Volume 11,* ed. Mark Timmons (Oxford: Oxford University Press, 2021), 91–111; Kauppinen's terms for the two are "Adventure" and "Service."

172 **"It is possible to imagine marriage":** Berry, *The Unsettling of America,* 124.

CHAPTER 19—RESONANCE

174 **"But for now we are young":** Neutral Milk Hotel, "In the Aeroplane over the Sea," track 3 on *In the Aeroplane over the Sea,* Merge Records, 1998, compact disc.

175 **He never treats happiness:** By never treating happiness as a mood that can be conjured at will, Qohelet distinguishes himself sharply from modern methods of mindfulness and at least some advocates of positive psychology. For an insightful, though perhaps cranky, critique of positive psychology and its effect on modern society, see Edgar Cabanas and Eva Illouz, *Manufacturing Happy Citizens: How the Science and Industry of Happiness Control Our Lives* (Medford, Mass.: Polity, 2019).

175 **"social acceleration": the modern condition of living:** See especially Rosa, *Social Acceleration.*

176 **social acceleration is the problem:** Rosa, *Resonance,* 1, "If acceleration is the problem, then resonance may well be the solution." The following quotation is from page 168 (italics removed). For Rosa's full sociological and philosophical exposition of resonance, see, of course, *Resonance.* (A concise synopsis is in the chart on page 174.) For a concise, further developed exposition of resonance through four exemplary characteristics of being affected, self-efficacy, adaptive transformation, and uncontrollability, which my paragraph summarizes, see Rosa, *Uncontrollability,* 30–39. For the details: On some aspect of the world speaking to you, see *Resonance,* 185; the four following verbs (moves, reaches, touches, calls) are from *Uncontrollability,* 32; the two following citations are from page 33; the example of climbing a mountain is from pages 34–35; and the following two citations are from page 37 (emphasis original). Other discussions of resonance's uncontrollability are in "Available, Accessible, Attainable," 47, and *Resonance,* 451. The citation beginning "it cannot be accumulated" is from *Resonance,* 38, from which also the favorite song illustration is adapted.

176 **Rosa regards modernity as both a catastrophe:** For modernity as both crisis of resonance and the provider of its enabling conditions, see Rosa, *Resonance,* 355. The subsequent quote is from page 373; the list of com-

mon spheres of resonance and the point that they are threatened by modernity's constitutive conditions is from page 171; the point about being short on time from page 416; assertion, aggression, and competition are from *Uncontrollability,* 38; and the promise of competition is from *Resonance,* 417–18. The point about not grasping for resonance as gain draws on page 382, and the citation beginning "In sociological terms" is from *Uncontrollability,* 59.

178 **Rosa treats alienation as a crucial background:** See Rosa, *Resonance,* 174, 188.

179 **Second, resonance is too fleeting:** The citations in this paragraph are from Rosa, *Resonance,* 415 and 185 (italics removed).

179 **"the idea of a responsive world":** Rosa, *Resonance,* 265.

180 **"YOU: You're a professor?":** Charles W McKinney, Jr. (@CharlesWMcKinn2), X, June 7, 2023, 8:48 P.M., https://x.com/CharlesWMcKinn2/status/1666608210868830209.

180 **"Man lives not only on this earth":** Gordon, "Nagel or Camus on the Absurd?," 26–27.

181 **If you hold that the nature of ultimate reality:** I adapt this point from Timothy Keller, *Making Sense of God: Finding God in the Modern World* (New York: Viking, 2016), 67. For an insightful, sustained exposition of this theme, see Gavin Ortlund, *Why God Makes Sense in a World That Doesn't: The Beauty of Christian Theism* (Grand Rapids, Mich.: Baker Academic, 2021), 57–112.

"THROUGH THE DARKEST OF CRISES"

185 **"Apart from emulative envy":** Joseph Epstein, *Envy: The Seven Deadly Sins* (New York: Oxford University Press and the New York Public Library, 2003), 4–5.

CHAPTER 20—FEAR

188 **"Waves were better than anything":** William Finnegan, *Barbarian Days: A Surfing Life* (New York: Penguin, 2016), 71. The quote that follows is from pages 18–19.

189 **"I perceived that whatever God does":** Ecclesiastes 3:14.

189 **What has Qohelet seen in this assembly:** My analysis of Ecclesiastes 3:14 here is indebted to Jason S. DeRouchie, "Shepherding Wind and One Wise Shepherd: Grasping for Breath in Ecclesiastes," *Southern Baptist Journal of Theology* 15, no. 3 (2011): 4–25, at 15.

190 **"Guard your steps when you go":** Ecclesiastes 5:1–2.

190 **He follows these cautions:** Ecclesiastes 5:4–6.

190 **"For a dream comes with":** Ecclesiastes 5:3, 7.

191 **"Though a sinner does evil":** Ecclesiastes 8:12–13.

191 **"The end of the matter":** Ecclesiastes 12:13.

191 **We could translate more literally:** See, among others, Barbour, *The Story of Israel,* 172; Fox, *A Time to Tear Down,* 362.

191 **To fear God is to fulfill your humanity:** Bartholomew, *Ecclesiastes,* 371.

191 **"What does man gain by all the toil":** Ecclesiastes 1:3 (see the repetition of the question in 3:9). The citation that follows is Ecclesiastes 1:13.

192 **The last two sections of the body:** Ecclesiastes 11:7–10; 12:1–7. The hinge verse is 12:1.

192 **This kind of fear:** This sentence paraphrases a portion of the sermon outline of C. H. Spurgeon, "A Fear to Be Desired," The Spurgeon Center, November 7, 1878, www.spurgeon.org/resource-library/sermons/a-fear-to-be-desired/#flipbook.

192 **Qohelet surveyed all and judged:** Here I riff on the insightful comments of Andrew G. Shead, "Ecclesiastes from the Outside In," *Reformed Theological Review* 55, no. 1 (1996): 24–37, at 33.

192 **Fearing God is not an alternative:** Similarly Shead, "Reading Ecclesiastes 'Epilogically,'" 70.

193 **societies "can be said to be driven":** Rosa, *Resonance,* 122. The following discussion of external and internal objects of fear is informed by page 123.

194 **"All of us fear what we cannot":** Dugdale, *The Lost Art of Dying,* 102.

194 **To fear God is to trust:** I would not have been able to put the point this way without the provocation of Heschel, *Man Is Not Alone,* 92, "God is of no importance unless He is of supreme importance, which means a deep certainty that it is better to be defeated with Him than be victorious without Him."

194 **"this horizon, this fear line":** The phrase and the block quote are from Finnegan, *Barbarian Days,* 18; the subsequent citation is from page 335.

195 **"Though he slay me, I will hope":** Job 13:15.

CHAPTER 21—JUDGMENT

198 **"Moreover, I saw under the sun":** Ecclesiastes 3:16–17.

199 **"Though a sinner does evil":** Ecclesiastes 8:12–13. My reading of these verses is closest to Bartholomew, *Ecclesiastes,* 290–91, though I regard Qohelet's conviction of a coming final judgment as an implicit resolution of the contradiction that he deliberately leaves intact in his text. See also Bartholomew, *Ecclesiastes,* 293, "What makes this section particularly interesting is that the juxtaposition appears to be done consciously in v. 12 and v. 13, with v. 12a drawing the reader's attention to the contradiction and thereby making the reader aware that the author is aware of the contradiction." Implicitly acknowledging the confessional epistemology that resolves the contradiction between what Qohelet sees and what he knows is Eaton, *Ecclesiastes,* 140, "The injustices of life are open for all to see; the Preacher's reply is not an observation, but the answer of faith."

200 **"Rejoice, O young man":** Ecclesiastes 11:9. For a survey of scholarly interpretation of the reference to divine judgment in this verse, see Ball, "*Hebel,* Joy, and the Fear of God," 142–45. His position, which I share, interprets "the call to recognize divine judgment as meant to ground and guide all of one's enjoyment, pursuits, and indeed, life" (145).

200 **"God's future judgment regulates":** Keefer, *Ecclesiastes and the Meaning of Life,* 165, which also informs my next sentence.

200 **And yet what Qohelet does say:** See Ball, "*Hebel,* Joy, and the Fear of God," 145.

201 **Qohelet presumably singles out:** As argued by, e.g., Richard Alan Fuhr, Jr., *An Analysis of the Inter-Dependency of the Prominent Motifs Within the Book of Qohelet* (New York: Peter Lang, 2013), 179–80.

201 **"Besides being wise, Qohelet also taught":** Ecclesiastes 12:9–14. I have altered the ESV's "the Preacher" to "Qohelet" throughout. The relationship between Qohelet's perspective (represented in the body of the book) and that of the so-called "epilogist," whom I have called Qohelet's editor (represented chiefly in the epilogue of 12:9–14) is contested. In my view, the epilogist endorses Qohelet's message; the epilogue serves as a coda, distilling one aspect of its central message and deriving from it a summary ethical injunction: Fear God and keep his commandments. For an exposition of the epilogue along these lines, in dialogue with the influential views of Fox, see Bartholomew, *Ecclesiastes,* 359–73. For an insightful reading of the verbal and thematic links between the epilogue and the body of the book, with convincing criticism of a variety of views that set them at odds, see Shead, "Reading Ecclesiastes 'Epilogically.'"

203 **"an act of moral discrimination":** Oliver O'Donovan, *The Ways of Judgment* (Grand Rapids, Mich.: Eerdmans, 2005), 7 (italics removed).

203 **"the whole totalitarian catastrophe":** From a colloquy recorded in Melvyn A. Hill, ed., *Hannah Arendt: The Recovery of the Public World* (New York: St. Martin's, 1978), 313–14; cited in Samuel Moyn, "Hannah Arendt on the Secular," *New German Critique* 105 (2008): 71–96, at 74n7.

CONCLUSION: PIERCED FROM ABOVE

205 **Here and now, we can't take our leave:** I borrow the image of Ecclesiastes as a photo negative from Short, *A Time to Be Born,* 100.

206 **But has anything entered the picture since:** Johann Georg Hamann, "Biblical Reflections," in *J. G. Hamann 1730–1788: A Study in Christian Existence, With Selections from His Writings,* ed. Ronald Gregor Smith (London: Collins, 1960), 136, "Ecclesiastes seems to have been chiefly written in order that he, the wisest of all seekers after wisdom, might point to the revelation of God in the flesh and the preaching of his kingdom as the sole new thing that would be significantly, universally and really new for

all the earth and would never cease to be new." (Cited in Atkinson, *Singing at the Winepress,* 200.)

207 **"new law in the Cosmos":** Percy, *Lost in the Cosmos,* 254.

207 **Jesus went about doing good:** Acts 10:38.

207 **Jesus was alienated:** The biblical passages cited or alluded to in this paragraph are, in order, John 1:11; Mark 3:21; Matthew 26:56; Mark 3:6; 15:10; Luke 23:1–24; Matthew 27:46.

208 **He became the waste of the world:** I owe this phrase to Ticciati, "Ecclesiastes," 265–66.

208 **"No man has power to retain":** Ecclesiastes 8:8. The following quote from Jesus is from John 10:17–18.

209 **aliens offer to rescue:** Percy, *Lost in the Cosmos,* 262.

210 **"For God will bring every deed":** Ecclesiastes 12:14.

ACKNOWLEDGMENTS

217 **" 'Cause there ain't no California":** Ilsey Juber, "No California," track 1 on *From the Valley,* Elektra Records, 2023.

© KARL MAGNUSON

BOBBY JAMIESON is a widely respected pastor, scholar, and award-winning author. Originally from San Francisco, Bobby began a career as a jazz saxophonist before redirecting into pastoral ministry. He has degrees from the Southern Baptist Theological Seminary and a PhD from the University of Cambridge, where he taught Greek and New Testament. Bobby served as an associate pastor of Capitol Hill Baptist Church in Washington, D.C., before moving with his wife and their four kids to plant Trinity Baptist Church in Chapel Hill, North Carolina.

ABOUT THE TYPE

This book was set in Garamond, a typeface originally designed by the Parisian type cutter Claude Garamond (c. 1500–61). This version of Garamond was modeled on a 1592 specimen sheet from the Egenolff-Berner foundry, which was produced from types assumed to have been brought to Frankfurt by the punch cutter Jacques Sabon (c. 1520–80).

Claude Garamond's distinguished romans and italics first appeared in *Opera Ciceronis* in 1543–44. The Garamond types are clear, open, and elegant.